Television and Everyday Life

Television is a central dimension of our everyday lives and yet its meaning and its potency vary according to our individual circumstances. Its power will always be mediated by the social and cultural worlds which we inhabit. In *Television and Everyday Life*, Roger Silverstone explores the enigma of television and how it has found its way so profoundly and intimately into the fabric of our everyday lives. His investigation unravels its emotional and cognitive, spatial, temporal and political significance.

Drawing on a wide range of literature, from psychoanalysis to sociology and from geography to cultural studies, Roger Silverstone constructs a theory of the medium which locates it centrally within the multiple realities and discourses of everyday life. Television emerges from these arguments as a fascinating, complex and contradictory medium, but in the process many of the myths that surround it are exploded.

Television and Everyday Life presents a radical new approach to the medium, one that both challenges received wisdoms and offers a compellingly original view of the place of television in everyday life.

Roger Silverstone is Professor of Media Studies in the School of Cultural and Community Studies at the University of Sussex. He is the author of *The Message of Television: Myth and Narrative in Contemporary Culture; Framing Science; The Making of a BBC Documentary*, and (with Eric Hirsch) joint editor of *Consuming Technologies: Media and Information in Domestic Spaces*.

Television and Everyday Life

Roger Silverstone

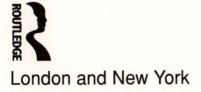

London and New York

First published 1994
by Routledge
11 New Fetter Lane, London EC4P 4EE

Simultaneously published in the USA and Canada
by Routledge
29 West 35th Street, New York, NY 10001

Typeset in Times by
Ponting–Green Publishing Services, Chesham, Bucks
Printed and bound in Great Britain by
TJ Press Ltd, Padstow, Cornwall

Printed on acid free paper

British Library Cataloguing in Publication Data
A catalogue record for this book is available from the British
Library

Library of Congress Cataloging in Publication Data
Silverstone, Roger.
   Television and Everyday Life / Roger Silverstone.
       p.   cm.
   Includes bibliographical references and index.
   1. Television broadcasting – Social aspects.
   I. Title.
   PN1992.6.S465   1994
   302.23'45–dc20   93–32143

ISBN 0–415–01646–0 (hbk)
ISBN 0–415–01647–9 (pbk)

For Jennifer

Contents

Preface

This is a work of media theory. But not disembodied theory. In it I try to approach television's significance in and for everyday life through lenses ground in, and refracted through, empirical research. I hope that the book will be the first in a series of volumes to emerge from ongoing, predominantly qualitative, research into the place of media and information technologies in everyday life, conducted under the auspices of the Economic and Social Research Council within its Programme on Information and Communication Technologies.[1] Perhaps I ought to explain why the first substantive product of this research is a book on, and in, theory and why I have not sought to integrate – in the best sociological tradition – theory and empirical data within a single text. There is no simple answer. Convenience, my own inadequacy, circumstance (I am an inveterate theoriser), are all relevant at a personal level. But more substantially the answer has to be that, as Tom Lindlof and Timothy Meyer (1987) have observed, one of the outstanding strengths of qualitative social research is precisely its ability to generate theory: and in particular to generate theory which is grounded in, and which seeks to explain, social process, to understand the density of lived relations.

The theory which emerges is, too, part of the process. It creates a dynamic of its own, feeding into the analysis of data and being challenged and changed by that data. In this sense, and for these reasons, this book can only be a provisional statement of an emerging position, but that should not necessarily invalidate it. It will, I hope, contribute to an ongoing debate about television and its place in the modern world.

Of course television is a medium of considerable power and significance in and for everyday life, but this power and significance cannot be understood without attending to the complex over- and under-determining inter-relationships of the medium and the various levels of social reality with which it engages. We need to think about television as a psychological, social and cultural form, as well as an economic and political one. We need to think about the medium as more than just a source of influence, neither simply benign nor malignant. We need to think about television as embedded in the multiple discourses of everyday life. And we need to understand what those discourses are, how they are themselves determined, how they interweave and, most crucially, how they are to be distinguished in terms of their influence relative to each other. This task of description and analysis requires both theoretical and empirical attention. I suggest in this book that it is through detailed analysis of the dynamics of everyday life on the one hand, and a theoretical account of the politics (in the widest sense) of everyday life on the other, that the most profitable route will be found.

There are continuities with some of my earlier attempts (esp. Silverstone, 1981) to confront this problem – though the problem itself seemed different then – and any close reading will recognise continuities of theme running from that early work, even in its very different methodological orientation. But there are also differences; differences which mark, I hope, a more sensitive understanding of the contradictions of television's status in the modern world. Indeed even if it is constructed differently now (and even if I have constructed it differently at various times) that problem remains the same. It is the problem, in all its social complexity, of the power and resonance of the media in our lives, articulating, albeit unevenly, their views of the world and limiting our capacity to influence and control their meanings; but equally offering the very stuff with which we can, and do, construct our own meanings, and through them (albeit equally unevenly) generate the raw materials for critique, transcendence, and change.

Running through the discussions that do follow, and almost with a life of its own, is the phrase 'essential tensions'. This phrase has emerged almost involuntarily while I have tried to work out what I wanted to say. It refers, of course, to a dialectic at the heart of social reality. This dialectic is that of the play and place of media in social life. It is a dialectic of freedom and constraint, of activity and passivity, of the public and private, and it is worked through at the interface of institutional forces and individual actions, historically situated and embedded in the contrary discourses of everyday life. It is in this context that any essentialist claim must be understood. Such essentialism does not imply an appeal to an unchanging social or political reality, nor is it a form of reductionism. It is an acknowledgement – for which I have no apology – that social life is, in all its manifestations, *essentially*, in constant and productive tension (see Murphy, 1972).

My arguments attempt to specify some of the elements of this precarious but compelling tension. Their plurality is not just a matter of weakness. Theory must be plural and open if it is to survive the challenges of the real and if it is, more specifically, to accommodate the contradictory and fragmenting world of late capitalism. What I am attempting in this book is a layered analysis of the structure and process of a set of complex and constantly changing relationships: television as medium, television as technology and television constructed and constrained by the rules, roles and rituals of the taken for granted yet entirely insistent everyday world. My view of these interrelationships takes the form of a kind of matrix: articulated through layers of ontology and individual psychology, domestic and suburban spaces, and industrial and technological structures, all of which are related, both in their collusion and contradiction, through the dynamics of consumption. Television, I argue, has to be understood in relation to all these things, because everyday life is formed through these things.

There is one possible contradiction in my own arguments that does need identifying more precisely, however. It lies in the focus on television itself. The ESRC PICT research is actually framed as a study of information and communication technologies in the home. I have myself argued that tele-vision is no longer an isolated media technology, (if ever it was) but one increasingly embedded into a converging culture of technological and media relationships that also involve computing and telecommunications. In this sense this book offers an historically transitional account. Television is its focus, certainly and justifiably, because television is still our focus – the focus of so many concerns about its power and influence and its place in our everyday lives.

I am conscious, however, that the arguments of this book might appear to become all too quickly an historical curiosity; that the dramatic changes in and around television technology and its regulation have already made much of what I have to say irrelevant and inaccurate. It is possible. It is possible if one believes that the whole range of present and future delivery systems – individualising, fragmenting and alienating as they plausibly might be – are indeed going to impact upon society like cultural napalm, burning their way through the soft and vulnerable tissues of a living, human, world. But, as I argue, new technological forms are not simply received, nor do they remain unchanged in their confrontation with the everyday. There is then a media politics to be pursued which must acknowledge that both security and creativity within an increasingly diverse and intrusive media environment are possible and desirable, even if they are, apparently, increasingly difficult to achieve.

Acknowledgements

This book has been a long time coming, but it is hopefully none the worse for that. Various parts of it have been read by Sharon Macdonald, Anthony Giddens, Marilyn Strathern, James Donald, Andy Medhurst, Janice Winship and Nancy Wood. I thank them all for their suggestions and comments. Some of the ideas have developed in undergraduate and postgraduate teaching both at Brunel and Sussex, and I am intensely grateful to all my students who have criticised and asked the difficult questions. Thanks too to those who participated in the HICT project at Brunel: Eric Hirsch, David Morley and Sonia Livingstone, and to Leslie Haddon, Research Fellow on the second phase of the project at Sussex. Thanks finally to Jane Armstrong, who commissioned the book at Routledge, and to Rebecca Barden who patiently waited for it. And thanks to Nathan Field.

The first chapter, 'Television, ontology and the transitional object', has appeared in *Media, Culture and Society*, Vol. 15, No. 4. I am grateful to its editors and publishers for permission to reproduce it.

Chapter 1

Television, ontology and the transitional object

[Man] can adapt somehow to anything his imagination can cope with, but he cannot deal with chaos. . . Therefore our most important assets are always the symbols of our general orientation in nature, on the earth, in society and in whatever we are doing.

(Langer, 1951, 287)

In my heart I will take my television set with me. I love you.
(Suicide note of New York schoolboy, Genero Garcia, who shot himself after his father banned him from watching television; *Sunday Times*, London, 20.2.83)

Running through recent (and not so recent) theorising on the nature of social life is a stress on the social as being a defence against anxiety. The solution to the classically defined problem of order, though not always constructed in this way, can be seen to be just that kind of defence. And it is a defence constructed, of necessity, at individual, institutional and societal levels of reality. Everyday life, it is argued, cannot be sustained without order – an order manifested in our various traditions, rituals, routines and taken for granted activities – in which we, paradoxically, invest so much energy, effort and so many cognitive and emotional resources. In the ordering of daily life we avoid panic, we construct and maintain our identities, we manage our social relationships in time and space, sharing meanings, fulfilling our responsibilities, experiencing pleasure and pain, with greater or lesser degrees of satisfaction and control, but avoiding for the most part the blank and numbing horror of the threat of chaos. The institutions that we have inherited and which we still struggle to maintain: family, household, neigh-bourhood, community, nation (increasingly vulnerable perhaps and in-creasingly open to challenge as a result of social and technological change) are those institutions that have historically been the containers of, and provided the resources for, our ability to sustain that defence. That ability itself is grounded in turn in our ability, within the activities of our daily lives, to preserve a sense of the continuity and reliability of things, to provide, as best we can, the necessary distance between us and the various threats to that continuity, either by denying them completely or by absorbing them, in one way or another, into the fabric of our lives.

In the modern world the threats of chaos and our ability to defend against them are, it is often argued, magnified by industrial and technological changes. This modern world, the world of, in Anthony Giddens' terms, 'space-time distanciation' (see below) is a world of the dissolution of pre-modern relationships grounded in what Alfred Schutz (1973) would call 'the vivid present': the experience of face-to-face interactions in familiar, manageable and relatively unchanging space and time. It is a world massively transformed by the threats of nuclear holocaust, of environmental disaster, but also by our vulnerability to the exigencies of national and international politics, and by the paradoxes of a planetary communication system that connects and disconnects us in the same breath to a world which is otherwise entirely out of reach.

There are those who argue, indeed, that this modern world is itself being radically transformed, only this time precisely by the combination of media- and information technology-led changes that express themselves within politics (the emergence of both a global politics and the revival of localism and regionalism), economics (the restructuring of mass production and the increasing power of the consumer) and culture (the domination of the mass media and the creation of a self-referential neither-norist fusion of fantasy and reality: the hyper-real).

In this chapter I intend to consider the ground base of television's place in modern or (post-modern) society. I intend to discuss television as an ontological and phenomenological reality, and I intend do so as a result of two related observations.

The first is television's veritable dailiness. How is it that such a technology and medium has found its way so profoundly and intimately into the fabric of our daily lives? How is it that it stays there? I believe that the answer to these two questions must rely to a significant extent on the way in which one comes to understand the nature of everyday life; and an understanding of everyday life must in turn be premised on an understanding, however imperfect, of the conditions of its own possibility: that is on an account of the preconditions for the possibility of social life as a whole. Phenomenology, sociology, psychoanalysis, and anthropology all address these issues in their various ways and in drawing on, and to some extent trying to synthesise, their various explanations I am trying to provide an account of what I have to call the *experience* of television: the experience of television in all its dailiness, in all its factuality.

The second is the recognition of a serious gap in the research. Recent reviews of research on the mass media have identified both the need for, and the difficulties of, understanding the complex and interweaving factors that are likely to attend the processes of mass mediation in general and media reception in particular. They have been identified as including personal social circumstances and psychological dispositions, general habits of media use, beliefs or expectations in the benefits to be gained by media use, the consequential acts of media choice and assessment, and their relationship to other aspects of people's lives (McQuail, 1987, 25). The problem, however, lies not so much in the identification of these factors or indeed in their study as isolated phenomena but in providing a framework for their integration.

Those same reviews tend to abstract the dynamics of media reception from the social environment in which it takes place. Much of the research on which they report does likewise. Even those that do take that social environment seriously fail to offer a theoretically informed account of the way in which media are integrated into the fabric of everyday life. They fail adequately to come to terms with the significance of the media in general, and television in particular, in what Stephen Heath calls 'its seamless equivalence with social life' (Heath, 1990, 267). The everyday escapes, and in that escape television escapes too.

In this chapter I want to approach television from as basic a level as it seems possible and reasonable to do. Watching television and discussing television and reading about television takes place on an hourly basis: the result of focused or unfocused, conscious or unconscious attention. Television accompanies us as we wake up, as we breakfast, as we have our tea and as we drink in bars. It comforts us when we are alone. It helps us sleep. It gives us pleasure, it bores us and sometimes it challenges us. It provides us with opportunities to be both sociable and solitary. Although, of course, it was not always so, and although we have had to learn how to incorporate the medium into our lives (Spigel, 1990, 1992) we now take television entirely for granted. We take television for granted in a way similar to how we take everyday life for granted. We want more of it (some of us); we complain about it (but we watch it anyway); but we do not understand very well (nor do we feel the need to understand) how it works, either mechanically or ideologically (Hall, 1977, 325). Our experience of television is of a piece with our experience of the world: we do not expect it to be, nor can we imagine it to be, significantly otherwise (Schutz, 1973, 229).

The palpable integration of television into our daily lives: its emotional significance, both as disturber and comforter; its cognitive significance, both as an informer and a misinformer; its spatial and temporal significance, ingrained as it is into the routines of daily life; its visibility, not just as an object, the box in the corner, but in a multitude of texts – journals, magazines, newspapers, hoardings, books like this one; its impact, both remembered and forgotten; its political significance as a core institution of the modern state; this integration is both complete and fundamental.

Some part of an explanation for that completeness can be sought through an examination of the writings of those who have attended to the structure and dynamics of everyday life, even if they have not focused on the role of the mass media as such in those dynamics. In what follows in this chapter I will draw on some of that literature, specifically in relation to what I think are three key and interrelated contributions to the study of the phenomenology of the social world as they bear on the experience of television. The first is Anthony Giddens' account of the relations between consciousness, self and social encounters in his attempt to characterise the structuration of everyday life. Here I will focus on his various discussions of what he terms the problem of 'ontological security'. The second is D.W. Winnicott's psychoanalytic account of the emergence of the individual and in particular of his discussions of transitional phenomena and potential space. Third, and to some extent synthetically, I will discuss some of the literature that addresses various aspects of the routinisation of social life, specifically in relation to tradition, ritual and myth.

A word of caution is in order. Beginning an argument about the status of television in everyday life in this way, that is through attention to what I have already described as the fundamental or basic levels of social reality, runs the serious risk of becoming reductivist and essentialist. It can be read as claiming that all aspects of the phenomenon of television can be (must be) related to this level of social reality. It can also be read as implying that an explanation of a complex social and historical phenemonon lies not in the realm of action and cultural variation but in the murky waters of physical or biological necessity. It then becomes an easy step to talk about television as if it was fulfilling certain fundamental human needs (which of course to some extent it does) and social functions (which equally of course it does). But the implication of this might be that we can only see television in its immutability: we are condemned to seeing it as invulnerable to criticism, and because it is so deeply engrained in the social world, unchanging and unchangeable.

This is not what I intend or hope to achieve in this chapter or in the book as whole. What I am doing, of course, is offering an account of the presuppositions about human nature which underlie my argument, as they underlie – though normally fairly deeply buried and unexplicated – the explanations of most social phenomena. My argument, in relation to television, is that it is precisely because television has colonised these basic levels of social reality that we need to understand it better. Without that understanding we will mistake the basis of its power and misjudge the difficulties in changing or controlling it. But equally, a concern with these fundamental levels of social reality is generated, and I believe warranted, precisely as a result of those social and historical conditions which are, arguably, threatening them. I am not implying that because television is so deeply embedded there is nothing we can do to change it, or that political, economic and social factors of a more tangible kind are not equally crucial for understanding its significance. On the contrary. It is because it is so deeply embedded, and because those political, economic and social factors are themselves so powerfully interwoven in television's existence that we need to give even greater attention to the medium as a complex and multiply determined force in modern society – for better and for worse. I will return to these issues in the final chapter of the book.

TELEVISION AND ONTOLOGICAL SECURITY

Anthony Giddens' discussion of what he terms 'ontological security' is a central component of his overall project of providing a theoretical basis for the understanding of social life in the modern world. That theory, which he calls structuration theory, takes both its start and its end points from the familiar but intractable core problem in sociology: the problem of structure and agency. It is not my intention to discuss what has become an extremely extensive and intensive body of work. But in abstracting one element of it, I need to acknowledge that I may be guilty of a decontextualisation that shifts or undermines its status in his own writing.

Giddens defines ontological security in the following way:

> [Ontological security] refers to the confidence that most human beings have in the continuity of their self-identity and in the constancy of the surrounding social and material environments of action. A sense of the reliability of persons and things, so central to the notion of trust, is basic to feelings of ontological security; hence the two are psychologically related. Ontological security has to do with 'being' or, in the terms of phenomenology, 'being-in-the-world.' But it is an emotional, rather than a cognitive, phenomenon, and it is rooted in the unconscious.
>
> (Giddens, 1990, 92)

There are a number of different, but equally important, elements in what he calls the 'project' (1989, 279) of ontological security. Let me consider a number of them.

The first is the necessary interrelationship between ontological security and trust, as individual and social aspects of the same basic and universal phenomenon. Before I can have confidence in you, Giddens is saying, I have to have confidence in myself. But, as we shall see, having confidence in myself requires a developmental process in which I have learnt to have confidence in others. This mutually reflective process of I–me–you relations is fundamental to the constitution of society, (the title of one of Giddens' recent books), indeed of all societies, and it is well explored in classic social, social-psychological theory and psychoanalytic theory (Mead, Cooley, Erickson, Laing, Winnicott etc.). But Giddens' version of it is not just an abstraction, and its own ontological claims cannot be confined to the ethereal visions of grand social theory. For, as he argues, both trust and ontological security are the product of an active engagement in the world, of an active engagement in the events and patterns and relationships of everyday life. That active engagement is physical; it requires bodily presence, face-to-face interactions, communication, language. It is cognitive; it requires under-standing, memory, reflexivity, an awareness of position in time and space. And it is affective; our relationships to material objects, to other people and to symbols are grounded in unconscious processes, but can only be sustained through a confidence, born of experience, in the certainty of the world – that is, in a kind of faith. This is a kind of faith because confidence has to be sustained through its dependence, particularly in modern society, on 'a sense of security in responses of others removed in time and space' (Giddens, 1989, 278).

Trust, the precondition, for ontological security and for our capacity to sustain an active anxiety-controlling engagement in the everyday world is defined as: 'confidence in the reliability of a person or system, regarding a given set of outcomes or events where that confidence expresses a faith in the probity or love of another, or in the correctness of abstract principles (technical knowledge)' (Giddens, 1990, 34). That confidence in turn implies the ability to manage, counteract or minimise the various threats and dangers that appear to challenge us, both as individuals and as collectivities. It is the *sine qua non* of social life.

Our individual and collective ability to trust is a consequence of upbringing (see below). But it is something which has to be sustained in the routinised activities of daily life; activities that require constant attention and sophisti-cated, albeit taken for granted, skills:

> This work and that of others upon the minutiae of everyday talk and interaction strongly suggest that what is learned in the formation of basic trust is not just the correlation of routine, integrity and reward. What is also mastered is an extremely sophisticated methodology of practical conscious-ness, which is a continuing protective device (although fraught with possibilities of fracture and disjunction) against the anxieties which even the most casual encounter with others can potentially provoke.
>
> (Giddens, 1990, 99)

In modern societies, Giddens argues, the circumstances in which our onto-logical security is maintained are of a significantly different order to those of pre-modern societies. Prompted by social and technological change, which together have had the consequences of attenuating many, if not most, of our significant relationships away from the face-to-face encounter towards those mediated by abstract tokens or the expertise of others, the creation of ontological security is a function of space–time distanciation. In modern societies, which are decreasingly reliant on kinship relations and in which locality (neighbourhood, community) no longer has the same significance as the source and support of daily routine, we have become increasingly reliant on relational networks and mechanisms whose workings we cannot see or feel as part of our own physically located patterns of daily life. Money, air travel, media content are all, in their various ways, trusted. They only work, of course, because they are trusted. Giddens' argument is that we have learnt (as it were) to 'trust from a distance' as a result of our earliest experiences of childhood, but that our capacity to do so is constantly vulnerable to threat, a threat that is increasingly derived not from natural hazard but from socially created risk. Giddens also suggests that our confidence in these new 'abstract' and attenuated trust mechanisms is 'not for the most part psychologically satisfying' (Giddens, 1989, 279).

Giddens' model of the experienced social world consists, therefore, in a dialectic of space and time, presence and absence, and in the routines that emerge and are sustained in order to hold the various elements of the dialectic together; routines that exist to protect individuals and collectivities from unmanageable anxieties, anxieties that accompany, indeed that define, situations of crisis.

In offering his account of the links between unconscious processes, conscious actions and the sustainable routines of everyday life, Giddens draws on a wide range of social and psychoanalytic theory. A number of comments are in order. The first is that it is perfectly possible to read him as offering a model of social life which is over-ordered, over-rational, and paradoxically over-threatened. There is some justification for each of these readings. His model of the social is of a routinised, defended social order. His model of the unconscious is one in which reason triumphs over the complex and irresolvable conflicts of the psyche. His model of modern society is one in which the level of risk and uncertainty is an ever-present and palpable threat. His judgement of the fragility of ontological security in conditions of modernity as compared to the pre-modern seems exaggerated. His evaluation of the quality of contemporary life seems contradictory and scarcely justified. Yet each of these objections, while partially true, should not be allowed to mask what I think is the value of his theory – at least for the purposes at hand – which is to provide the beginnings of an analytic rather than a descriptive account of the structure of everyday life.

Of course, the world as we and others experience it will not match point by point Giddens' characterisation of it. Actually we do often live, as he himself acknowledges (1984, 50), in a world of broken patterns, non-rational or duplicitous actions, irresolvable conflicts and unpredictable events – in liminal as well as in secure environments. Yet those of us who do manage (or manage for much of the time) the challenges and risks of everyday life do so because we have, as individuals and as members of social groups, the resources – our senses of trust and security – which are grounded in our experiences of predictable routines in space and time.

The irony of Giddens' position, of course, is that he only belatedly considers the media as significant factors in creating modernity (Giddens, 1991, 23–7) and equally is only just beginning to recognise the relevance of his theory to an understanding of the media. This will be my concern and I want to pursue it by considering and extending two aspects of his argument in a little more detail.

My argument will go in two directions. The first is backwards, as it were, towards the psychodynamic conditions for the establishment of a basic sense of trust in the developing infant. But in considering the circumstances of these early years I expect to widen Giddens' perspective by considering not only the development of ontological security in the experience of basic trust, but also the development of a sense of the symbolic which can be seen to accompany it. I shall suggest that in the theories of the English psychoanalyst, D.W. Winnicott, and indeed within that body of psychoanalytic thought known as object relations theory, there lies the seed of a potentially powerful explanation for the space that television occupies in culture and in the individual's psyche.

The other direction is also one marked by Giddens, but this time one that, although substantially developed in his analysis of the patterned constraints of everyday life, still fails to reach the crucial significance of the media and television for everyday life under conditions of modernity. This concerns the central role of routine in everyday life; habit, seriality, framing, and of course the media's role in defining and sustaining these routines.

TELEVISION, POTENTIAL SPACE AND TRANSITIONAL OBJECTS

D.W. Winnicott offers a theory of the individual and of the psyche which is based on a rejection of the classical Freudian model of ego psychology. Instead of the individual being seen as a structured bundle of unconscious processes and instincts whose explanation and analysis requires a deep immersion in the inner workings of the mind, Winnicott suggests that the individual is a product of the facilitating environment of his or her early years; the early years in which the developing child must learn, through experience and through his or her relationships with others, a sense of self. Winnicott's narrative account of these early years provides the basis for what has been called 'object relations' theory. Its significance within psychoanalysis is that it requires consideration of the individual not as a monad, or in isolation from others, but on the contrary, precisely as both the product and producer of symbolic acts of communication. Its significance in this context is the same. Winnicott and others within what has become the English school of psychoanalysis (Kohon, 1986) have provided an opening within psychoanalysis for the consideration of the social, and of course at the same time they have provided an opening within the study of the social for the consideration of psychoanalytic and psychodynamic processes.

At the root of Winnicott's account of the development of the individual lies the relationship between the the baby and its mother, a relationship focused, both literally and symbolically, on the mother's breast. The key to the successful emergence of the individual is, in Winnicott's view, the ability of the child to separate from the mother. That ability is itself conditional on the quality of the caring environment provided for it, above all in terms of its reliability and consistency (as well as its intensity). The child can separate from the mother if there exists in the relationship enough trust and security for him or her to do it safely. But that separation is neither a simple nor an insignificant process.

Separation, indeed, also involves connection. An individual's ability to see him or herself as separate from another is based on a willingness to recognise at the same time the links with that other. Independence involves dependence. The emergence of the individual as ontologically secure requires both a distancing and a closeness in his or her relationships with others and a complementarity of inner and outer security. Inner and outer, the worlds of subjective and objective reality, have to be distinguished but also related. How is this achieved? What are its implications?

Winnicott argues that the emergence of the individual is a process involving both social and symbolic dimensions, substantially grounded in the experience of space and time, and substantially relevant to an understanding of the emergence of culture. The separation of the individual, the creation of the individual as a social subject, involves the emergence of a space – a potential space (perhaps more accurately a space for potential) in which the work of separation, the separation of 'me' from 'not me' can take place. This potential space is a transitional space in a number of senses. It is a space, as we shall see, in which the first objects emerge in the perception of the infant. The first objects are the first symbols. The first symbols are the product of the first creative acts. And the first creative acts are the first encounters with culture. This space consists, then, in the intermediate area between infant and mother, between subject and object. It is the space within which the infant both tests reality and begins to be able to fantasise, to imagine, to dream, and to play.

The key to the unlocking of this process and of the various elements of it which make it such a deceptively simple one are to be found in Winnicott's discussion of the first possession. The first possession starts with the newborn infant's fist-in-mouth activities and leads eventually to an attachment to a teddy, a doll, a blanket; to what Winnicott calls a transitional object. This object is the focus of a great deal of emotional and cognitive activity. It is the first mark of the infant's recognition that he or she is in some sense separate from the mother. It is the focus of all the powerful emotional energies, desires and fantasies which have been attached to the mother as an extension of the infant, but which are increasingly vulnerable because the mother goes away. This object becomes vitally important to the infant for use at the time of going to sleep, and as a defence against anxiety. It becomes a comfort and a comforter. It is taken everywhere, cherished for its familiarity, a magical object embodying the continuities of care but also the infant's emerging powers of creativity. In terms of a simple metaphorical substitution, which is what it is, the transitional object stands for the breast (as indeed the breast 'stood for the mother' previously), but in the space created by the metaphor it is the object through which the infant begins to distinguish between him/herself and the mother (or as Winnicott puts it, 'between me extensions and not me'), and equally important, between fantasy and reality. The space is the space of illusion: the capacity to imagine, the capacity, indeed, to create meaning. As Winnicott suggests:

> From birth . . . the human being is concerned with the problem of the relationship between what is objectively perceived and what is subjectively conceived of, and in the solution of this problem there is no health for the human being who has not been started off well enough by the mother. *The intermediate area to which I am referring is the area that is allowed to the infant between primary creativity and objective perception based on reality testing.* The transitional phenomena represent the early stages of the use of illusion, without which there is no meaning for the human being in the idea of a relationship with an object that is perceived by others as external to that being.
>
> (Winnicott, 1975, 239, italics in original)

Winnicott identifies this intermediate area of experience with the individual's subsequent capacity to become involved in any creative activity; in the arts, religion, 'imaginative living and . . . creative scientific work' (ibid., 242).

In his discussion of the relationship between transitional phenomena or objects, the emerging individual, and culture, Winnicott is, therefore, making a number of interrelated points (1974, 118). The first is that cultural experience is located in the potential space between the individual and the environment (originally the object). This is also true of play, the first expression of cultural experience. The second is that each individual's capacity to make use of this space is determined by life experiences that take place very early on in an individual's existence. From the very beginning the infant has intense experiences in the potential space between the subjective object (the emerging him or herself) and the object subjectively perceived (the not-me or the other). This potential space is at the interface between there being nothing 'but me' to experience and there being other objects and phenomena outside my control. Every baby has both good and bad, favourable and unfavourable experiences within this potential space. Initially, dependence is maximal. The potential space happens only 'in relation to a feeling of confidence' upon the part of the baby – on his or her ability to trust or to be encouraged to trust – and on the confidence generated by a dependable mother-figure or by environmental elements. Confidence (trust) consists in the introjection (the interiorisation) of evidence of that dependability. Finally, in order to study the play and then the cultural life of the individual, Winnicott argues 'one must study the fate of the potential space between any one baby and the human (and therefore fallible) mother-figure who is essentially adaptive because of love' (ibid.).

I want to apply some of these arguments to television, but before I do there are a number of points to be made arising from my discussion thus far; points that will also, hopefully, make connections with my earlier discussion of ontological security.

The first is by way of a gloss on the kind of argument that Winnicott presents. It may not be necessary to point out (but then again it may be) that Winnicott's talk of mothers and breasts can be seen as both literal (there are real mothers and real breasts and both are objects of intense emotion) and metaphorical; that is the carer may not be a 'mother' as such, and the breast may well be a bottle. Equally his apparent concern with the materiality of the transitional object should not be taken too literally. Not all of us will drag blankets around like Linus in Schultz's cartoon; the space created by the work of the mother-figure, when it has indeed been created, can be filled in all sorts of ways. Winnicott may or may not have believed in the need for an authentic mother or an authentic breast: his characterisation of the 'good enough mother' is sufficiently ambiguous to leave the question open. But it matters not for his argument. What does matter, of course, is the consistency of care and the kind of care an infant receives, and the need to understand the relationship between that care and the capacity of the developing child to establish his or her individuality, to separate off from the mother-figure and to begin to become an independent agent in the world.

The second is perhaps more difficult to deal with. It concerns Winnicott's obvious clinical concern with pathology and health. Once again I think it is possible to distance oneself from the authority of the clinical gaze without sacrificing the main burden of the analysis. By this I mean the following. What Winnicott is pointing to, and I shall be discussing this again in a moment, is the very fine line between pathology and health in matters of creativity, culture and individuality. Dependence and independence are separated by a hair's breadth and yet are totally interdependent; creativity and addiction are expressions of that mutuality. Equally the boundary that separates the individual from those that surround him or her is equally fragile and vulnerable. The line between the good enough mother (or mother figure) and the one who seems to have failed is equally fine and contentious. Once again, though, the strength of Winnicott's position for this discussion is not so much the clinical judgement but the recognition that the environment is a crucial factor in understanding the fundamental development of the individual as a social and cultural agent, and most importantly as a psychodynamic one.

This point releases a third. The challenge that Winnicott poses to sociology is real: different in its focus and more tangible than that posed by Freudian psychoanalysis, and, in a different way, by Lacanian theory (see Giddens, 1991). For Winnicott is presenting a descriptive and an analytic account of the creation of the subject as a social and symbolic unit (not, *pace* Lacan, as a subject fragmented by and through the symbolic) who can of course be damaged and destroyed, but who can develop (and most often does develop) into a viable social actor. He is also presenting an account which requires the social to be taken fundamentally *into* account. But not in a simple relationship of cause and effect.

Potential spaces, transitional phenomena, are just those: potential and transitional. In both cases they speak to the dialectic of dependence and freedom, trust and insecurity, creativity and sterility, potency and omnipotence which mark the particular problematic of action in everyday life. Within this space, and through these – ultimately cultural – phenomena, individuals come to some kind of terms with the subjectively perceived, objective circumstances of their early and then their later environment. Winnicott's psychodynamic theory is therefore also a sociological theory. And its appropriation here is not, once again, a slip into reductionism but a challenge to understand society and culture in terms of its construction by individuals in environments which are not often of their own making.

The equation which is being offered here is one which Giddens has already, but in a different register, provided. It is an equation of trust, security and the capacity to act, both individually and socially. To this Winnicott adds, explicitly, the capacity to create. He draws in culture, but he also, through his discussion of transitional objects, draws in media.

> I have used the term cultural experience as an extension of the idea of transitional phenomena and of play without being certain that I can define the word 'culture'. The accent indeed is on experience. In using the word culture I am thinking of the inherited tradition. I am thinking of something that is in the common pool of humanity, into which individuals and groups of people may contribute, and from which we may all draw *if we have somewhere to put what we find*.
>
> (Winnicott, 1974, 116, italics in original)

I sympathise with Winnicott's troubles with the definition of culture. His last emphasis above, however, provides a powerful metaphor for understanding culture as something in which we all participate, but with different degrees of competence and with different degrees of freedom. Equally the phrase 'if we have somewhere to put what we find' does imply that we need to understand the dynamics of that participation.

Crucial to this participation is the transitional phenomenon, the transitional object. The point I want to make here is this. Winnicott draws attention to the central role the transitional object has both for the child's development and for the creation in the newly separating individual of a sense of identity and security within a challenging world of self and others. In the normal scheme of things the emotional significance of the early, intensely cathected object is reduced, eventually, to insignificance. The space it occupied is filled by other cultural activities and forms which continue the work of providing relief from the strain of relating inner and outer reality (indeed, as he points out (1975, 240) the task of reality acceptance is never complete). This cultural work continues, with its consequent satisfactions and frustrations, and with the continuing reliance on objects and media to facilitate it. I want to suggest that our media, television perhaps preeminently, occupy the potential space released by blankets, teddy bears and breasts (Young, 1986), and function cathectically and culturally as transitional objects. As such, they are, of course, vulnerable to the exigencies of our own individual upbringing as well as to the environments in which they are both produced and consumed. And vulnerable also to the precarious balance of pathology and health towards which Winnicott is clinically so sensitive, and to which I also must briefly once again pay attention.

The link between Winnicott's arguments and my own, and the status of media as transitional objects can usefully be illustrated, in the first instance, by drawing on one of Winnicott's own case studies: the case of the string (1965). The case concerned a seven-year-old boy with an obsession with string. He was constantly tying chairs and tables together; he would tie cushions to the fireplace, and prior to his being seen by Winnicott he had been found tying a string round his sister's neck. Winnicott interpreted this behaviour as the boy's attempt to deal with his fear of his mother's separation (the mother had been separated from the boy for considerable periods on more than one occasion): 'attempting to deny separation by his use of string, as one would deny separation from a friend by using the telephone' (ibid., 154). The boy's symptoms were alleviated as a result of the mother's ability to discuss her son's anxieties with him.

Winnicott comments on the symbolic significance of string as an extension of all other techniques of communication. String, symbolically and materially, is for joining things together: 'it helps in the wrapping up of objects and in the holding of unintegrated material'. This is its common significance, yet for this boy its significance was exaggerated and his use of it seemed abnormal. Its use was associated with a sense of insecurity and the idea of a lack of communication. String had become not so much a joining medium but one associated with the denial of separation. 'As a denial of separation string becomes a thing in itself, something which has dangerous properties and has to be mastered.' For Winnicott this case was useful both in exploring pathology in relation to transitional phenomena and as an example of the development of a potential perversion. In later comments (1974) he notes that the boy was not cured and developed new addictions, including addictions to drugs, during his adolescence.

How does this case help in the understanding of the media? As part of his later comments Winnicott asks whether an investigator making a study of drug addiction would pay proper attention to the psychopathology evident in the area of transitional phenomena. My argument, in relation to the use of television, both pathological and non-pathological, creative and addictive, is explicitly the same. But there is more to it, I think, than matters of pathology, though such matters loom large in any discussions of the medium, these days and always. There are a number of observations which can be made. The first is a general, sociological rather than psychoanalytic, one about addiction. The addiction to string may be an exception (and indeed Winnicott does not explain why the child's relationship to string is itself addictive, or leads to further addiction), but quite clearly the regular cycle of moral panics associated with the introduction of new media is most often associated with the fear of addiction (see Shotton, 1989; Spigel, 1992 on television). Addiction is plausibly, as Giddens has suggested in correspondence, a particularly modern pathology, since it emerges out of the often unmanageable demands for self-autonomy that life in modern society creates. Addiction and obsession are transferrable (they attach themselves to multiple objects and practices), but it seems that they are most pervasive (and often also most troubling) when the media provide their focus. More particularly the string case illustrates that the same object can be used both positively and negatively, and that addiction and creation are very closely related to each other. But it also illustrates the ways in which an understanding of the use of such a medium as string can be grounded in the early experiences of childhood, precisely in relation to such issues as security, separation and the desire for communication. If string is a very simple medium indeed television, of course, is another story.

CULTURAL SPACE IN GENERAL AND TELEVISION IN PARTICULAR

Potential space – the space in which identities are formed with or without the involvement of transitional objects, in an environment of trust or the absence of trust – potential space is the place in which the seeds of culture are sown. But Winnicott acknowledges that the seeds are sown in paradoxical ground:

> the essential feature in the concept of transitional objects and phenomena . . . is *the paradox, and the acceptance of the paradox*: the baby creates the object, but the object was there waiting to be created and to become a cathected object . . . we will never challenge the baby to elicit an answer to the question: did you create that or did you find it?
>
> (Winnicott, 1974, 104, italics in original)

This is a fundamental paradox indeed. It runs right the way through any and every discussion of culture or creativity. And it runs very powerfully through all discussions of the role of television and of the television audience. I will return to it in my last chapter. For the moment, however, it is important to note that while we may not wish to question the child, we do have to question the implications of that paradox as it works its way through the experience of culture and especially the experience of television (see Hodge and Tripp, 1986, Ch. 3; though note that theirs is substantially a cognitive–Piagetian based analysis).

The present question however is this. What is it about television that makes

it such a potentially significant transitional object? The question is a reasonable one because television, like string, is neither an infinitely malleable nor
a neutral object. In his pathological engagement with the string, the boy in
Winnicott's case study used something which already had both a practical and
a symbolic significance. Television also comes pre-packed as it were: a
complex communication of sound and image with already powerful reality
and emotional claims.

Perhaps the first observation to be made is that television will become a
transitional object in those circumstances where it is already constantly
available or where it is consciously (or semi-consciously) used by the mother-
figure as a baby sitter: as her or his own replacement while she or he cooks the
dinner or attends, for whatever length of time, to something else, somewhere
else. The continuities of sound and image, of voices or music, can be easily
appropriated as a comfort and a security, simply because they are there.
Television's availability, then, is clearly one aspect, but there is also another.

Winnicott's account of the creation of the transitional object depends on a
kind of reality testing in which the infant is presumed to follow a sequence in
relation to it. The sequence begins with the infant's relating to the object, then
'finding it', and then, at least in fantasy, destroying it, but since it survives
destruction (it exists despite all my efforts to deny it) it can be used, adored
and depended upon. Television survives all efforts at its destruction. It is, in
Williams' (1974) terms, in constant flow, and switching it off (in anger, in
frustration, or in boredom) does not destroy it. We can switch it on again and
it demonstrates its invulnerability and its dependability. Any challenge we
might make to its content, our rejection or acceptance of its messages is, I
want to suggest, based in this primary level of aceptance and trust. Television
is, as many observers have noted, constantly present. It is eternal. This quality
of the medium is one that also guarantees its potential status as a transitional
object even for those who may have grown up without it. My argument, of
course, is not that television is outgrown. On the contrary it can and does
continue to occupy potential space throughout an individual's life, though
obviously with different degrees of intensity and significance.

But this capacity to provide a permanent presence and, in so doing, a
colonisation of potential space is not simply a function of the quality of the
technology. Many technologies, particularly communicating or informing
technologies (Young, 1986; Turkle, 1986) do indeed have the capacity to
generate a degree of dependence, security and attachment in a similar way to
television; each case is potentially both creative and addictive. But these
attachments are over-determined by the content of the media, and in
television's case through its schedules, genres and narratives. Television is
a cyclical phenomenon. Its programmes are scheduled with consuming
regularity. Soap operas, weather reports and news broadcasts, perhaps
above all, provide a framework for the hours, days and weeks of the year
(Scannell, 1988).

There is what I might call an ontological circle in play. The regularity and sequentiality of television programming is often justified on economic grounds (Smith, 1976), and while evidence suggests that it is rare that an individual will watch every episode of a series (Goodhardt, Ehrenberg and Collins, 1975) or every news broadcast, there are profound economies of scale and scope to be had by a continuing run within television. These economies can of course themselves be understood as a response to the deeply felt needs of audiences and viewers for continuity; needs that are in turn made more pressing perhaps by virtue of the increasingly stressful or threatening world in which we live; a world which is, of course, for most of us only seen on television. So those needs are being massaged or reinforced by the programmes themselves which, in almost every case, are involved in the creation and mediation of anxiety and in its resolution. For example the weather, the most consistently watched television programme (Mellencamp, 1990), provides constant reassurance (even in times of bad weather) both of the ability to control the elements (albeit only through talk and graphics and, particularly on US weather shows by reporters who rival air hostesses both in their claims for the ownership of the object, 'I have today a few clouds for you', and their ability to project confidence), and to encourage or reassure the viewer that tomorrow will be (basically) all right. Likewise in the case of soap opera; soaps have been understood as constant masticators of social realities, provoking and reassuring within a complex narrative and through the medium of strong and identifiable reality claims (Livingstone, 1990).

But it is the news, I think, which holds pride of place as the genre in which it is possible to see most clearly the dialectical articulation of anxiety and security – and the creation of trust – which overdetermines television as a transitional object, particularly for adult viewers.

News has long been recognised (Wright, 1968, 1974) as a genre whose function is reassurance as well as surveillance. In a fascinating study of a fascinating situation, Turner *et al.* (1986) have charted the role of the media in contributing to the social reality and security of those living on or alongside the San Andreas Fault in California. The study was undertaken before the recent (1988) earthquake, but it reveals a finely balanced cycle in the news programming of anxiety generation (mostly in terms of reporting the latest predictions or 'scientific' evidence in relation to possible future movements of the fault) and reassurance (in which scientific experts are debunked or the tension resolved in some other way). This is, of course, an intense example of the essential tension within the news: both in the narrativity of anxiety creation and resolution and in the dominance of form over content ('How come they call it news if it's always the same?' asks a child in a *New Yorker* cartoon; see Park, 1940; Galtung and Ruge, 1965).

Reassurance is not provided only, of course, in the content of reporting. On the contrary. Yet the levels of anxiety that could be raised (and of course may well be either inevitably or deliberately raised) are ameliorated both in terms of the structure of the news as a programme (the tidying of papers, mutual smiles and silent chat following a 'human interest' story complete news bulletins, except under exceptional circumstance of crisis or catastrophe, all over the world), and in terms of its reliability and frequency. It is no surprise that perhaps the first international single strand satellite cable channel was CNN's News, providing a twenty-four-hour commentary (reassuring by its very persistence) on the events of the world. On the other hand 'real' news, news of catastrophe, is often the occasion for the interruption of the regular programming (a catastrophe of another kind for those committed to a regular pattern of viewing, and an example of the tendency towards homology in the forms and content of television). The gradual withdrawal of the reporting of the event into the regular news programmes is, once again, evidence of its incorporation into the familiar and hopeful, distancing and denying (Doane, 1990, 235) structures of the daily schedule. News is addictive, the more so when the world is unsettled. News is a key institution in the mediation of threat, risk and danger, and on Giddens' terms as well as Winnicott's, central to our understanding of our capacity to create and maintain our ontological security. And it is this, as well as (or as much as) its significance as its role as a provider of information (a term which itself needs careful attention), which needs to be understood if we are to recognise the basis for television's persistent importance in everyday life.

Finally there is the issue of illusion. This is an extraordinarily complex phenomenon and one to which I can scarcely do justice here. For Winnicott the transitional object is both the focus and the mediator of the constant shifting between illusion and disillusion that marks the beginnings of reality testing and the emergence of the individual as a viable social actor. The mother's job, in his terms, is to provide the basis for the illusion in the child that she is part of the child and then (in weaning) to provide the basis for disillusion. The transitional object, the location of the first not-me experiences, is the locus of both; it offers a secure site for the exploration and test of the complex relations between reality and fantasy.

Recent discussions in the literature on children's relationship to television (Palmer, 1986; Hodge and Tripp, 1986) have drawn attention to the creative work engaged in by children in relation to the medium; to the appropriation of, for example television's fantasy images into the world of private fantasy and to the creation for themselves of a comfortable physical environment in which to watch. As Palmer (1986, 133, 67) herself notes: 'Observations of children show them to be manipulators of the set. They enjoy switching it on and playing with it. They are confident and able in adjusting the set to find their programmes, but they rarely switch it off.' Television is the focus of games, play and acting out. Palmer, in particular, argues for the importance of television in a child's life precisely as a mediator of reality and illusion and (both for good and ill) as a crucial resource in the reality testing activities of the child.

However television is not just a child's medium. Clearly the arguments about its status as a transitional object have to continue to be relevant to the adult experience of the medium as well. Many observers (Postman, 1987; Hartley, 1987) have regarded television as, in significant respects, infantalising or regressive. Watching television, it is argued, is a regressive experience which drags the adult into a comatose, infantile state of uncritical attention; or, in another version of the argument, through the mode of address of the programmes themselves, television creates a paedocratic regime (Hartley, 1987) – infantalising and disempowering the viewer. I will deal in more detail with these arguments in a later chapter. At this point I need to point out only that the implication of my argument too is that television must offer a regressive experience, if by regressive is understood a return to some earlier phases of an individual's development or to a withdrawal to a dream-like state (Laplanche and Pontalis, 1973, 386). However in neither sense of the term need it be assumed that what is being described is necessarily pathological. It can be, of course. But it need not be.

ROUTINES, RITUALS, TRADITIONS, MYTHS

If the subject cannot be grasped save through the reflexive constitution of daily activities in social practices, we cannot understand the mechanics of personality apart from the routines of day-to-day life . . . Routine is integral both to the continuity of the personality of the agent, as he or she moves along the paths of daily activities, and to the institutions of society, which *are* such only through their continued reproduction.

(Giddens, 1984, 60)

Routines, rituals, traditions, myths, these are the stuff of social order and everyday life. Within the familiar and taken for granted, as well as through the heightened and the dramatic, our lives take shape and within those shapes, spatially and temporally grounded and signified, we attempt to go about our business, avoiding or managing, for the most part, the traumas and the catastrophes that threaten to disturb our peace and our sanity. It is not always easy. Not only are we faced with the persistent contradictions and irresolvable challenges of daily life – problems of death, identity, morality – but the bases on which our security is grounded shift with each twist of the modern or post-modern screw; with industrialisation and post-industrialisation, with shifts in population, social structure, technology and cultural values. These shifts and their ontological effects have been much discussed in recent years (Lasch, 1977; Berger *et al.*, 1974; Ignatieff, 1984). Significant among prime causes are, it is often argued, the media, above all television (Postman, 1987; Mander, 1978).

But, for most of us most of the time, everyday life does go on, and it is sustained through the ordered continuities of language, routine, habit, the taken for granted but essential structures that, in all their contradictions, sustain the grounds for our security in our daily lives. These comments may seem jejune. They are nevertheless central to our understanding of the place of the media, not just as disturbers (their most common characterisation), but also as sustainers, of social reality. I would like in this final section of the chapter to change register and move attention away from the individual and the psychodynamic to the collective and the social, but to do so in a way that preserves the basic concern: the ground base of social life and the crucial importance of the symbolic in making sense of it.

Ontological security is sustained through the familiar and the predictable. Our commonsense attitudes and beliefs express and sustain our practical understandings of the world, without which life would quickly become intolerable. Common sense is sustained by practical knowledge and expressed and supported by a whole range of symbols and symbolic formations. The symbols of daily life: the everyday sights and sounds of natural language and familiar culture; the publicly broadcast media texts on billboards, in newspapers, on television; the highly charged and intense private and public rituals in domestic or national rites of passage or international celebrations; all these symbols, in their continuity, their drama and their ambiguity, are also bids for control (see Martin, 1981, 70 on working-class culture). Defensive or offensive, they are our attempts, as social beings, to manage nature, to manage others, and to manage ourselves. They have their roots in the individual's experience of the basic contradictions of social life: the independence–dependence, identity–difference problem which Winnicott analyses; and they also have their roots in the collective experience of sociality, in the demands of co-presence or face-to-face interaction (Goffman, 1969), in the emotional charge of the sacred (Durkheim, 1971) and in the demands of and for structure expressed in all our cultural forms, prototypically in myth (Lévi-Strauss, 1968) and ritual (Turner, 1969).

What is the issue here? It is the place of television in the visible and hidden ordering of everyday life; in its spatial and temporal significance; in its embeddedness in quotidian patterns and habits, as a contributor to our security. Television as object: the screen providing the focus of our daily rituals and the frame for the limited transcendence – the suspension of disbelief – which marks our excursions from the profane routines of the daily grind into the sacred routines of schedules and programmes. Television as medium: extending our reach and our security in a world of information, locking us into a network of time-space relations, both local and global, domestic and national, which threaten to overwhelm us but also to provide the basis for our claims for citizenship or membership of community and neighbourhood. Television as entertainer and as informer: providing in its genres and its narratives stimulation and disturbance, peace and reassurance, and offering within their own order an expression and a reinforcement of the containing temporalities of the everyday.

> Since social life has some order, yet moves continuously – on the grand scale through historical time – on the micro-scale through each hour, its movement requires a great deal of subtle meshing between the regular and the improvised, the rigid and the flexible, the repetitive and the varying. Social life proceeds somewhere between the imaginary extremes of absolute order, and absolute chaotic conflict and anarchic improvisation. Neither the one nor the other takes over completely.
>
> (Moore and Myerhoff, 1977, 3)

The routines and rhythms of everyday life are multiply structured in time and space. The daily patterns of work and leisure, of getting up and going to bed, of housework and homework: the clock times, free and indentured, are themselves embedded in the times of biography and the life-cycle, and in the times of institutions and of societies themselves – the *longue durée*, slow and glacial (Scannell, 1988, 15). Everyday life is the product of all these temporalities, but it is in the first, in the experienced routines and rhythms of the day, that time is felt, lived and secured. And time is secured in the equally differentiated and ordered spaces of everyday life: the public and the private spaces; the front-stages and the back-stages; the spaces of gender and generation, domesticity and community.

Television is very much part of the taken for granted seriality and spatiality of everyday life. Broadcast schedules reproduce (or define) the structure of the household day (itself significantly determined by the temporality of work in industrial society (Thompson, 1968; Horkheimer and Adorno, 1972), particularly of the housewife (Modleski, 1983). Narrative patterns themselves, the essential recursiveness of beginnings, middles and ends, and of action and characterisation, offer a homological expression of, and a model for, the paramount narrativity of experience (Ricoeur, 1984). Broadcast national events articulate calendar time: at Christmas, Thanksgiving, Coronation (Shils and Young, 1953) or Royal Wedding (Dayan and Katz, 1992), Cup Final or Superbowl (Real, 1982). Similarly our everyday spatiality is grounded in the patterns of everyday life as we move together and separate around the single or multiple television sets in bedrooms, sitting rooms, bars and public arenas. And it is grounded in the shifting relationship of global and local which television articulates and refashions (Meyrowitz, 1985), extending reach and shifting boundaries both phenomenologically and materially.

Everyday times and spaces can, in the main, be thought of as profane. We can and do distinguish them from those events, predictable or manageable (like birthdays or weddings, births and deaths), which are the focus of more or less satisfying domestic rituals, and also from those events, either predictable and manageable or dramatically unsettling and terrifying, for whose ritualisation we depend on television. The shift into the 'as-if' (Vaihinger, 1924) world of television both in its factual and fictional programming is both a part of, and not a part of, the everyday (see Turner (1969), on the betwixt and between-ness of the liminal as a characterisation of ritual). Even within the pattern of the domestic day, certain times, certain programmes, are marked and protected, as special. During those times or programmes the pattern of the day is both preserved and interrupted. Phones are not answered. Meals are not cooked. Dishes are not washed. These paradoxically 'daily' rituals are firmly integrated into the structure of everyday life. But even those that are not so easily integrated, those that challenge and disturb and which therefore provide the focus for a ritualised or ritualising response can be seen to be articulated into daily life (often) through television and television culture. Christmases, which are both intensively domestic and extensively public, are celebrated around the television set. Weddings, which increasingly are being video-recorded, are therefore being overdetermined as ritual by their incorporation into television culture. And crises and catastrophes, the natural or the man-made disasters, are 'managed' by the highly regularised and ritualised structures and flow of the news (Mellencamp, 1990; Alexander, 1986). All these events are expressions of the medium's capacity to mobilise the sacred and to create what anthropologists have called 'communitas'; the shared experience, however fragile, momentary and synthetic, of community.

Traditions may change but tradition remains. As Giddens (1990, 105) argues: tradition 'contributes in basic fashion to ontological security insofar as it sustains trust in the continuity of past, present and future, and connects such trust to routinised social practices'. Once again this argument holds both for private and public traditions, the increasingly interdependent traditions of both family and nation. As Scannell suggests:

> as fast as particular ceremonies and symbols lose their resonance and are relegated to the lumber-room of history, others replace them. In the process of modernisation ritual and tradition shed their intimacy with religion as new secular traditions were rapidly and prolifically invented. Nowhere was this more diligently pursued than in the reconstruction of images and emblems of nationhood.
>
> (Scannell, 1988, 16)

Scannell points to the increasing ritualisation of nationhood in which broadcasting was materially involved. But these new traditions were not those just of the media. They were, if they were to have any meaning, also to become the traditions, and the pleasures, of the hearth (Frith, 1983). Television may have provided a new content for domestic and national rituals, but it essentially preserved both their traditional form and their function.

Preserved, too, were and are the familiar and barely disguised forms of narrativity within television programmes which, in both factual and fictional expressions, provide a secure framework for the representation and control of the unfamiliar or threatening. This mythic character of television has often been noted. It refers to the persistence of familiar oral forms of storytelling –

to the structured narratives of folklore present in news, drama and documentary; to the particular functional significance of forms of storytelling as articulating the endemic and irresolvable contradictions of the host society; and it refers also to the ideological character of images and stories which naturalise and disguise the reality of the historical and the man-made (Barthes, 1972).

Patricia Mellencamp offers a particularly interesting example of the process of mythification in her discussion of television's treatment of catastrophe (catastrophe can have for television the same significance as Garfinkel's experiments with trust have in relation to the structure of the everyday: both reveal, through their challenge, the character of the taken for granted). What makes this example so interesting here is both the exploration of a factual rather than a fictional form (and of the status of 'information' as a social and symbolic force) and the exploration of the representation of catastrophe through a discussion of the amelioration of anxiety:

> Like a doctor detailing medical procedures to a patient before and after surgery, information [on or about catastrophe, RS] here provides a therapeutic service, a ritual akin to prayer or chanting. Cloaked as an epistemé, a desire to know, it soothes our anxiety, protecting us from fear. Thus, information, the raison d'être of coverage, becomes story, therapy, and collective ritual. Later it will be known as myth.
>
> (Mellencamp, 1990, 248)

These are themes to which I will return. Suffice it now to let me draw together some of the threads of this first chapter and attempt a summary of this first stage of my argument.

Television is part of the grain of everyday life. I have tried in this chapter to provide an account of how that might be considered to have come about. Not as a result of some arbitrary or political imposition of a medium on a resistant culture (though that will also be part of an explanation under certain circumstances) but as the result of its occupation of the particular spaces and times of a basic level of social reality. I stress space and time, and will continue to do so, for good reason. There are no real surprises in offering these two categories as primary ones in an attempt to understand the preconditions for the possibility of social life and for an individual's place and competence within it. The juxtaposition of the two theories of Giddens and Winnicott is an attempt to provide a theoretical matrix for my own efforts at charting the territory, since Giddens' metaphors and preoccupations are principally temporal and Winnicott's are principally spatial. The media – television of course preeminently – are (probably by any definition and certainly in practice) mediators of both space and time, and are produced and consumed in space and time. The quality of space and time in each case is significant both materially and symbolically.

Yet television is so much a funadamental part of our everyday life that it needs to be understood, I have suggested, both at a psychodynamic as well as at a sociological level. The identification of psychoanalytic theory in general, and Winnicott's theory in particular, as a plausible basis for offering an explanation (rather than, at least initially, more strictly psychological explanations) is because of its ability to offer an account of the development of the individual that brings together the social and the symbolic on the one hand and an understanding of the dynamics of conscious and unconscious processes on the other. Giddens offers a similarly structured account. Television is absent in the work of both, but it requires, perhaps no less or no more than other social products, but nevertheless crucially, the same multivalent approach. This has been my argument. It grounds all that follows.

Chapter 2

Television and a place called home

Television is a domestic medium. It is watched at home. Ignored at home. Discussed at home. Watched in private and with members of family or friends. But it is part of our domestic culture in other ways too, providing in its programming and its schedules models and structures of domestic life, or at least of certain versions of domestic life. It is also a means for our integration into a consumer culture through which our domesticity is both constructed and displayed.

Recent research has begun to take television's domesticity seriously. It has attempted to understand the social dynamics that take place around the television set and that construct it as an element in the private culture of the home: gendered, aged, multiply dispersed in differently occupied spaces, differentially connected to a secondary technology – the computer or the VCR – and serviced by an increasingly large selection of broadcast and narrowcast channels. Television has become embedded in the complex cultures of our own domesticity. We can no more think of television as anything other than a necessary component of that domesticity than we can think of our domesticity without seeing both in the machine and the screen a reflection and an expression of that domestic life.

That domestic life, both in ideal and reality, is however not just a sociological but also a cultural and an historical phenomenon. It is, to a significant degree, the creation of a bourgeois class newly risen to commercial and cultural prominence in the early nineteenth century. That class was able to create and display a private world, separate from the world of affairs; a world in which personal pleasures and social preoccupations could be sustained and protected, shielded from the attentions of the public. In this (domestic) interior a different world could be created; a world of images, desires and illusions. As Walter Benjamin, writing about the emergence of the private citizen under Louis-Philippe suggested:

> For the first time the living space became distinguished from the place of work. The former constituted itself as the interior. The office was its complement. The private citizen who in the office took reality into account,

required of the interior that it should support him in his illusions. This necessity was all the more pressing since he had no intention of adding social preoccupations to his business ones. In the creation of his private environment he suppressed them both. From this sprang the phantasmagorias of the interior. This represented the universe for the private citizen. In it he assembled the distant in space and time. His drawing room was a box in the world theatre.

(Benjamin, 1976 (1983), 176)

The modern interior is still as Benjamin described it. It is still a place where the illusions of control, the ability to 'assemble the distant in time and space' are fundamental, even in their absence. But it is, in all respects, a much more complex and contradictory place (e.g. Putnam and Newton, 1990; Tomlinson, 1990a). Perhaps it always was. It is no longer, of course, only a bourgeois place. It is gendered and highly differentiated according to geography, class position and culture. It can be a place of conflict and despair as well as of peace and security. It can be a haven or a prison. And our interiors are not just physical spaces. They are social, economic, cultural and political spaces. And they are technological spaces. And in all these dimensions our domesticity is unsettled and vulnerable, extending beyond the physical spaces of the house, or the social relations of the family, into a world of change, of movement. Running through the dynamics of these complex shifts and instabilities, informing them, supporting them, reflecting them, reflecting on them and reassuring us about them, is television.

In this chapter I shall be concerned with the domestic interior and with television's place within it. I shall argue that although we need to preserve our concern with television as a domestic medium, and understand its contribution to that changing and fragmenting domesticity, we should recognise that domesticity is itself problematic. The boundaries around house and home are not equivalent, nor are they impermeable. Our domesticity is the product of a historically defined and constantly shifting relationship between public and private spaces and cultures, a shifting relationship to which television itself contributes. That domesticity is at once a phenomenological, a socio-cultural and an economic reality.

These dimensions of domesticity can be addressed through various differently focused conceptualisations, each expressing, though by no exclusive demarcation, one element of that reality through which we still appear to want to distinguish the private from the public world. I will identify these different dimensions of our domesticity as home, family and household.

There is a certain irony and difficulty in this undertaking, since home, family and household are, in much current writing, only there to be denied. In a post-modern world of movement, fragmentation and globalisation, the always ideological securities attached to the claims of home (Massey, 1992), the equally ideological support of patriarchy embedded in the family (Barrett,

1980), and the complex economic systems that create (but equally have often undermined the integrity of) the household, are all seen as breaking down. Yet by the same token they survive, albeit not unchanged or unchanging. Teasing out television's role in the dynamics of these changes is no easy thing to do. Yet the nature of that domesticity in which we (in all our differences) receive the medium, has to be understood. For it is there, in all its cultural, social and economic dimensions, that television culture is received and reconstructed.

HOME

Home is a construct. It is a place not a space. It is the object of more or less intense emotion. It is where we belong. Yet such a sense of belonging is not confined to house or garden. Home can be anything from a nation to a tent or a neighbourhood. Home, substantial or insubstantial, fixed or shifting, singular or plural, is what we can make of it.[1]

Agnes Heller sees home, however, quite simply as a base:

Integral to the average everyday life is awareness of a fixed point in space, a firm position from which we 'proceed' . . . and to which we return in due course. This firm position is what we call 'home' . . . 'Going home' should mean: returning to that firm position which we know, to which we are accustomed, where we feel safe, and where our emotional relationships are at their most intense.

(Heller, 1984, 239)

The home is easily idealised. In part, that is its function in everyday discourse. And it is quite easy to see under what circumstances home can be considered, and becomes, a place to be left, avoided or denied. It is equally possible to see home as offering multiple and indeterminate references. In those various references, both literal and metaphorical, what is being articulated is a construct, materially conditioned by circumstance (of migration or stasis) and culture, but a construct which gains its power, which makes its claims, through an emotional attachment to place – to some place at some time.

Yet its idealisation has a function, and as such it has consequences for the conduct and evaluation of our everyday lives and for our feelings of security, attachment and loss. Home is a powerful concept. To characterise someone as homeless is to imply some kind of moral lack or weakness. Attachment to place and being able to be placed are crucial elements in contemporary life, the more so as we begin to recognise how vulnerable and difficult our lives are becoming.

It is this power granted to place and articulated through ideas and ideologies of home that many geographers have identified as a key if not to modernity then at least as a key to a critique of modernity. As Edward Relph suggests:

Probably it is true that modern man is . . . a homeless being, and that there has been widespread loss of attachment to home places. But the dismissal of the significance of home . . . is too sweeping; there are surely more stages of association with home places than complete attachment and complete unattachment.

(Relph, 1976, 40; see Berger *et al.*, 1974)

Underlying any discussion of the home is a prior distinction. It is the distinction between place and space (Relph, 1976; Seamon, 1979; Buttimer, 1980). That distinction is an expression of an experiential difference between those areas of the world, large or small, for which we have no feeling and those for which we do. Places are human spaces, the focus of experience and intention, memories and desires. They are not abstractions. They are, perhaps above all, important sources of individual and communal identity (Relph, 1976, 141). Edward Relph suggests that in our daily lives we may be largely unaware of the ties that bind us to places, but that does not alter their significance. Places will be located in our sensibilities for a variety of different reasons associated with our own presents and pasts or the presents and pasts of others. We relate to places, he suggests, in the same way that we relate to people: because places without people are no longer places, places are essentially and completely human:

But if we are really rooted in a place and attached to it, if this place is authentically our *home*, then all of these facets are profoundly significant and inseparable. Such home places are indeed foundations of man's existence, providing not only the context for all human activity, but also security and identity for individuals and groups.

(Relph, 1976, 41)

There is a fearful romanticism in all of this, but there is a reality too. And it is a reality which can be understood not just when spaces and places are compared, but when the notion of placelessness is introduced. Placelessness involves the leaching of humanity from places. It refers to an environment without significant places and also to an underlying attitude which does not recognise significance in places. 'It reaches back into the deepest levels of place, cutting roots, eroding symbols, replacing diversity with uniformity and experiential order with conceptual order. At its most profound it consists of a pervasive and perhaps irreversible alienation from places as the homes of men' (Relph, 1976, 143.) The struggle between place and placelessness is a struggle, perhaps, between modernity and post-modernity (Berman, 1983, Harvey, 1989). But it is also an everyday struggle, as we fight to create and maintain place and home in a world of increasing placelessness.

Home is therefore a relational concept. For the geographer Anne Buttimer, home is intimately connected with what she calls the 'horizons of reach'. The relationship between home and reach is an expression of 'the lived reciprocity of movement and rest, territory and range, security and adventure, housekeeping and husbandry, community building and social organisation' (Buttimer, 1980, 170). Reach is important and once again it is a complex notion involving both physical, social and imaginative extensions of the individual from base, roots and the familiar routines of daily activities in space and time. Home is the base for our actions, and it is the place to which we return, but its significance and its power is dependent on how far we have travelled and how long we have been away.

Clearly the nature of the reciprocity between home and reach has shifted quite dramatically historically. And 'reach' is now something disengaged from physical movement (Giddens, 1984). It is infinitely extended through our involvement with the mass media (Harvey, 1989). However it is possible to question how far that extension of reach, as one expression of the consequences of technologically induced post-modernity, has actually transformed, or threatened to transform, the nature of our domesticity and, in particular, our attachment to home. As Doreen Massey (1992) points out (and as Marjorie Ferguson (1990) has argued in a different context) the new forms of social, temporal and spatial relations embodied in the communications media have yet to transform the lives of most of us.

Home, then, is a manifestation of an investment of meaning in space. It is a claim we make about a place. It is constructed through social relations which are both internal and external and constantly shifting in their power and significance. Home, in geographical theory, but also in object relations theory is a potential space, as Doreen Massey recognises in her elucidation of its gendered quality (a gendering engendered, in her argument, by the different relationships formed between mothers and boy and girl children) (Massey, 1992, 14).

David Seamon (1979, 78ff.) sees home as the product of physical presence, familiarity, ritual, possession, control and restoration. His phenomenology offers an account of subjective perceptions of home derived from empirical study. However his respondents constructed those perceptions without, it would appear, recognising that what they were describing was still an ideal. They failed to recognise home as both full of conflict and political. None of the elements of at-homeness can be understood without recognising that homes can also be prisons. And that the reality of home life (as opposed to the idealisation of home) can be, and often is, intensely disputed, and intensely exploitative.

In particular the meanings of home are vulnerable to changes in life experience. Judith and Andrew Sixsmith (1990), in their discussion of the home-life of the unemployed and the elderly, suggest that 'home' can be divided into three experiential domains: the personal which they describe as a private space, an escape, a place of and for, memory and solitude; the social, a place for family life; and the physical, a place of comfort and security. Each of these domains can be both positively or negatively experienced. For the unemployed especially home can, indeed, become a prison. In many ways, they suggest, 'positive and negative experiences of home are two sides of the same coin: refuge or prison, privacy or isolation. Thus "home" is not something that is given directly from the environment, but is a function of the person–place dialectic' (ibid., 24).

This characterisation of the home as a complex and conflictful place is reinforced by Jennifer Mason (1989) in her study of long-married couples. The home is the site of the intersections and articulation of public and private meanings and realities, and she too recognises that home is a material, spatial, temporal, social and a 'metaphysical' (ideological or moral) entity (ibid., 103). Home also involves gender and power relations:

> The home, what it is, what it means, and how it is experienced, does not just happen, or get structurally determined, but is the product of negotiations by people who operate within certain constraints.
>
> (Ibid., 104)

Television and other media are part of home – part of its idealisation, part of its reality. The dimension of home that involves positive feelings of security and belonging are both challenged and reinforced by a medium that brings the world into the interior. New media or unacceptable images are threatening, and television is something that has to be controlled, if only on behalf of the children. Yet the 'box in the corner' is, in our dependence on it, a crucial link to a shared or shareable world of community and nation (Anderson, 1983) and, as such, acts to extend the boundaries of home beyond the front door. Television may be received 'at home' but 'home' itself is both constructed through, and constructs, other realities, and television is implicated in all of them.

Let me suggest three interrelated ways in which this is so. The first concerns the relationship between home and reach; the second between home and hearth; the third between home and identity.

Walter Benjamin was writing about reach in the quotation that began this chapter. More recently Joshua Meyrowitz (1985) has discussed television's contribution to changing the relationship between home and reach, and in particular on its impact on those – women and children – who are, at various stages of their lives, literally housebound. 'Television, and other electronic media', he suggests, 'bring [the hostile society of the outer world] into the home and change both the public and domestic spheres' (ibid., 223); and again: 'Television . . . now escorts childen across the globe even before they have permission to cross the street' (ibid., 238).

This has, Meyrowitz argues, a particularly significant impact on gender identities and relationships since what is being brought into the home, and what the 'home' can now reach is the public world of men and masculinities. What is involved is a breaking down of boundaries – those between the sexes in what he terms a 'situational androgyny', and those between public and private spaces. The home is no longer, if it ever was, the preserve of women, nor an unambiguously female domain. Television, together with other electronic media, dislocates place from space and as a result 'the home has, in many ways, become a part of the larger world which we have merely "roofed over and lighted fire in"' (ibid., 225).

These are familiar and provocative arguments involving, as they do, an inflection of McLuhan's idea of the global village. For the same idea, and the same ideal, are embodied in both village and home. Both are addressing the problem of reach and our media's effect on it. However the elisions are unacceptable. So too, in both McLuhan and Meyrowitz, are the scale of the generalisations and the profligacy of the conclusions. Extension of reach does not necessarily involve greater control, nor is reach itself an unambiguous concept, for it is the quality of the contact – the quality of the touch – that surely is the issue.

And at issue too are the claims that can be made on behalf of television that it can and does have the power to shift such deeply engrained values and habits. It will consistently be my argument throughout this book that such a position, though it contains elements of plausibility, is untenable as it stands (see Ferguson, 1990). To be convincing it requires properly to be integrated into the phenomenology of television, and into an understanding of the variety of experienced and empirical worlds – in this case the home – in which it is received.

Home and hearth is perhaps a less contentious matter. Whereas arguments around television and reach plausibly have to do, almost entirely, with its status as a medium, the 'hearth' can be seen to be something which is created both by the physical existence of the TV as an object, often at the focal point of the family room, and by its programming; that is, in the more or less conscious efforts of the early broadcasters, both on radio and television, and particularly in the UK, to create an atmosphere conducive to the sustenance of home (Frith, 1983; Scannell and Cardiff, 1991).

> Broadcasting means the rediscovery of the home. In these days when house and hearth have been largely given up in favour of a multitude of other interests and activities outside, with the consequent disintegration of family ties and affections, it appears that this new persuasion may to some extent reinstate the parental roof in its old accustomed place, for all will admit that this is, or should be, one of the greatest and best influences on life.
>
> (C.A. Lewis, 1942, quoted in Frith, 1983, 110)

As Simon Frith argues, the power and pleasures of early broadcasting lay in its ability to flatter, to deceive, to create through the modes of its address the familiar: familiar voices at familiar times received, it was presumed, in familiar places, and providing a substitute, perhaps, for the stories read beside the fire.

Hearth and reach in these arguments are not easily assimilated concepts since they refer to quite contradictory aspects of television's contribution to home and domesticity. Lewis seems to be making two presumptions. The first is that existing homes and hearths provide a safe container for broadcasting; the second is that broadcasting also provides a safe container for the home. But the extension of reach is, as Meyrowitz notes, not just a matter of safety. It is likely to change existing patterns and values of home life, and, potentially, is even more threatening to the security and comfort of the hearth.

New forms of television delivery systems, as well as multiple receivers in individual households, are likely of course to change even this.

Finally to the question of home and identity, and television's role within that. These are big issues, and perhaps more even than before, concern needs to extend beyond the confines of the domestic. Increasingly it is being argued that questions of identity, and the relationship between identity and location, space and place, are crucial ones in a fragmenting world of migration, dispossession and post-colonialism. Identity is an essentially contested concept, meaning different things to different people at different times, and shifting its significance geographically, historically and socially. We might wish simply to postpone such a discussion completely, recognising both the complexities and pluralities associated with the term, except that, in the domestic context of home, there are a few things that can still usefully be said.

Television provides a link between home and identity in a number of ways, both in its status as a domestic object and through its mediation of images of domesticity which can be seen to be reflective or potentially expresssive of images of home. As Czikszentmihalyi and Rochberg-Halton (1981, 144) suggest:

> The importance of the home derives from the fact that it provides a space for action and interaction in which one can develop, maintain and change one's identity . . . The home is a shelter for those persons and objects that define the self; thus it becomes, for most people, an indispensable symbolic environment.

Czikszentmihalyi and Rochberg-Halton are concerned with the meaning of objects in the home (see also Dittmar, 1992). With arguments that echo those of object relations theory, they identify the important role media technologies play in helping adolescents 'solidify their selves through control of psychic processes' (Czikszentmihalyi and Rochberg-Halton, 1981, 118). In their discussion of television, however, they muddle relations to the set, as an object, and relations to it as a medium, to its programmes, so their conclusions about its status in the home are confused and confusing. Insofar as its significance as an object is concerned, they report a high valuation of it, particularly in relation to sense of self (and particularly for men). However their judgement that televisions are not good vehicles for binding people to their own past because of the rapid obsolescence of a TV set, mistakes the significance of medium and message and completely underestimates both the role of television as a status object in the home (Leal, 1990) and the capacity of memories of television programmes to provide a basis for individual reflection and a shared sense of the past.

Television also provides images of home, homemaking and domesticity (Haralovich, 1988), which in turn can be seen to provide an, albeit highly ideological, resource for individual and domestic identity formation within the home. Haralovich, in particular, shows how images of the homemaker ('the housewife', though the shift in terminology is instructive) in soaps and sit-coms (and in advertising) in the early years of post-war television in the United States, provided an ideology of domesticity which would encourage women to accept a gender identity appropriate to their required role in society; a role supported and sustained both through changes in domestic architecture and the further development of the suburb (see Chapter 3 below) and her mobilisation as a consumer into the post war economy (see also Chapter 5 below).

These aspects of television's role in the construction of home extend beyond the phenomenological, and involve a much wider range of concerns. For home is not just an abstraction and, idealised or not, successful or not, it is produced by individuals within families or other domestic arrangements; within dynamic and complex social units and for the most part behind closed doors.

FAMILY

'Television today is an integral part of the family household – almost another member of the family' (Gunter and Svennevig, 1987, 4). But what, in this context, is the family?

If home can be considered a phenomenological reality, then family can be considered a social one. For David Schneider (1980) the family is a unit of sexual reproduction and as such distinguishable from other social units consisting of relatives. Wilson and Pahl (1988), on the other hand, argue that families can be considered as an action set, a source of social solidarity and gossip and also as a very practical source of material help in coping with problems. Families also provide social identities and basic social coordinates for their members (ibid., 249). Quoting Pitkin (1985, 16), they suggest that 'The family is not a thing to be understood in its composition so much as it is a system of relationships that change over time'; the study of the family should be the study of process. And they conclude that the family should be understood in the terms in which family members themselves define it.

There is no doubt that actually trying to define what a family is is quite an impossible undertaking (see Bernardes, 1986; Wilson and Pahl, 1988). Equally impossible is the likelihood of reaching a conclusion about its significance and status in contemporary society, fought over as it is ideologically, fought through as it is socially.

Fragile or fraught in any individual case though it may be, the family is nevertheless the social unit in which most of our early consumption of media takes place. The relationships that define it, the myths, stories and values that sustain it, the conflicts or crises that threaten it, provide one of the basic social environments in which individuals struggle, on a daily basis, with the problems of everyday life. When media consumption takes place in the family, therefore, it takes place in a complex social setting in which different patterns of cohesion and dispersal, authority and submission, freedom and constraint, are expressed in the various sub-systems of conjugal, parental or sibling relationships and in the relationships that the family has between itself and the outside world. These relationships are played out in variously cramped or expansive, highly differentiated or undifferentiated domestic spaces; and they are played out through variously organised or disorganised, routinised or chaotic domestic temporalities. They are played out in public and they are played out in private. Patterns of media consumption – especially television viewing – are generated and sustained within these social, spatial and temporal relations.

Families create homes and live in households. And it is on the family that much recent research on television has been focused (Morley, 1986; Lull, 1988, 1990; Hobson, 1982). This research is beginning to take seriously the significance of the family as a socio-cultural unit of some complexity, and has sought to understand the use of television within a context of gender relations (Morley, 1986), within the family as a commmunicative system (Lindlof and Traudt, 1983) and in psychodynamic terms (Rogge and Jensen, 1988).

Yet these researchers need to recognise, though some do not, that families are problematic entities, not only in terms of their composition but also in terms of their changing character in modern society. In the UK, for example, only 32 per cent of household units consist of families in the sense of containing adults with children, and while this is still the single largest household unit statistically, it remains the case that around two-thirds of households contain social groups (or individuals) that do not fit the model of the nuclear family. Lone-parent families are rapidly growing in number. So too is the number of households of only one individual.

Equally the boundaries around a family are not clear cut. I have already noted, following Wilson and Pahl (1988) and Bernardes (1986), that the family should be seen as a dynamic social entity extending, potentially and actually, beyond the confines of house and home and really only to be understood, both historically and dynamically, as a process (see Bott, 1971). Researchers in television and the family are also beginning to recognise this and talk of interpretative communities (Lindlof, 1988) to indicate that even at the level of television watching family relations extend into non-kinship networks. Families must be seen as being embedded in a wider set of social relationships, just as the activity of watching television is embedded in the social relationships of the family.

In a review of systems theory and family theory, based principally, but highly suggestively, on the literature in family therapy, Gill Gorell Barnes offers a characterisation of the family as a system in the following terms:

> [as] the patterning of intimate relationships organized over time. In the process of organization, certain behavioural sequences will be selected and conserved and others ruled out. Over time, the sequences within the pattern will be associated with perceptions, thoughts and feelings which constrain members of the family in different ways. The more that the group interact on a regular basis around certain repeated events, the more it is likely that systemic aspects of pattern influence their interrelationships.
>
> (Barnes, 1985, 226)

The perception of the family as a system, while it accurately identifies a primary characteristic of any ongoing social entity, is a perception which is not confined to family therapists. It is not unproblematic of course, for in any individual case it is precisely the status of the individual family as a system which is often at issue. But it provides, potentially quite precisely, a framework both to describe and to analyse a family's uniqueness both as a viable and as a vulnerable social unit, and of course it provides a framework for the comparison of families one to another (see Minuchin, 1974). Above all it offers a route for inquiring into the rule- and role-governed nature of family life and into the ongoing capacity of a family to present itself to itself and others as more or less coherent, more or less self-contained, more or less special.

It is this capacity to regulate and order its own inner life that defines, for David Reiss (1981) the central element in his comprehensive attempt to provide a model for understanding the family. That capacity is in turn predicated on the sharing of a basic set of core assumptions about the world, assumptions which are shared despite disagreements, conflicts and differences between members of the family. Indeed Reiss suggests (1981, 1) that membership of the family is itself based in an often unconscious or inexplicit acceptance of, and a belief in, these abiding assumptions.

Reiss' approach to the family is one which is guided and informed, of course, by his therapeutic interests. But perhaps rather more strikingly than many other similarly derived approaches, it takes seriously not just the differential capacity of families to manage and sustain themselves as social units as a result of their internal structures and dynamics, but also the relationship the family has with its immediate social and cultural environment. This relationship, Reiss argues, is essentially a dialectical one in which the family is active in its transactions with a dominating social world: 'Our approach accords considerable adaptability and creativity to the family itself, at the same time recognising the enormous influences and strong forces in its social world' (ibid., 4). The central component of the Reissian model is therefore the attempt to conceptualise (and for clinical purposes also to operationalise) what it is that makes a family a family. But it does so without insisting on a rigorous boundary around it (often a problem with systems-oriented approaches); it also recognises that family construction and maintenance is an ongoing project sustained in and through the dynamics of social relations both within the household and outside it.

Reiss comes to understand the family through the notion of paradigm. Drawing, as so many have done in other fields, on Thomas Kuhn's use of the term in his attempt to characterise the history and epistemology of science, he describes the family paradigm as the 'central organiser' of the family's shared constructs, sets, expectations and fantasies about its social world. Each family's transactions with its social world is, he suggests, guided by its own paradigm, and families can be distinguished one from another – by the differences in their paradigms (ibid., 2). Family paradigms are the product of, and embody, the families' particular success (or failure) in weaving from the raw materials of their contradictory experiences and their conflicting emotions a more or less consistent basis for action (ibid., 379). In the therapeutic setting, Reiss argues, this perception allows the clinician to address the family's own conception and construction of the world as a basis for understanding family life and, presumably, for intervention. In the context of the present argument it provides another element of the framework for understanding the crucial significance of the social and cultural setting in which television is received.

However before considering this directly in more detail, I need briefly to return to Reiss for an important discussion of the centrality of the management of space and time as factors in the ability of families to create and sustain their family paradigm.

In a complex but fascinating analysis Reiss distinguishes between family ceremonials (both consecration and degradation ceremonials) and what he calls pattern regulators. The first are infrequent but highly significant ceremonies, charged with feeling, symbolic, episodic, but requiring a high level of family participation. The second are the taken for granted daily routines which a family uses to regulate space and distance amongst its members and between the family and the outside world. Reiss proposes that the central ceremonials both shape and stabilise the minute and subliminal pattern regulators of everyday family life. This relationship between ritual and the taken for granted is a familiar theme in sociology (e.g. Goffman, 1969), as is another of Reiss's crucial perceptions, that it is in action that knowledge, attitudes and beliefs are both embodied and affirmed as true (Thomas, 1966):

Interaction patterns in family life enable all members to experience their own values and assumptions as if they were unquestionable components of outer reality. This transformation enables the family paradigm to serve as guide or framework for action-in-the-real-world by all members, which further reinforces their conviction in the objectivity of their assumptions.

(Reiss, 1981, 228)

Family interaction patterns, then, embody the family paradigm, and through them the family sustains or fails to sustain itself as an ongoing social unit. This stress on ritual and on the consistency of pattern in social action has implications for our understanding of the place of television in family life. I argued in Chapter 1 that both public and private forms of ritual are implicated in the management and acceptance of broadcast television, and that the taken for granted certainties of both broadcast schedules and daily routines – which are of course both spatial and temporal – create the framework within which the normality and security of everyday life are sustained.

Space and time are inextricably intertwined. The quality of the temporal culture of the family's relationships is expressed in its attitudes to the past, present and future embodied in speech or in the particular characteristics of the household economy (ibid., 233).

Following Kantor and Lehr (1975), Reiss distinguishes between 'orienting' and 'clocking'. Orienting refers to the reference points in time which a family uses to conduct its affairs. Families can be shown to have dominant orientations: to either past, present or future. Past orienting is remembering, re-experiencing, or re-enacting – a living in the past or a preoccupation with the history or tradition of the family. Present orientation has to do with the here and now, with what is being experienced or actually felt or being undertaken. And future orientation, perhaps a stereotypical middle-class trait, is emphasised in anticipation, imagining or planning ahead – to deferred gratification. Temporal orientation can be expressed in household furnishings, contacts with kin, patterns of friendship, what is saved or thrown away, as well as in relationships to television and technology (Silverstone, 1993). Time orientation is also expressed in the particular economy of the family household, where credit, saving or accumulated wealth indicate orientation to present, future and past respectively.

Clocking involves a different but related set of considerations of time. Clocking is, according to Kantor and Lehr (1975, 82) the regulation of sequence, frequency and pace of immediately experienced events from moment to moment, hour to hour and day to day. Clocking entails a whole series of activities which in turn involve sequencing and the setting of frequency, duration and scheduling. They result or do not result in a pattern of synchronisation in which family or household members come together or pass each other, according to a pattern which is set and engrained in their daily routines, and which also meets both the organisational demands of everyday life and the cultural demands of their particular orientation to the world. All of this is not just a matter of synchronisation. There is often conflict about matters of time (and control over space) within families and households. But there is equally no question that a family's clocking pattern is not the basic mechanism by which it structures itself as a viable social unit. Kantor and Lehr (1975, 86) suggest that clocking, the organisation and management of time within the family, reveals 'what the family considers most important'.

The quality of the spatial culture of the family is, in a parallel fashion, expressed in the ways in which families set and maintain the boundary between themselves and the outside, regulating in numerous ways the material and symbolic passages across that boundary – 'boundary maintenance'. It is also expressed in the regulation of internal space, the space of personal distance and privacy within the family, and in the family's conception of the physical and emotional arrangements of its world: '[The] family's arrangement of internal space clearly reflects how it as a group conceptualises or understands the world outside the family' (Reiss, 1981, 237). Synchronisation is a matter, then, of both temporal and spatial ordering.

The different ways in which families organise and express their space–time relations in their daily and ritualised interactions become the basis for a typology of families in Reiss' work, in terms of the differential expression of a family's coherence, integration and points of reference (ibid., 209ff). I am not, for the moment, going to pursue this typology here. Suffice it to say, though, that my excursion into the realms of family therapy has provided an important route into an understanding of family process, at the level of daily social interaction as well as at the level of the long-term stability and consistency of patterns of social interaction.[2] It has also provided a route into an understanding of some of the key questions relating social action to those beliefs, attitudes, values and cognitions that comprise a family's collective articulation of its capacity to sustain itself as a viable social unit.

I now want to relate these questions and issues specifically to the place of television in the family.

TELEVISION AND THE FAMILY

The issues raised both explicitly and by implication in my discussion of the family thus far are beginning to be taken into studies of the significance of television in the family. Rather than being perceived, monochromatically, in terms of a displacement of other activities (see Himmelweit et al., 1958; Robinson and Converse, 1972) or, in a blanket sense, destructive of family relations (see Morley, 1986), it is beginning to be seen both as a focus of family activities and as a resource. An understanding of its status as a resource, of course, goes back to the 'uses and gratifications' research in the 1950s (Katz and Lazarsfeld, 1955), but despite their interest in the primary group, their research centred on the individual, and on the individual within the context of a reference group which was not principally the family, but rather the neighbourhood or the community.

There are a number of themes within these discussions which I wish briefly to address here, though I will return to them more fully in Chapter 6. One can approach the argument in one of two directions. The first is from the point of view of the family. In this case the issues concern television's role as a component of a family system. The pattern of use of television within a family will have consequences for the way in which the family constructs and sustains itself as a social unit in time and space.

The other is from the point of view of the medium. In this case the issues concern the construction and reconstruction of television through the differential patterns of activity or passivity, choice, interest, commitment or attention, that frame and fragment it, and thereby contain and define its impact within the family. In both sets of often interweaving discussions, the concerns have been with the family as a system and as a context for media consumption, a system and a context powerfully inflected by the domestic politics of gender and age as well as by a sensitivity to ethnographically derived details of the social uses to which television is actually put.

From the point of view of the family the starting point for a discussion of television is its status within a rule-governed social environment (Goodman, 1983; Lull, 1980a) in which television carries the burden of a number of different functions within the family. An understanding of how the family incorporates television into its patterns of daily activity is, argues Irene Goodman (1983), a good point of entry for understanding the family system as whole, in the same way as mealtimes might once have been. Drawing too on family systems research she argues that the use of television is a function of a constantly evolving family unit; television can and will be used as 'a companion, scapegoat, mediator, boundary marker between family members, to schedule other activities, as a reward or punishment, as a bartering agent, and so on . . . By studying the role that TV plays in the realisation of these other purposes, we are in effect looking at TV use as a tool for understanding family interaction' (ibid., 406). But more than that, by looking at television use in this way we are also in effect insisting on a much more powerful mediatory role for the family in relation to television content than otherwise (see Brody and Stoneman, 1983). This, in turn, has profound implications for our understanding of the power of television in modern society, for in granting the family (or household or other primary group) such significance we are identifying a cultural space in which the media's messages are themselves mediated.

This line of research has been pursued by a small number of scholars, principally working within an ethnographic, interpretive, tradition. James Lull has pioneered an approach and pursued empirical investigations in the United States and in China (1980a and b; 1988; 1990) which have led him to offer a typology of television's functions within the family. His work provides a touchstone for enquiries into the systematic and systemic relationship between television and family life.

Other studies have drawn attention to the relationship between television and family time (Bryce, 1987), television and family gender relations (Morley, 1986) and television, more broadly in the context of family process (Rogge and Jensen, 1988).

Jennifer Bryce explores families' use of television through a framework of temporality derived from Edward Hall (1973). His distinction between mono-chromatic time (emphasising schedules, segmentation and promptness) and polychromatic time (characterised by several things happening at once) provides the basis for a study designed to enquire into television's integration into the particular temporalities of different families. An understanding of the dynamics of the distinct character of a family's temporality provides a clear route, Bryce argues, into an understanding of television's place in family life:

> Television viewing, like all other family activities, cannot escape the power of the family's organisation of time . . . The sequencing of viewing, its place in the mesh of family activities, reflects a choice, an organisation, a negotiation process about which very little is known.
>
> (Bryce, 1987, 122–3)

Whereas Jennifer Bryce focuses on the quality of time use within the family, David Morley (1986) focuses on the quality of gender relations within the family. Two concerns link them. The first is with the way in which a domin-ant pattern of social organisation in the family structures the household's relationship to television, and the second concerns the relationship between the private expression of time and gender and its public articulation. Morley explores gender and power within the family. Across a whole range of finely tuned dimensions of viewing practice (the power and control over programme choice, viewing style, the planning or unplanning of viewing, the amounts of viewing, television related talk, programme and channel preference, solo and 'guilty' viewing) he finds a significant difference between men and women in the families he studies. He interprets this in an important way, arguing that such differences are not to be related to biology but to the particular character of gender relations that have emerged within patriarchal society, as a result of which the home itself has become highly gendered. Men dominate the television at home because home is where they relax, where they are looked after, and where, after a long day's work, they bring their own publicly legitimated masculinity into the woman's working domain. That gender is a significant factor in the domestic relations around the television set is undeniable, but as Morley himself acknowledges (1986, 174), not by itself and not unproblematically. The stage a family has reached in its life-cycle, the significance of age, class and ethnicity as well as gender, and the particularities of family history and culture make the situation a much more complex one than he begins to describe.

This complexity is approached in a most instructive and enlightening way in a study reported by Jan Uwe-Rogge and Klaus Jensen (1988). They, too, take a systems approach in their study of German families, but do so both by casting their net to include family history, biography and family myth (see Byng-Hall, 1982) and by taking into account a family's relationships to technology in the home more broadly. Their families are perceived to live in complex material, symbolic and constantly changing but routinised and ritualised, domestic settings. Their use of the media is a product of that environment and cannot be understood apart from it. Families construct for themselves their own media world, a display of their own competence as media consumers and of their knowledge and appreciation of programmes and technologies. Rogge and Jensen (1988, 103) draw attention to the way in which the imaginary worlds of the media can become a primary experience, becoming substitutes for missing elements in 'the emotional and inter-personal spheres'. They also draw attention to the ways in which fundamental changes in the social position of the family, for example unemployment, or life events, will affect the patterns of media use within it. They pay particular attention to the situation of the single parent family. They suggest that an understanding of the family's use of the media must be based on an understanding of two aspects: its content and its form. In relation to the first:

> media activities can be understood as an attempt to construct a meaningful relationship between the media program and reality as actually experienced. Conscious, subconscious, or preconscious wishes play an important role in the way people use the media. The media are interpreted against a background of everyday life as it is lived and experienced; they are used to cope with everyday problems, either in the main or in the short term.
>
> (Ibid., 1988, 94)

The media are, they suggest, entirely taken for granted. As such they become functional, part of the family system. Family members feel unable to live without them. They become the focus of a great deal of emotion. 'People seek contact with the media partly because the media appeal to and allow access to feelings such as fear, joy and insecurity . . . the media provide remedies for loneliness; they are used to create "good" feelings and to define human relationships' (ibid., 95).

Television becomes, then, a member of the family in a metaphorical sense but also in a literal sense insofar as it is integrated into the daily pattern of domestic social relations, and insofar as it is the focus of emotional or cognitive energy, releasing or containing tension for example, or providing comfort or a sense of security. It also becomes a member of the family insofar as it is expressive of the dynamics of a family's interaction, the dynamics of gender- or age-based identities and relations, or the dynamics of its changing position in the world, as children grow up and leave home or as heads of families become unemployed or die.

But the internal structure of the family is no more a product of life within the private space of home than are their media. And the phenomenology of home and the social life of families still leaves at least two dimensions of the domestic world unaccounted for. The first is the representation of the family on the television screen itself. The second is the role of the household as an active participant in the economic, social and cultural life of the public sphere.

FAMILY TEXTS

Lynn Spigel (1992) traces the rise of the situation comedy on the television screens of post-war America. In doing so she provides an account of the ways in which this particular genre, a hybrid product drawing on both legitimate and vaudeville theatrical traditions, became a staple of American television of the time. It offered family entertainment within an increasingly formulaic mould. The formula claimed a certain kind of aesthetic realism in terms of its ability to provide recognisable images of contemporary family life, but it also preserved a self-conscious and reflexive theatricality, reflecting on the artificiality of everyday life, and preserving the screen as a proscenium arch. In doing this television created a genre which had a much wider historical resonance. As Spigel points out, it preserved something of the same kind of domestic culture that had been established by Victorian middle-class households. In an echo of Benjamin's observation which began this chapter she also points to the bourgeois sitting room as the site for the theatrical construction of the family:

> In fact, at midcentury, bourgeois Victorians were so fascinated with theatricality that they literally turned their parlors into theatres, staging plays with friends and family members in their homes . . . these 'parlor theatricals' were sold in books that people purchased and adapted to their own use at parties. Using their front parlor as a proscenium space and their back parlor as a backstage area, Victorians constructed theatrical spaces, even adorning entrance and exit ways in the home with curtains and other decorations.
>
> (Spigel, 1992, 162)

The home as theatre is an idea that survives on and through television, but it is a family theatre, in which families participate both as audiences and players. Spigel comments too on another aspect of the reflexivity of the genre. These programmes offered an opportunity for Americans to see how the fictional TV families came to terms with television, both as performers (Burns and Allen were enormously inventive in their taming of the new medium) and as consumers (episode after episode of family sit-coms included scenes around the television set, and discussions of its significance for family life).

I have already referred to Mary Beth Haralovich's (1988) analysis of the ideological significance of family sit-coms during a sightly later period (the late fifties), linking their popularity to the specific historical demands to re-establish family life in the US after the war, and to provide models of appropriate domesticity, particularly for the housewife (or homemaker) newly ensconced in suburbia. These family sit-coms provided a less theatrical and more realistic version of family life, offering a kind of naturalism which would demand a less self-conscious identification of viewer to screen, and a version of the suburban family increasingly represented through the lives of the young.

There are a number of different issues raised by these examples, apart from the obvious problems of periodisation. The first is one that Spigel (1992, 163) herself raises when she suggests that: 'Postwar Americans . . . must, to some degree, have been aware of the theatrical, artificial nature of family life'. Maybe, maybe not. At issue, of course, is the methodological and substantive question of being able to read ideological implications from the analyses of texts, as well as making assumptions about how they will be read and the values and attitudes of those reading them. But it is also a question of being able to recognise a more complex representational world than might at first be imagined. This complexity resides in the variety of images of the family even within the sit-com genre; it resides in the genre's historical development and its responsiveness to a wider set of ideological concerns; it resides in the representation of families outside the genre and the skewing of the image of the family relative to the world of real families; and it resides in the way in which idealised models of family life have provided an invisible structuring of sit-coms based in other settings.

All these issues are addressed, in one way or another, in the literature. With respect to the first and second, Ella Taylor (1989) has analysed the inter-relationship of social, political, industrial and ideological factors that in the post-war years resulted in the particular and changing character of the episodic series and situation comedy. She identifies both the industry's increasing need for a middle-class, middle-brow, mass audience, as well as the chronic but differently focused anxieties about the status of the family in American society as key determinants of the emergent genres. Their politics, as well as the politics of the TV families, fluctuates too between a solid and reflective reinforcement of middle-class white values, to ones which, either in the espousal of alternative family structures (*The Golden Girls*, *My Two Dads*) or in other ways (*All in the Family*), provide a more critical gloss on the status of the family in American society.

The genres too have become increasingly blurred in outline, as family series and sit-coms take on, both seriously and parodically, versions of feminism or versions of ethnicity. Taylor's analysis and critique of *The Cosby Show*, to take a case, exemplifies the complex dialectics of politics, ethnicity, domesticity and generalised anxiety, that appear relevant to an understanding of its particular leached blandness. *The Cosby Show* offers one version of family that can really be understood only through an analysis of its place within contemporary politics, its relationship to a generic history, and its function as one element in a mythic television discourse (Lévi-Strauss, 1968) which has the problem of the family at its centre.

With respect to the third dimension of the family's representation on television, Gunter and Svennevig (1987) review a number of studies that have attempted to chart the degrees of distortion and exclusion that main-stream television images generate relative to the variety of family types and experiences present in contemporary society. In reporting on research con-

ducted in the US, the UK, Hungary, Australia and Denmark, they point to a
number of predictable conclusions, pertinent, for example, to the under-
representation of working-class and black families; the continuing manifestation of patriarchy within family life; the ideology built into the differential representation of wealthy families, who are usually unhappy, compared
to poor families who, (surprise, surprise) are usually seen as contented; and
the presence of family conflicts which tend to be between spouses or siblings
rather than cross-generational.

The problem of course with this and other analyses of content is that of
their interpretation. As Gunter and Svennevig (1987, 49) themselves point
out: 'the significance of television families for the audience and the lessons
about family life which they present, can only be inferred'. There is no
guarantee, as many analysts have recently noted (esp. Liebes and Katz,
1991), that audiences will see programmes, or families on programmes, in
predictable ways.

The final dimension of the family's representation on television is that of
its structural presence in other settings. Ella Taylor (1989) and Paul Kerr
(1984) have both pointed to the ways in which families have provided a model
for the social organisation of the workplace. *The Mary Tyler Moore Show*,
*M*A*S*H*, *Lou Grant*, *Hill Street Blues* and many others have seen in the
family a version of social life that has wider relevance. The family is a
mechanism for humanising the otherwise alienating worlds of work. But there
is more to it even than this. In the transition from home to work family
becomes community in which the *gemeinschaft* values that have their origin
in the family are extended and transformed. In this transition, Ella Taylor
appears to be suggesting, the tortured complexities of the family are being left
behind in a compensating image of the workplace as home.

Once again it would be pointless to try and adjudicate between these
competing images of family or their ideological significance. What I want to
stress is that television's status as a domestic medium and its role in our own
perceptions of domesticity – especially in this case of the family – are
inextricably, though always inconclusively, linked to the images and narratives that appear on its screen. Situation comedy, especially, has offered those
images and narratives. What we do with them of course is still an open
question. I will return to it.

I want now however to focus on the final dimension of television's role in
our domesticity, and that is in relation to the economics, politics and culture
of the household.

THE HOUSEHOLD

Homes and families are fluid categories and variable entities, vulnerable to
subjective redefinition and cultural and historical differentiation. Households
are similarly conceptually and empirically variable. They too can be con-

sidered as processes (Wallman, 1984, 20), but processes of a different order. Whereas families are based on kinship, households are based on propinquity. But more than that, households can be considered as economic units: they are resource systems. As Sandra Wallman argues:

> A model of households as resource systems . . . conceives households as being differently bounded in respect of different resources available to them, the resources they choose to deploy, and the kinds of value they vest or invest in them for particular purposes in local or cultural contexts of various kinds.
>
> (Wallman, 1984, 21)

Wallman identifies land, labour, capital, time, information and identity as the six necessary resources which are the focus of a household's actvities, and whose analysis defines the particular characteristics of a household's variation and viability. Yet, as she acknowledges and as she makes explicit, households are more than simply economic units. Households with broadly similar economic or material circumstances will vary enormously in terms of their styles of life and their tastes.

> People everywhere need food, shelter, companionship and self-esteem; livelihood anywhere is a matter of balancing a household economy and getting on with the neighbours. The point is only that there is not just one way of defining or achieving one set of ends.
>
> (Wallman, 1984, 41)

Studies of families and households in industrial society have tended to conflate the status of the two institutions. Equally conflated, though perhaps less seriously, are the household and the home.

Families and households have become more or less synonymous, since the industrial revolution is believed to have fractured the extended family as both a social and a productive unit. The nuclear family, mistakenly believed to be uniquely a product of that revolution (Laslett, 1965), was a unit in which social, spatial and economic boundaries coincided. Two-generation units, with the male householder as the breadwinner, living within a more or less self-contained physical space and becoming economically self-supporting became, increasingly (ideologically), the norm. Needless to say this portrait is neither historically accurate nor sociologically adequate. Not only did such a social organisation precede the industrial revolution, but other forms of family unit, particularly extended and multi-generational families, survived that revolution. Equally, in more recent times, households consist of many different kinds of social units, containing larger and smaller numbers of individuals differently related or associated with each other but sharing the same domestic space, and indeed they consist of individuals on their own.

In the present context the distinction between family and household is one that has also been insufficiently marked in the literature. Studies of television in the home have tended to be, as should now be clear, studies of families (Morley, 1986; Lull, 1988) and have concentrated principally on television's place in the internal structure of the family's social relations. Of course there are very good reasons for this and I have already referred to, and endorsed, them. Nevertheless it is the case that a consideration of television's place in the economic structure of the household (which may or may not be a family household) is less often a preoccupation, and there is very little research on the significance of television in single-parent households, or in shared flats, for example.

The distinction between household and home is of a slightly different order. Homes, as I have suggested, are more than just houses. The home is the product of our practical and emotional commitment to a given space, and as such it can be seen to be a phenomenological reality in which our identities are forged and our security maintained. For Saunders and Williams (1988) the home is the 'crucible of the social system':

> It is the base point around which local and national politics is organised and which in essence provides the starting basis for the allocation and distribution of resources, the collection of statistics and much else besides. It is all of these things, certainly, but first and foremost it is the nodal point of our society, the locale through which individual and society interact.
>
> (Saunders and Williams, 1988, 84)

Saunders and Williams do not adequately separate the social, the phenomenological and the political economic dimensions of domesticity. Though there is no gainsaying their argument for the significance of what they call home, they fail to see that there is a need to distinguish between home as a product of social practices and those practices themselves. Home is what is produced or not (we feel or do not feel at home in the spaces we occupy and create); it is produced as the result of productive and reproductive work by its members, and also by a whole range of other activities, principally consumption activities, that have as their end product a more or less powerful statement of identity, ownership and belonging. Households are the social, economic and political systems in which that work takes place (see Pahl, 1984). As Saunders and Williams (1988, 82) themselves remark: 'Few men, women or children are islands, for it is through their membership of household units that they are integrated in one way or another into the wider complex of social institutions which comprise their society.' It is to the quality and dynamics of this integration and to television's place within it that I now want to turn.

In order to address this question, I want to draw on a conceptualisation of the household as a moral economy (Silverstone et al., 1992).

The moral economy refers to the capacity of households actively to engage with the products and meanings of the public, formal, commodity- and individual-based economy and to produce something of their own as a result of that engagement. Descriptions of moral economies appear in a number of different contexts and in a number of different guises in various literatures.[3]

E.P. Thompson (1971) uses the term to describe the persistence of traditional forms of economic activity among the rural and urban poor of the eighteenth century in contradistinction, and sometimes in direct opposition, to the emerging dominance of the market, particularly in food and agricultural produce. Behind the activities of the mobs in the eighteenth century was a set of traditional beliefs and values which comprised an alternative view of economic behaviour. This version of economic behaviour was fundamentally opposed, by virtue of its grounding in a sense of the common weal, to the individualising calculations of the market. The new market economy was perceived by those on the wrong side of it to be a de-moralising economy, denying traditional practices as well as traditional principles of economic behaviour. The conflict between the two economies was of course thrown into high relief at times of dearth or threatened famine. Thompson's analysis also throws into high and dramatic relief the nature of the conflict between traditional and modern forms of economic behaviour. What it also does, of course, is to reveal in what ways forms of economic life other than those defined by the market can be sustained – even if, as in this case, they are acutely vulnerable.

David Cheal (1988) makes a similar case in his discussion of the continuing significance of the gift economy in modern society. He uses the term moral economy to refer to a system of social (rather than simply, or only, economic) transactions:

> which are defined as socially desirable (i.e. moral) because through them social ties are recognised and balanced social relationships are maintained . . . In a moral economy, trust is generated as a result of members sharing a common way of life. Individuals' commitments to fulfil their customary obligations to others make their actions predictable, and thus keep the complexity of the social environment at a low level.
>
> (Cheal, 1988, 15–16)

The system, principally but not exclusively, of domestic gift-giving in advanced societies provides, suggests Cheal, both an alternative and a supplement to the institutionalisation of the market, above all insofar as it provides the basis for an extended reproduction of social relations (ibid., 19).

Neither Thompson nor Cheal, however, consider in detail the nature of the interrelationship between the moral and the formal or market economies, nor their particular relationship to the household. The two economies operate either side by side (Cheal) or in opposition (Thompson). There is little sense of the dynamics of their interrelationship, nor of its location in a specific domestic setting.

It is both in relation to the dynamics of that interrelationship and to its location at the boundary between private and public spheres, that the work of

Jonathan Parry and Maurice Bloch (1989) on the meanings of money and the morality of exchange is so suggestive. In introducing their recent collection of papers, Parry and Bloch explore the range of cultural meanings that surround monetary transactions and argue that money does not have a defined and dominating set of meanings in all societies, nor does it impose uniformity on all aspects of socio-economic life. An understanding of the significance of money requires an understanding of the transactional system within and through which exchange takes place. Money, in its passage through such a system, changes its meaning, and its meaning becomes a product of differential social action associated with the different beliefs, values and cognitions of those who come into contact with it:

> the meanings with which money is invested are quite as much a product of the cultural matrix into which it is incorporated as of the economic functions it performs as a means of exchange, unit of account, store of value and so on. It is therefore impossible to predict its symbolic meanings from these functions alone.
>
> (Parry and Bloch, 1989, 21)

The meanings of money are subject to transformation as it crosses social and cultural boundaries, above all as it crosses the boundary between the public world of individual- and commodity-based transactions and that of the private world of domestic reproduction, where a different set of values associated with the longer term interests of the social or cosmic order is dominant. Viviana Zelizer (1989) also talks of 'special monies' in this domestic context, suggesting that regardless of its sources 'once money had entered the household [US family households during the years 1870–1930], its allocation, calculation, and uses were subject to a set of domestic rules distinct from the rules of the market. Family money was nonfungible; social barriers prevented its conversion into ordinary wages' (ibid., 368).

The meanings of money are therefore negotiable. They are negotiable not in arbitrary ways, but in ways that mark their engagement in the fundamental problems and projects of human existence and everyday life: 'the symbolism of money is only one aspect of a more general symbolic world of transactions which must always come to terms with some absolutely fundamental human problems' (Parry and Bloch, 1989, 28).

But it is, of course, not just money which can be addressed in this way. As I shall go on to suggest, their argument has precise (both predictable and obvious) parallels in the literature on the mass media, both in terms of the emergence of a similar damning morality surrounding money and media (both have been and still are seen as the roots of all evil), and in terms of our understandings of the meanings of media in modern society: that in their exchange, they too are negotiable, and that an understanding of them also requires us to understand the transactional orders through which they pass.

And this applies not just to money or media, but to objects and commodities too. As Igor Kopytoff (1986) argues, objects pass through economies like individuals pass through life. In the formal economy they are part of a generalised and homogenising system of exchange: they are commodities. But then as they are bought and owned they become part of an individualising, singular world of private consumption: they change their meaning accordingly. Objects move, in modern society, from one domain to another. They have a biography in the same way individuals do:

> In the homogenised world of commodities, an eventful biography of a thing becomes the story of the various singularizations of it, of classifications and reclassifications in an uncertain world of categories whose importance shifts with every minor change in context. As with persons, the drama here lies in the uncertainties of valuation and identity.
>
> (Kopytoff, 1986, 90)

The moral economy of the household is therefore both an economy of meanings and a meaningful economy; and in both of its dimensions it stands in a potentially or actually transformative relationship to the public, objective economy of the exchange of goods and meanings. The household is, or can be, a moral *economy* because it is an economic unit which is involved, through the productive and reproductive activities of its members, in the public economy and at the same time it is a complex economic unit in its own right. Recent studies of the domestic division of labour (Pahl, 1984; Morris, 1990), and of the management and control of family money (Pahl, 1989), as well as of the household's resource system (Wallman, 1984), have opened up for close examination the hitherto hidden recesses of economic life within the home in terms of the relationship between households and employment, in which issues of class position, gender and life-cycle, as well as local economic conditions loom large; in terms of the domestic division of labour as such, dependent as it is not only on the engrained divisions and ideologies of work and domesticity in the public sphere, but modified internally both by family ideologies, family politics and culture, as well as by technical change (Cowan, 1989; Gershuny, 1982); and in terms of the position of the household in the networks of kin and friendship within and beyond the local neighbourhood (Bott, 1971; Wallman, 1984).

The household is, or can be, a *moral* economy because the economic activities of its members within the household and within the wider world of work, leisure and consumption are defined and informed by a set of cognitions, evaluations and aesthetics which are themselves defined and informed by the histories, biographies and politics of the household and its members. These are expressed in the specific and various cosmologies and rituals that define (or fail to define) the household's integrity as a social and cultural unit.

In the context of the family-household this aspect of the moral economy bears a close resemblance to Reiss' description of the family paradigm.[4]

Other expressions of the moral economy of the household in family culture can be found discussed by Basil Bernstein (1971) in his concern with family socialisation and language, Pierre Bourdieu (1984) and his discussion of the habitus (see below, Chapter 5), and Mary Douglas (1973) in her drafting of grid and group.

I am suggesting therefore that households are both economic and cultural units, and that although their material positions set profound limits on the opportunities available for consumption and self-expression, within those limits and in some ways sometimes transcending them, households can define for themselves a private and a public moral, emotional, evaluative and aesthetic environment – a way of life – which they depend on for their survival and security as much as they do on their material resources. To understand the household as a moral economy therefore is to understand the household as part of a transactional system dynamically involved in the public world of the production and exchange of commodities and meanings, the world of work and leisure, of social and economic resources. But that involvement is not simply a passive one. At issue is the capacity of the household or the family within it to create and sustain its autonomy and identity (and for individual members to do the same) as an economic, social and cultural unit. At issue too – particularly in modern society – is the household's ability to display, both to itself and to others, its competence and its status as a participant in a complex public economy. The tensions generated between public and private worlds, and the contradictions of individuality and collectivity, and of standardisation and singularisation, which result and which are daily demanding of resolution in the practices of everyday life lie at the heart of the condition of modernity.

There are two things briefly to be said about this conceptualisation of the household as a moral economy. The first is that it is not intended as an evaluative term. The moral economy of the household is what is achieved, in some way or another, by any and every household as a result of its efforts to sustain itself as a social and cultural entity. It is the equivalent of, but distinguishable from, Giddens' 'project' of ontological security, Reiss' family 'paradigm', and Wallman's resource 'system' (and Bourdieu's 'habitus', see below, Chapter 5). In each case an attempt has been made to define a level of coherence, a baseline for describing and accounting for the viability or lack of viability of families and households as participants in the wider world of social life. In characterising households in this way I am not suggesting that there is a single morality which enables us to define sickness or health, normality or pathology, in relation to specific households or family life. The questions which are raised are not, principally, evaluative; they are descriptive and analytic.

And the second is that it is not intended as a reification, nor should it become one. Empirically families and households will create many different, more or less integrated, more or less contradictory and conflictful, and more or less changing, versions of their own private cultural and economic spaces. Those variations and their distinctiveness relative to the values and rules of behaviour manifest in the public sphere, are not predefined, nor are they necessary. In a limiting case the moral and the public economies would be indistinguishable. In another it might be quite impossible to identify in a given household anything remotely recognisable as a moral economy. Yet the particular conjunction of culture and economics, of symbolic and material resources, that the term moral economy insists upon, and the transactional relationship to the world of public goods and meanings that it suggests, are central for an analysis of the role of television in everyday life. I shall be developing this analysis on two further occasions in this book (pp. 97ff. and pp. 122 ff.).

Suffice it to say at this point that television has a dialectical relationship to the moral economy of the household. On the one hand the particular characteristics of a household's moral economy will define how television is actually used: how it is incorporated into the daily pattern of family or domestic life; how its use is structured by the gender- and age-based relationships of the family at a particular stage of its life-cycle; or how it is mobilised into the household's sense of its own domesticity, its own sense of home. And equally the kind and level of resources a household can call on will also affect how television comes to be used, both in terms of the household's spatial arrangements, in terms of the accepted patterns of the household's time use, and in terms of such simple but crucial factors as the number of television sets or channels available within the domestic space. On the other hand television itself, as medium and as message, will extend and plausibly transform a household's reach: bringing news of the world of affairs beyond the front door; providing narratives and images for identification, reassurance or frustration; affecting or reinforcing the household's links with neighbourhood and community; and locking the household ever more firmly into an increasingly privatised and commodified domestic world.

THE DOMESTIC

Finally, then, to the question of the domestic itself as an encompassing – as a political – category, one which subsumes home, family and household, and one which is an expression of the relationship between public and private spheres. Public and private have evolved, historically, together (Sennett, 1986, 89ff), and as they have developed it is the domestic that has suffered (Donzelot, 1979). In an industrial society dominated by production and the exchange of commodities; in a capitalist society of bourgeois and increasingly privatised social relations, the domestic has, it is often argued, become marginalised and politically insignificant. The domestic is being seen as increasingly isolated and removed from the mainstream of modern society, and only reachable through technical and heavily mediated forms of communication. Television has been a principal factor in this still shifting boundary between the public and the private, particularly in its structural capacity to merge public and private behaviours (Meyrowitz, 1985, 93ff.).

The domestic is indeed subject to increasing regulative pressures and, certainly in an age of broadcasting, it can be seen to have become the object of a consistent attempt, through scheduling and ideological discriminations, to mobilise it into a subservient relationship to the temporal and patriarchal structures of an increasingly sclerosed public sphere. Yet the domestic dies hard. Publicly expressed identities and values are produced and reproduced in the domestic (Mason, 1989, 120). The domestic is the site and source of our activities as consumers (and also as citizens (Fontaine, 1988, 284)) and through consumption (see Chapter 5), paradoxically but plausibly, it is becoming increasingly significant in the modern, public sphere.

The domestic has become a complex and contradictory reality. So too has the modern interior. Both are sites of the intersection of a whole range of practices: economic, political, aesthetic. As the bourgeois increasingly retreats to his or her private living space, a retreat demanded, perhaps, by the increasing pressures and uncertainties of life in the modern world, the 'box in the world theatre' assumes greater and greater importance in the fabric of everyday life. Home – the home – assumes a new and more contradictory significance as the location where the competing demands of modernity are being worked out. Do-it-yourself decoration and house improvement, the increasing personalisation of media and information technologies, consumption itself in all its various manifestations, the intensification of the home as a leisure centre, as well as a place of paid work, all signify its changing status (Tomlinson, 1990).

It is this notion of the domestic, and of television's role in its definition and its change, that is now raised. Domesticity is a relational concept: the product of the mutuality of public and private spheres, but the product too of the suburban hybridisation of modernity. It is to this – the suburban – dimension of television and everyday life that I now want to turn.

Chapter 3

The suburbanisation of the public sphere

One more refinement of the precinct home was achieved when . . . Levitt not only managed to supply television as a standard item, but also to build it into the living room wall so that it qualified as an item of household equipment that could be financed on the mortgage. Next to the hearth, the bright beady eye of the baby-sitting machine reassured both children and adults that the scant physical community of the mass-produced sacred huts was redeemed by the magical electronic community created by national television.

(Dolores Hayden, 1984, 105, writing on the post-war development of the American suburb)

This chapter has two starting points. One lies in the work of Raymond Williams. The other is to be found in some observations of the British anthropologist Marilyn Strathern. From this double-headed beginning I want to suggest that television is both historically and sociologically a suburban medium. And that it is through this characteristic – literally 'of and for the suburb' – metaphorically and ideologically 'suburban' – that television finds itself at the centre of a whole range of relationships and identities, both public and private, global and parochial, domestic and non-domestic, which mark out the territory of the everyday. I want in this chapter to construct television as a political entity, but a political entity with a small 'p', that is fully implicated in the interweaving of both the small-scale and the large-scale manifestations of ideology and control that provide the framework of life in modern society.

Raymond Williams (1974) traces the origins of radio as a broadcast medium to the specific changes in industrialising society, changes that together generated 'in a number of ways and drawing on a range of impulses from curiosity to anxiety' (ibid., 22) an incipient demand for new information and new kinds of orientation in the world. Substantial movements of population, originally from country to city; the political and economic expansion of empire and industry; the liberation, with the early telegraph and telephone technologies, of the movement of information from its dependence on physical transport, all together, he suggests, provided the conditions for the emergence of a new technology (radio) and a new medium (broadcasting). The new technology did not require broadcasting. The new technology did not emerge in isolation. Williams points out that radio was (and could have remained) a medium for two-way interaction (as the telephone did remain, despite a thirty-year flirtation with it as a broadcast medium in Budapest (Marvin, 1988, 223–8)). Its incorporation as a medium for transmission from a centralised source to individual homes was not an inevitable consequence of the technology but the product, among other things, of the lead taken by the manufacturers of radio receivers in the development of the new medium in the years immediately following the First World War. As Williams (1974, 25) points out, radio (and television too)

> were systems primarily devised for transmission and reception as abstract processes, with little or no definition of preceding content . . . It is not only that the supply of broadcasting facilities preceded the demand; it is that the means of communication preceded their content.

Radio, during the twenties and thereafter, took its place amongst a whole new range of what came to be known as 'consumer durables' – principally other technologies – which included the motor car, the motor cycle, the camera and domestic electrical technologies. This socially defined set of technological developments took shape alongside (Williams is careful not to ascribe a causal relationship) the development of the now entirely familiar material and symbolic fabric of modern living. This fabric, Williams observes, contained two paradoxical yet strongly connected tendencies: mobility (and here the private car was the key factor of course) and the increasingly self-sufficient family home:

> The earlier period of public technology, best exemplified by the railways and city lighting, was being replaced by a kind of technology for which no satisfactory name has yet been found: that which served an at once mobile and home centred way of living: a form of mobile privatisation. Broadcasting in its applied form was a social product of this distinct tendency.
>
> (Ibid., 26)

And the suburb, though he does not say so in so many words, was, and is, its embodiment.

The 'need' for such a technical and social solution to some of the new conditions of modernity was anticipated in the dramas of the mid- and late nineteenth century, characterised by Williams as being constructed for the first time around dramatic situations in which 'men and women stared from [the family home's] windows, or waited anxiously for messages, to learn about forces out there which would determine the conditions of their lives' (ibid., 27). Here is the obverse of what Benjamin describes as the 'box in a world theatre'. The media's facilitation of increased reach generates anxiety as well as a complementary desire for control. But control is pursued through aesthetic strategies (see Benjamin, 1970), since, of course, more direct ones are increasingly unavailable. The media are, as both Benjamin and Williams note, central to this undertaking, and central too in the mediation of anxiety and reassurance, real dependence and illusory control that I have already begun to identify as lying at the heart of an understanding of contemporary everyday life.

For the first time, then, in the early years of this century, the home became the focus for aesthetic concern and the home (at least as Williams describes it here) became, both in drama and reality, the product and the focus of a new – increasingly efficient and encompassing – communication and information order. Television was heir to all of this. Its own technical development echoed that of radio. Here too the technology preceded content; but television could be, and was in the UK after the Second World War, slotted into a cultural, technical and economic framework which had already been well established through the institution and institutionalisation of the BBC.

Television, and radio before it, was clearly, then, both a technological expression of, and a response to, a set of wide-ranging changes in capitalist industrial society. The movements of populations into cities, and then, from the late 1880s on in Britain, gradually (and then increasingly rapidly) (Girouard, 1985) into suburban developments on the edge of cities, was facilitated by communication technologies such as the car, the telephone, the radio. The private home was linked to, and became fundamentally dependent on, a whole network of technologically derived services (Mumford, 1938, 467). But the individuals within private homes were free to come and go as they pleased, as well as (as I have noted), increasingly free to bring the world into their living room.

But if television (and radio before it) was created for the suburb, and if it has become suburban in that sense, then it would be fair to point out that it is not always watched in suburbs. On the contrary. It is watched in all sorts of different places, at home and abroad. I want to suggest therefore that television is not just the product of the suburbanisation of the modern world, but is itself suburbanising. In order to make this point reasonably clearly I need to turn to my second starting point.

Marilyn Strathern (1993), in a paper in which she addresses the relationship between the increasing technologisation of modern life and our attitudes to (and our theories about) nature and culture, draws attention to an essential hybridisation built into the very fabric of modernity. This hybridisation which she variously refers to as 'creolisation' (following Hannerz, 1988; 1990) and 'suburbanisation', expresses the central dynamic of contemporary Euro-American culture: the constant process of intermixing and interweaving, of creativity and constraint, of individuality and collectivity that marks the specificity of modern or post-modern culture.

Families and kin are themselves ambiguously set across these divides: they can be thought of as entities within tradition, something unique and specific which provides a basis for a shared sociality, or they can be seen as concatenations of individuals, either working together or moving away. Here is another expression, perhaps, of the idea of mobile privatisation as both a metaphorical and literal description of something more general and more far-reaching. The 'technologisation' and the 'denaturalisation' of the twentieth century extends its influence to other dimensions of social life. The point I think that Strathern is making is that this creative tension between stasis and movement, tradition and novelty, is intrinsic to, and a fundamental part of, twentieth-century culture, and to its various embodiments in social relations.

Culture consists, too, in our ability to think through these relationships, to find analogies for them, and to express them. Lying at the heart of Western perceptions of culture has been a primary distinction between nature and culture. It seems that we need to be able to distinguish between bodies and machines, between things that live and things that work, between the rural and the urban, between (though this is a slightly different register) reality and fantasy. In each case the two terms are defined in relation to each other. But this is now breaking down. Modernity (and I think also post-modernity) consists, Strathern seems to be suggesting, in the conflation and elision of these distinctions: a conflation and an elision which is itself, of course, cultural.

In modern society it is the city – the melting pot, the cosmopolitan (the urban cosmos, the microcosm) which symbolises so much of this awareness of the intermixings of culture. The city has provided a powerful focus for our critiques of, and our fantasies about, our place in society and culture. It is often seen as a realm of artifice, of technology, of the embodiment of the cultural as opposed to the natural – the urban as opposed to the rural. Yet the city is the locus, not of a hybridisation but of an 'unnatural juxtaposition'. The melting pot does not melt; the city is constructed in and through difference, in and through diversity.

Not so the suburb: 'Suburbia is neither urban nor rural. It may represent both; but when it is reproduced *as* suburbia, comes to represent neither' (191); it is neither creole nor cosmopolitan, 'for a mix that does not depend on distinction is no longer a mix'. Suburbia constitutes a new, a different, reality in which the crucial distinctions of culture – and the crucial but constantly shifting distinction between nature and culture – are absorbed into each other, to be lost under the weight of culture, of the artificial, of the technological. The suburb expresses that particular quality of modern culture in its own denial of perhaps the traditional difference between nature and culture: in its merging of nature and culture into a culturally created nature: into nature man-made. This collapse of the distinction between nature and culture which the suburb effects can be seen also to be represented *by* the suburb. The collapse of this crucial distinction – the collapse too of the distinction between bodies and machines as metaphors for each other (dramatically illustrated in the problems posed for us by the new reproductive technologies in which neither the body nor reproduction as such can remain untarnished by technology) – are symptomatic of a version of culture which is in essence hybrid, which is fundamentally suburban.

What I want to take from this discussion is the following: to see the suburban both as an historical product, a built environment constructed to provide a way of being which is neither rural nor urban, and which is both supported by and supports particular political, economic and social relation-ships – a form of life; to see the suburban as an idea and as an ideal – a dream for those wishing to escape the density of the city or the emptiness of the country, and a nightmare for those who regard the suburb as a sterile hybrid, the bastard child of unculture; to see the suburban as a symptom of, and as a metaphor for, a dominating trajectory of the culture of the twentieth century in which the ambiguities of that hybridisation (the ambiguities of progress and regress, isolation and connection, the private and the public, the global and the parochial, the individual and the collective, the real and the fantastic) are for ever intertwined.

And finally, to see television as of a piece with each of these three versions of the suburban: historically developed alongside the development of suburbia and reinforcing and enabling suburban existence by its presence; providing in its programmes – particularly in soap opera – images of the suburb, and offering objectifications of the dreams and nightmares of suburbanism within its own dominating mythologies; and, perhaps most crucially, as an institution and as a medium – in its forms and contents – as an engine of hybridisation, of the vigorous sterility of suburbanising culture as it creates, displays and mythically resolves all the ambiguities of modernity.

Now in pursuing this argument and in trying to hold on to these three levels of television's suburban character I run a number of risks. I don't imagine that I will avoid all of them but it is worth bearing in mind what they are before I step off the cliff.

The first is the risk of historical inaccuracy. The suburb is neither, in any sensible historical sense, a product of television, nor is television, literally, a product of the suburb. Suburbs preceded the introduction of television by some hundred years; television found its place within a suburban environment but was by no means as directly influential on the creation of those suburbs as advances in transportation and communication technologies which preceded its introduction. In pursuing the relationship between the suburb and television historically and sociologically (and following Raymond Williams in so doing), I want to characterise the relationship between the two more in terms of what Max Weber (in an entirely different context) talks of as an 'elective affinity'. The suburb and television are to be approached in their ideal typicalities in order to extract something of the central aspects of that relationship.

Second, there is the risk of reductionism. Television, I am arguing, is a suburban medium. It is suburban in its institutionalisation as a broadcast medium. It is suburban in the form and content of its programming. It is suburban through its incorporation into the fabric of everyday life. It is suburban in its expression and reinforcement of the particular balance of isolation and integration, uniformity and variety, global and parochial identities and cultures, that are, indeed, the mark of the suburban existence. Through these various manifestations of suburbanness, television is, to be sure, reduced. Yet television is not to be understood only in this way. The suburban character of television represents the socio-political aspect of the medium alongside, but also crucially dependent upon, its status both as a domestic and a psychodynamic phenomenon. I will go on in subsequent chapters to consider its status as technology and as the object of consumption.

Third, there is risk of a kind of universalism, and in particular of merely restating the characterisation of television as the *deus ex machina* of postmodernity. Jean Baudrillard (1981), in particular, offers an analysis of the medium's role in creating a culture of eternal self-reference and simulation. This is a version of hybridisation certainly, but it is one that takes little account of sociological or historical processes. Baudrillard expresses a view of the consequences of the medium which, in its own failures to make distinctions, is itself symptomatic of the condition he criticises. I hope to avoid falling into the same trap. I return to a discussion of his analysis of television later in this chapter.

The remainder of this chapter will consist of the following discussions: a brief account of the rise of the suburb as an international phenomenon and expression of modernity; a discussion of the relationship between suburbia and communications; an account of the problem of what I will rather loosely call the suburbanisation of the public sphere and television's role in creating it; a discussion of the soap opera as television's suburban genre, *par excellence*; and finally a discussion of hybridisation and simulation as ways of accounting for the particularity of television's suburbanness in postmodern culture.

SUBURBAN PASTS AND PRESENCE

In the city, Mars and Vulcan had become friends. Venus, neglected, sought the consolations of domesticity in a distant suburb.

(Mumford, 1938, 210)

The first suburb was probably built in Calcutta during the late 1770s. Chawringhee Road was the site of the development of well-ventilated freestanding houses, 'good habitation(s) in an open airy part of town' which William Hickey recommended as essential for the life of the employees of the

East India Company at the time. These houses, increasingly with verandahs, soon became the fashionable mean between houses in the centre, and the garden or country residences – 'bungilos' – away from the city (Girouard, 1985, 242). Both the form and content of the suburb, both its function and its aesthetic, derived from this colonial beginning. Suburbs were rapidly to spread first to Britain and to the early suburbanisation of London, and then further afield. As they spread they expressed the changing political economy of Western capitalism: an increasing amount of surplus capital and surplus time, initially for the upper and middle classes, then belatedly, for others in the population. The suburb was the product, Thorns (1972) argues, of five separate but related factors: increased mobility, congestion in the cities, increased availability of land (and funds) for building, the emergence of Town and Country Planning legislation (in Britain) and the engendering of social aspirations which associated the suburb with respectability, a high status and an essentially middle-class way of life.

The history of the suburb is at once a history of a built environment, socially, culturally and economically distinctive but also socially, culturally and economically dependent, a history of an idea and a history of an ideal. The first London suburb, in St John's Wood, contained gracious Palladian and neo-colonial cottages and villas, both detached and semi-detached, with their own chapel, inn, assembly rooms, pleasure garden and cricket ground. By 1813–14 it had developed into a complete suburb popular with people who 'wanted to live cheaply, quietly or conveniently for visits into or out of central London – which meant artists, architects, writers, retired East India Company officials and rich men's mistresses' (Girouard, 1985, 277). Not far away, Regent's Park was being developed, modelled on the city of Bath, but inscribing once and for all the ideal intermixing of country and city – urban development around a park – which was to provide the model of much mid- and late Victorian development of middle-class suburbs both around London and increasingly on the edges of the industrial cities of the Midlands and the north of England. The suburb was an attempt, by and for the middle classes, to get the best of both worlds: the country and the city. The early examples can be presumed to have inspired those who sought this particular hybrid utopia in specific acts of social engineering. Ebenezer Howard, the founder of the Garden Cities Association wrote in 1898, in what became a seminal treatise, that: 'Town and country must be married and out of this joyous union will spring a new hope, a new life, a new civilization' (quoted in Appelby, 1990, 22).

But the bulk of suburbia, both in this country and elsewhere was unplanned (Oliver *et al.*, 1981). And even if the ideal was middle-class, the residential and domestic environments often were not. Crucial for all suburban development were advances in transport, both public and then private. Railways, omnibuses, trams, and then the motor car, all, both in Britain and the United States, released a population from its locational dependence on the city. The separation of home and work became increasingly attenuated. Both time and space were split between production and consumption, work and leisure (King, 1980). Whole cities, perhaps most extremely, Los Angeles (Brodsly, 1981), grew rapidly, spreading low-density housing and low-density culture across enormous expanses of suddenly valuable real estate. The ideology of home ownership, the demand for single-family houses, the urgent need to provide cheap housing for the demobbed soldiers, particularly in the US after the war, all contributed to the growth of the suburb, all contributed to the creation of the suburb as the dominant form of housing in Western society in the twentieth century.

The patterns of suburban growth obviously varied from country to country. And in particular the British and the American experience differed, in terms of its timing (US suburbia was an almost entirely twentieth-century creation), in its character (much more consistently middle-class in the US) and in its planning (the various attempts through the garden city and new town experiments, as well as the involvement of the State in trying both to control unplanned development and provide homes for working people in Britain) (Thorns, 1972; Harvey, 1989). None of this was conducted, however, without a set of ideals and values that enshrined the suburb as an escape from, and a solution to, the ills of industrialisation. On the margins of the city, absorbing the countryside, providing single family household units for the middle class and those aspiring to become middle-class, the suburb offered a standardised dream, embodied in standardised units (prefabrication of buildings and components became the norm) within which, however, individuals could, and did, express their own individuality (see Miller, 1988).

This tension between standardisation and individualisation, between uniformity and diversity (a tension which I have already identified in my earlier discussion as being at the heart of culture) appears most forcibly as a characterisation of suburbia in Seeley et al.'s (1956) study of Crestwood Heights, a middle-class suburb of, presumably, Toronto.

The name itself, Crestwood Heights (although in fact it is a pseudonym in the study), is emblematic. It signifies the sylvan and the romantic, 'the suburb that looks out upon, and over, the city, not in it or of it, but at its border and its crest' (ibid., 1). The inhabitants of Crestwood Heights, middle-class all, depend on the city economically, but are economically in a position to buy into the North American dream, through their ability to purchase the privacy and the sunlight, the spacious houses and the gardens of the suburb, their cars, their freedom to travel, their sense of conquering both time and space. They can draw on the cultural excitment of the City and the peace and tranquillity of the not-too-distant wilderness of Northern Ontario. But they can return from both to the material and technological comforts of home: mass produced but individually consumed: customised in use and in display:

Here, then, is the raw material from which the dream may take on a form and shape. But selecting and rejecting elements, each family or person builds a special version, a particular cultural pattern, like and yet unlike the neighbours. The process is never fixed and final, for one learns to make new choices and new combinations endlessly.

(Ibid., 10)

Middle-class suburban life – child centred, competitive, sociable (but also lonely), exclusive, dependent on a particular balance of female domesticity and male social and geographical mobility, security and ambition – provides a concrete embodiment of a modern utopia (e.g. Gill, 1984) or for many, a dystopia (Sennett, 1986, 296–7; Mumford, 1938; Lodziak, 1986 etc.). Yet other suburban and neo-suburban developments: the Levittowns for the returning servicemen and aspiring middle classes in Long Island, Pennsylvania and New Jersey; the overspill estates for the working classes to relieve the pressures of the declining inner cities; the unplanned ribbon developments or commuter villages (what Thorns (1972, 88) calls 'the reluctant suburb'); industrial suburbs, both planned and unplanned, where domestic housing, and the population, is closely linked to a single local industrial complex; the garden suburbs; garden cities and new towns – all in their various ways, are expressions of this ideal.

Ideals will rarely match realities and these ideals are, of course, problematic in a number of different ways. And ideals themselves have consequences. For the history of the suburb is a history both of inclusion and exclusion, and above all it has involved the exclusion of all those who might tarnish that ideal, especially ethnic minorities, from full, and often any, participation in it. Furthermore, similarity in life-style does not necessarily lead to, nor is it synonymous with, community. Sociability and neighbourliness within the suburb do seem to be a product very much of similarities both in culture and position in the life-cycle. And they seem to break down when either or both of these are not present (in a new suburb of mixed ethnic groups, for example (Richards, 1990), or in a second- or third-generation suburb with families at different stages in their life-cycle). Equally the ideal, or expectation, that suburban life is in some essential sense middle-class and therefore likely to impose, environmentally as it were, a middle-class life-style on its non-middle-class residents is open to some dispute (see Wilmott and Young, 1960; Goldthorpe, *et al.*, 1969).

Yet in all these cases, what is not in dispute is the central importance of house and home. Those desirous of moving to the suburbs express those desires principally in terms of their ownership and occupation of their own private space (Richards, 1990): the house and garden, the garage and driveway, which provide, in microcosm, their own domestic hybrid.[1] The house, as I have already argued in general terms, is home. It is both the site and symbol of the suburbanisation of modernity. The house is:

an impressive and intricate material apparatus, the possession of which makes possible the [suburban] way of life, from a physical and, even, more important, from a psychological point of view . . .

. . . the house is a valuable means of ensuring privacy in a crowded city; a vehicle for enforcing family solidarity and conformity; a place to practice and perfect consumption skills; a major item of personal property, which, for the head of the family . . . stands as a concrete symbol of his status and visible sign of his success.

(Seeley *et al.*, 1956, 45–6)

Within the suburban house and around it, defining the conditions of its possibility, is to be found a complex set of social and cultural relations organised in time and space and through gender. The division of labour, of production and consumption, of public and private spaces and identities, of public and private times, of availability and privacy, sociability and separateness, work and leisure, is perhaps symbolised through the unique product of industrial capitalism, the weekend. As Anthony King (1980, 205) describes it, the weekend was a new temporal concept released by the material and symbolic surpluses of advancing capitalism:

defined in relation to place, a place different from the normal location of work and residence. The weekend was not simply a duration of time but also a spatio-temporal unit. The link was established by new modes of travel – the railway, the bicycle and the car. With the separation of work from residence, it had also a social dimension. The 'working week' was spent in town, in the company of office colleagues, the 'weekend' at home (or occasionally at the 'cottage'), in the company of wife and children.

King is writing, principally, about the emergence of the country cottage and bungalow as second homes; an initial and exaggerated expression, it might be suggested, of the dichotomisation of city and country that the suburb subsequently synthesised. But in that initial separation all the elements of suburbanisation are already clear.

The suburb (and the suburban household) is constructed in close proximity to the world of work and the world of the city. It can only really be understood within the particularities of industrial society's political economy. And as such it has to be understood in all its punishing paradoxicality: as politically both liberating and oppressing; as culturally both creative and sterile; and as sociologically both including and excluding. Within the household, both time and space are marked in terms of private and public domains; temporalities are fixed by the gendered tasks of daily, weekly and annual routines. The suburban home is for male leisure and female work. It has become possible, as many commentators have described, as a result of developments in technology – particularly transport technology. It has been sustained as an economic unit, in all its contradictions, by other technologies: the refrigerator, washing machine, vacuum cleaner (Cowan, 1989). It also has been sustained as a symbolic unit by communication technologies, of which the telephone (Pool, 1977; Moyal, 1992) and the television are preeminent.

THE SUBURBS AND COMMUNICATION

Clearly the suburb is a product of technological changes, particularly in transport and communications. Williams however, in his characterisation of the mobile privatisation inscribed within the recent generation of communication technologies, points to a powerful tension that lies at the heart of suburban life: a tension between mobility and stasis; individuality and collectivity; private and public life. If the early transport technologies: the omnibus, the tram, the light and underground railways, and the motor car provided both a mechanism for the dispersal and reconsolidation of populations, the second generation of communication technologies provided, in their parochial and global space–time distanciation, a reinforcement of the way of life already well developed in the suburb. To anticipate somewhat, it can be seen that the space for television had been created by a social and cultural fabric already prepared; a fabric – of natural and man-made fibres – which, in its fundamental hybridisation, provided an environment for the more or less determined acceptance of all the compromises and contradictions offered by the new medium.

Margaret Morse, in an extremely stimulating analysis, characterises this hybridisation in terms of *nonspace*:

> a nonspace of both experience and representation, an elsewhere which inhabits the everyday. Nonspace is not mysterious or strange to us, but rather the very haunt for creatures of habit. Practices and skills that can be performed semi-automatically in a distracted state – such as driving, shopping, or television watching – are the barely acknowledged ground of everyday experience. This ground is without locus, a partially derealized realm from which a new quotidian fiction emanates.
>
> (Morse, 1990, 195–6)

Television viewing, in Morse's discussion, has its analogies in the acts of driving and shopping, and in the other, particular, symbolic and material manifestations of suburban life: the freeway and the shopping mall. This is important, I believe, and in essence correct, though the notion of nonspace suggests a kind of cultural vacuum which I would wish to deny. Television viewing, driving and shopping, analogically and mutually, define, rather, a potential space, a hybrid space, within which individuals, families and neighbourhoods can create in different ways something of their own culture and their own identities: spaces for dreaming as well as spaces for action. Those spaces are the product of technological and social changes, but they are also continuously reconstructed in the daily activities of those who attend to them – distracted maybe, but nevertheless committed participants in the ongoing struggles of everyday life.

Yet suburbs are both consequence and cause of changes in the means of communication. The early growth of the London suburbs is significantly a history of the improved system of public transport which allowed commuting to take its place as the suburb's *sine qua non*. The first omnibus was introduced in 1829. By 1834 there were over a hundred omnibus services to South London alone. The first suburban railway line in London (between London and Greenwich) opened in 1836, the Metropolitan Railway in 1863 and the first underground in 1890. Cheap fares were offered to encourage working men to leave the inner city. The tram was electrified in 1901, the omnibus motorised in 1909. It has been estimated that there were 250,000 daily rail commuters in the London area by 1900. During the twentieth century suburban railways expanded and suburban roads were built, to link suburb and centre and also suburb to suburb. The motor car had arrived. Clearly other factors were relevant to the growth of suburbs (Thorns, 1972, 35ff.). But equally clearly, and not just in London, the increasing mobility of an urban population provided the crucial catalyst for suburban development, both in the UK and elsewhere in the world.

In Los Angeles, that supremely suburban city, the story is similar, though of course also very different both in its timing and its character. As David Brodsly suggests, Los Angeles was almost entirely the product of railway and freeway development, a suburban city held together by a lattice of concrete mediations, an urban sprawl, an urban scrawl:

> The power of the freeway system to shape a metropolitan sensibility cannot be understated [sic]. The freeways have almost single-handedly expanded the realm of the accessible, and thus they have enlarged what most people recognize as their metropolitan environment . . . As a result of new freeway construction and of highway improvements, the area of land within a thirty minute drive from the civic centre rose from 261 square miles in 1953 to 705 square miles by 1962, an increase of 175 per cent . . .
>
> In the metropolis distance becomes a function of time.
>
> (Brodsly, 1981, 32–3)

Los Angeles is a suburban metropolis. It is, he suggests, 'a living polemic against both the large industrial metropolis and the provincial small town . . . a society integrated by rubber tyres' (ibid., 33, 37). The freeway connects a set of points, spaces not places, and the metropolis that it has created has become only a context for dwelling, a space of passage. Journeys are measured in terms of time, the time taken, the time spent, in the impenetrable privacy, at once domestic and suburban, of the car.

But the car, in particular, and its extension in the road network that has been designed to accommodate it, is not just a material artifact, a techno-logical object. It lies at the centre of a socio-economic and symbolic system

(Lefebvre, 1984, 100). Above all it can be seen to be embedded in almost every aspect of the suburban way of life, mutually reinforcing and being reinforced by, the symbiosis of nature and culture, the public and private, which define the suburb's specificity.

James L. Flink (1988) talks of the automobile–refrigerator complex. The car, together with the range of domestic technologies that had the refrigerator at its head, transformed shopping and food preparation. The consequences were profound both for the retail trade (the supermarket replaced the local store) and for domestic life (though how far the 'housewife' was liberated by such a development is moot (Cowan, 1989; Gershuny, 1982)). The kitchen, suggests Flink, began to lose its status as the centre of the household. More people ate out, and ate fast. The consequences were also profound for domestic architecture and domestic life, particularly in the United States, where the automobile encouraged leisure time away from the home. The front porch and the parlor were eliminated. Rooms became less specialised and the garage moved to the front, and then became an integral part, of the house. '[The] prominence of the driveway and direct entry into the kitchen from the garage turned the suburban home into an extension of the street' (Flink, 1988, 167).

The suburban house may have become an extension of the street, but the car became an extension of the suburban house. Boundaries between public and private spaces had become less distinct, more permeable, transparent even. Indeed the new suburban houses had large picture windows from behind which the equally large picture windows of the neighbours could be seen, and from within which the objects by which the household most wanted to express its own status and identity could be revealed for all to see.[2]

If the dispersion into the suburb can be laid at the door of the automobile (and of earlier, public, forms of mass transportation), its consolidation can be ascribed to the electronic communication technologies: the telephone, the radio and the television, that followed. The suburb remains, of course. Still a hybrid. A materialisation in space and time of the fusion that culture has imposed on nature. The machine in the garden. Connection and separation. Mobile privatisation. The radio and the telephone left people where they were. No need to travel. Each household became the centre of a network: of broadcasting in which nations and neighbourhoods shared a common culture (Scannell, 1989); and of telecommunications in which households, through the activity, principally of the 'housewife', were linked to other households, both of kin and friendship (Moyal, 1989). Falls in the numbers of those attending the cinema are symptoms of the withdrawal of entertainment into the home. Increasing expenditure on do-it-yourself indicates another dimension of at-homeness which the media enable and reinforce.[3] With extraordinary prescience (though perhaps with a little bit of muddle) Lewis Mumford in 1938 foresaw it all:

With the return of entertainment to the house, through the phonograph, the radio and the motion picture [sic] – with the near prospect of television – the modern house has gained in recreational facilities what it lost through the disappearance of many of the earlier household industries. The radio and the telephone, moreover, have made the house no less a center of communication than was the old market place.

(Mumford, 1938, 467)

But it is not just the character of domestic space nor indeed the domestication of public space which new technologies made possible and which the suburb embodied. Perhaps even more signifcant was the change in the political environment that accompanied these social and technological transformations, a change, potentially of great significance, in the relationship between the private and the public sphere and in what I shall call the suburbanisation of the public sphere.

THE SUBURBANISATION OF THE PUBLIC SPHERE

The appearance of, and the subsequent decline in, or erosion of, the public sphere within capitalist society, and of the media's role in both its rise and fall, are subject to much debate. It is clearly not going to be possible to address all the issues or provide a fully satisfactory account here. Nevertheless the continuing status of the public sphere: a culturally and politically defined public space where the democratic process, the to-ing and fro-ing of informed and enlightened discussion, can be pursued unhindered and unfettered by the forces of the State or the compromises of the market, is of great importance both at a macro and a micro political level. At issue, among other things, is the quality of the politics of everyday life, of broadcasting and television's role, contemporarily, in providing a framework for that politics, and above all, from the point of view of my argument here, of the quality of suburban politics, and the politics of the suburb, that can be seen to have emerged during modern times. At issue too is the nature of privacy, and of privatisation, for the public and the private can only be defined in relation to each other. Public and private shift their character and their balance as social, cultural, and economic changes affect the institutionalisation and dynamics of power at both a structural and a quotidian level.

The starting point for any discussion of the emergence and supposed decline of the public sphere in capitalist society – for it is argued that the public sphere is a specific product of capitalism – must be the writings of Jürgen Habermas.

Habermas (1989) describes the emergence, initially in eighteenth-century Britain, of what he calls the public sphere as a direct consequence of the material and cultural freeing of the bourgeoisie with the advance of capitalist society. This new class gained the time and the material resources to engage 'in public' – in literature, in newspapers, in coffee-house discussions – with the world of affairs: their affairs. This public sphere occupied a space between the increasing domination of civil society by the State and the private realm of economic and personal relations, the latter of which became progressively privatised and withdrawn. The public sphere, or at least Habermas' idealisation of it, provided both the opportunity and the resources for the involvement of the private individual (all private individuals in principle) to engage in a politics of rational discussion, a politics in which the business of the State (and the state of business) could be subjected to analysis and debate. Central to the vitality of such a public sphere was the newspaper, originally a presenter of information, increasingly, during the eighteenth century, a forum for the expression of opinion.

Habermas argues that this brief flowering of the public sphere began to decline as the other institutions created by capitalism assumed greater dominance. The increasingly interventionist State, which took on more and more of the traditional responsibilities of civil society (welfare, education) and the increasing power of the market and of monopoly capitalism, squeezed the public sphere into insignificance. The commercialisation and 'massification' of culture, the control of information, the profound inequalities of access to public fora were the result. Citizens became consumers; the public sphere became refeudalised. The mass media, at first the essential support for free public debate, became the instruments of its suppression, as 'new techniques were employed to endow public authority with the kind of aura and personal prestige which was once bestowed by the staged publicity of the feudal courts' (Thompson, 1990, 113). The private citizen, the individual actor on the public stage, was relegated to the wings of a uniform and isolated domesticity:

> The shrinking of the private sphere into the inner areas of a conjugal family largely relieved of function and weakened in authority – the quiet bliss of homeyness – provided only the illusion of a perfectly private personal sphere; for to the extent that private people withdrew from their socially controlled roles as property owners into the purely 'personal' ones of their noncomittal use of leisure time, they came directly under the influence of semipublic authorities, without the protection of an institutionally protected domestic domain. Leisure behaviour supplies the key to the floodlit privacy of the new sphere.
>
> (Habermas, 1989, 159)

The phrase 'floodlit privacy' in this quotation perfectly captures another aspect of suburban life to add to Williams' 'mobile privatisation'. The suburb is reinforced as a social and cultural oxymoron. In this case it is manifested, architecturally in the dialogicality of the picture window, and politically, less in terms of a focus on the politics of the State than on the politics of status (Veblen, 1925).

There are a number of obvious criticisms of Habermas' characterisation of the public sphere, as well as a number of strengths. Its strengths, as Garnham (1986) points out, are those of insisting on the importance of a separate sphere distinct from the economy and the State, and the correlative importance of a strong and independent media, which can provide the essential support for a significant democratic politics. Its weaknesses are historical and sociological. The public sphere was never public in the sense that all members of the public had equal access to it. It was restricted, for all practical purposes, to bourgeois males. It is also individualistic in that it presumes both that the individual has full access to all the relevant information and debates, and equally that there are no mediating institutions within the public sphere whose task it is to manage or to control the movement of information within it (ibid.).

More substantially, however, Thompson (1990) challenges not just the historical accuracy, but also the present relevance of the Habermasian position. Whereas others (e.g. Elliott, 1982; Lodziak, 1986) have taken it as sufficient to provide the basis for a thoroughgoing critique of the 'politics of consumerism' within modern society, Thompson suggests that Habermas has not just got the history wrong, but that the present media environment provides for the continuing sustenance of the public sphere, though not in quite the terms that Habermas defined it. Since Thompson's arguments are important for my own position in relation to the suburbanisation of the public sphere, I will briefly review them.

He makes four points. The first is that Habermas' notion that the commercialisation of the mass media has led to a refeudalisation of the public sphere is belied by the contradictions embedded in modern communication, in which increasing visibility, multiplicity of channels and a better informed electorate, offer both increasing reach for the communicators but also increasing possibilities for resistance among their audiences. Second, Thompson (following much of recent media scholarship), suggests that Habermas underestimates the active engagement of media consumers, treating them as entirely vulnerable to the media's influence, and equally underestimating the new kind of fragility which political processes acquire in the era of mass communication.[4] Third, Habermas misunderstands the nature of ideology, seeing it exclusively (at least in his early work) in terms of false consciousness and the depoliticisation of everyday life. Finally the relevance of Habermas' version of the public sphere to contemporary society comes under scrutiny. Here Thompson suggests that Habermas' notion of the public sphere was grounded exclusively in an understanding of print-based culture. Electronic means of communication have radically altered the conditions under which public debate takes place. In addition, the complexity of national and international politics have made participatory opinion-formation at that level impossible, though participatory democracy at other levels can be maintained.

Thompson attempts to sustain a notion of the public sphere despite the significant changes which he notes have taken place in the political, cultural and technological life of modern society:

> Television and other media have generated a new type of public realm which has no spatial limits, which is not necessarily tied to dialogical conversation and which is accessible to an indefinite number of individuals who may be situated within privatized domestic settings. Rather than sounding the death knell of public life, the development of mass communication has created a new kind of publicness and has transformed fundamentally the conditions under which most people are able to experience what is public and participate today in what could be called a public realm.
>
> (Thompson, 1990, 246)

The public sphere alive or dead? Participation real or imagined? A new kind of publicness or an old kind of pseudo-publicness? These questions are not easily resolved and Thompson does not resolve them. He does not, above all, identify what that public realm consists of, nor does he consider what kind of power can be exercised within it.

What remains at issue is the compatibility or incompatibility between the particular character of contemporary mass media, its domestication, and an active engagement in public life: the compatibility or incompatibility between democracy and consumerism. Paddy Scannell (1989) argues that public service broadcasting, at least in the UK, has provided a framework for a genuine kind of public involvement in public life; in its reasonableness, not in its rationality. Public service broadcasting creates, in its variety, and above all in its mode of address – in its domestication of the public utterance – what he calls a communicative ethos in which a relaxed conversational style of presentation provides the basis for a particular production of the essential elements of contemporary public life:

> The world, in broadcasting, appears as ordinary, mundane, accessible, knowable, familiar, recognizable, intelligible, shareable and communicable for whole populations. It is talkable about by everyone. This world does not exist elsewhere. It is not a reflection, a mirror, of a reality outside and beyond. It is one fundamental, seen but unnoticed, constitutive component of contemporary reality for all.
>
> (Scannell, 1989, 152)

In this version of public culture, public utterances are domesticated and correlatively the domestic becomes part of public culture (ibid., 143). Broadcasting, in its provision of information and ideas, images and stories provides the stuff of everyday life: its gossip and its glue. Here is a new kind of – genuine – public sphere, according to Scannell, but a public sphere that is constructed at the local level, albeit with materials provided nationally or globally.

The suburb is where this culture is supposed to take shape. And this public culture is essentially suburban. Understanding it is not a matter, as Habermas and others have argued, of opposing a politics of the public sphere to the politics of consumerism, in which participation in a democracy is replaced by participation in a market. It is, rather, a matter of understanding how the particular politics of modernity is constructed out of the mix of mass-mediated public information (and public entertainment) and mass participation in the consumption of images, objects and ideas, and the way they are appropriated by individuals, households and groups in order to construct their identities and the bases for both individual and collective social action. It is this particular mix of the public and the private, of the individual and the collective, of the democrat and the consumer, that is forged in the activities of everyday life, and indeed has become the hall-mark of the hybridising life of the suburb (see Whyte, 1956, 280). This hybridisation raises questions about the democratic potential of the media in general and television in particular, for like so much of what takes place in and through the suburb, the tension of creativity and sterility, power and impotence which is expressed in suburban politics can often be seen to be very unequal. It is, or can be, democratic in name only.

As Lewis Mumford notes:

In creating a better biological environment, however, the builders of the suburb failed to take account of the need for a more adequate social environment . . . [the suburb] started a de-politicizing process that has been steadily spreading as the suburb itself has been spreading throughout our civilisation.

(Mumford, 1938, 217)

A number of case studies provide some indication of how the politics of the suburb has been played out. Suburban politics extends all the way from organised action within or on behalf of the 'community' to membership of clubs or organisations which may or may not have a declared political identity – but can and often do exert political influence, for example Parent–Teachers Associations. Suburban politics will also include, of course, in formally democratic societies at least, the vote. But a consideration of suburban politics also requires an acknowledgement of the absence of politics: or perhaps more accurately an anti-politics of withdrawal from the public sphere – of conformity, self-interest and exclusion.

At the heart of much of the politics, indeed of the life, of a suburb is the desire to avoid conflict. Baumgartner's study of an American suburb (1988) draws attention to what he calls 'moral minimalism', whose source is this very desire to avoid conflict. The suburb, as he characterises it, is an environment which combines transiency with homogeneity, and autonomy and independence with a relative absence of strangers. Avoidance is the main strategy that suburbanites adopt to deal with threats, conflicts or disturbances. Baumgartner paints a picture of a neighbourhood environment in which every aspect of social life – above all those dimensions of social life which create a sense of community – are missing. In a high status suburb, even the stranger – the most potent of threats – is dealt with in an insipid and disengaged manner: 'only when they can be assured that someone else will bear the full burden of moral authority, allowing them to remain completely anonymous and uninvolved, do suburbanites approve the exercise of social control' (Baumgartner, 1988, 127). He points to yet a further sociological paradox of suburban life: the mutual juxta-position of a kind of basic fragmentation and individualisation within social life with a high degree of order: 'The most apparently disintegrative tendencies of modern life actually breed a harmonious social order all of their own' (ibid., 134).

Baumgartner's view of suburban politics is, perhaps, overdetermined because of the blandness of the particular suburb which provides the basis of his investigation, but also because he seems to construct his view of suburban order principally in terms of its defensiveness in relation to threat. This is, of course, an important dimension of suburban political life, as Richard Sennett (1986, 301ff.) illustrates in his discussion of the defence of Forest Hills during the early 1970s. However, as Sennett himself describes, such defensiveness can also provide the basis for a coordinated and aggressive neighbourhood politics, a politics of moral outrage, territoriality and 'ghettoisation', as when this predominantly Jewish middle-class suburb was threatened by New York City's attempt to build working-class and potentially ethnically diverse housing within its neighbourhood. This is neither unusual nor unfamiliar. And suburban politics is only a democratic politics, often, within the narrow confines of the suburb itself. Not in my backyard.

But equally a perception of politics as defence may lead to an under-estimation of the significance of other dimensions of public life within the suburb. It may also lead to an overestimation of the suburb as the key determinant of aspects of the social structure of everyday life to be observed within it. In this sense suburban politics is also a class politics: so too is the politics within the suburb. For instance Thorns (1972) draws attention to the level of participation in organisations (from religious organisations to Parent–Teachers Associations to membership of local branches of national political parties) observed in a number of studies of suburban life both in the UK and the USA. Participation rates vary of course; but one striking factor is their more or less consistent skewing towards the middle classes. Middle-class suburbs reveal a higher degree of participation in 'neighbourhood' or 'community' activities than do working-class suburbs (Gans, 1967; Seeley et al., 1956); and within more heterogeneous suburbs, the middle classes exhibit a higher degree of participation than those who are nominally working class (Willmott and Young, 1960; Thorns, 1972). This is true both for membership and intensity of participation. It is perhaps less true, or less clear, for those (increasingly informal) activities that shade off into participation in public leisure activities, or in the shared sociability of the public or the private house. Evidence seems to suggest, however, that these activities are becoming increasingly privatised, especially compared to the pattern of social life in the city (Willmott and Young, 1960). And this privatisation is precisely what is at issue in discussions of the role of the media in the sustenance of the public sphere.

Finally, however, suburban politics also includes a more subtle but not necesssarily any less comfortable politics of identity – a domestic politics in which, above all, gender relations are centrally involved. These politics – the politics of housework (Oakley, 1974), the politics of television viewing (Morley, 1986), the politics of domestic space (Hunt, 1989; Mason, 1989) – are all expressions not only in the private domain, but also in the public one, of the constant negotiation and renegotiation of gender (and age-based) identities and relations: privately in the sitting rooms, bedrooms and kitchens of the home, publicly in the integrated or segregated gatherings of women and men in community associations, in the organising of child care, in the pubs or local party meetings.[5] As I have already pointed out the home is itself an essential component in the politics of status – the suburban politics *par excellence* – in which an engagement with the consumer products of the public sphere provides the basis for a subtle – and intensely gendered – struggle for the self.

I am of course arguing that an understanding of the dynamics of these various political processes must take television (and other media) into account. Specifically, now, I want to concentrate on three aspects of television's involvement. The first is through the genre which provides, perhaps most clearly, images of suburban life which both mythically and functionally, formally and substantively, can be seen to be offering images and models of the suburban way of life. The second is by considering some of the ways in which television, both in its scheduling and in the particular temporality of the soap opera's narrative itself, provides a framework for the temporal structure of the suburban day. And the third is by focusing briefly on the ways in which that genre, soap opera, provides the raw material for the glue of social intercourse in suburban (and indeed in other) environments: through gossip and the secondary discourses surrounding the plots and characters of the everyday stories of urban, suburban and country folk.

SUBURBAN TEXTS

In the last chapter I drew attention to the various ways in which television, principally through the situation comedy, provides models for family life, in its endless regurgitation of family dynamics both in the domestic and the work setting. The soap opera is a more complex form for my argument.[6] On the face of it, especially in the UK, it seems much more preoccupied with environments that are anything but suburban: the declining or revitalised working-class inner-city area on the one hand (*Coronation Street*, *East-Enders*), or the rural idylls of *Emmerdale* on the other. Only *Brookside*, the more real than real, Liverpool-based, soap opera has a location firmly fixed within the suburban heartland, though *Crossroads* could also be seen to have been located in suburbia and also embodying both profoundly suburban values and a kind of suburban ontology (in its name and even in the standard of its acting).[7] American soaps are, or were, much more consistently secure in a suburban (or small town) environment, a version of which provides the parodic stimulus for the recent *Twin Peaks*. The Australian appropriation of the genre could be described in broadly similar terms. Finally, more widely, and more internationally, the likes of *Dallas*, *Dynasty* and the rest, though not strictly speaking soap opera (which is an essentially parochial genre), offer a vision of what can be described as a kind of suburban hyper-reality, in which the various characters play out the new frontier, struggling with the tension of the transfer of the old Western, traditional, values into the new West: a potent mixture of place, tradition, family values and the frantic struggle for 'stability, happiness and success' (Newcomb, 1982, 171).

However, the argument that the soap opera is a suburban genre is not based necessarily, or only, on an examination of the content of single examples. What I want to suggest is that, taken as a whole, that is taken as a system in the Lévi-Straussian sense of the term, the soap opera provides, mythically, a cultural form in which the problems of the suburb and of the suburban are worked through. It is impossible, of course to demonstrate this conclusively. But I will try and explain what I mean.

Lévi-Strauss' (1969) analysis of the systematic nature of pre-Columbian mythology depends crucially on understanding each myth and each set of myths as part of a wider system which contains them all. Within this system the myths (individual stories or variants of stories) are related to each other through transformative relations. These transformative relations, the principles by which, Lévi-Strauss argues, the system is held together, provide a means whereby each mythic story can also be understood as growing out of a particular society and culture. The story-teller will draw on what is to hand in his or her own environment to fashion his or her own particular narrative, but according to rules that are familiar to the listeners and which also mark the story as a myth, that is as something which is both of, and beyond, everyday experience. The myths also function to provide a kind of commentary on the basic problems of existence in every society and all societies, dealing with matters of life and death, gender relations, nature and culture, the origins of things, in such a way as to reassure by the closure that each narrative offers.

The soap opera is not a mythic narrative in the simple sense in which Lévi-Strauss defines it, and I am not going to suggest that it is structured in the same way as the myths that he analyses: that is, with the same degree of narrative closure (see Geraghty, 1990). What I do want to suggest, however, is that both within each soap opera as an example of the genre,[8] and within the genre as a mythic system, the same kind of narrative and functional dimensions are visible. The system of soap opera includes within it narratives that are set in urban, rural and suburban settings. Between and amongst them the problems which suburbanness attempts to deal with, and of which it is itself a mythic (utopian or dystopian) resolution – the problems of nature and culture, of the rural and the urban, of the stranger and the friend, of gender and family relations and so on – are displayed and worked through, constantly and continuously. They become a kind of Greek chorus for the drama of everyday life.

In much of the literature on soap opera the key term which students of the genre have chosen to define is that of community (e.g. Geraghty, 1990 for a recent example). There is no doubt that this is an accurate assessment of much of what soap operas are about: yet community is a peculiarly disembodied notion, and the focus of soap opera is better posed as a problem of the modern community, that is in terms of the 'suburban community' which provides the framework both for the lives of its audiences (though by no means exclusively so: see Liebes and Katz, 1991) as well as of its characters. This community is constructed however not just in the content of the soap opera but in its form; in the secure, endless and structured recursiveness of the ordinariness and crises of the daily lives of its characters. The fictional populations of *EastEnders* and *Coronation Street*, as well as those of *Brookside*, no less than those of *Dallas* and *Dynasty*, and especially those of *Home and Away* and *Neighbours* are involved in a cultural exploration of the nature of the suburban – both of its heartland and its margins, its content and its forms. The suburban is worked through not just in each example of the genre but in the genre as a whole. This, I want to suggest, is its major significance.

Yet the argument can be pushed a little further. The soap opera is, principally, a female genre. Historically created for women at home who were perceived to be the principal audience of the radio programmes and the principal consumers of the soap powders that were advertised within them, they were scheduled at times when the housewife could listen without being too distracted from the chores of her daily routine – chores that were themselves expressions of the distracted and fragmented labour of housework. Tania Modleski (1983) has made this perception a central part of her understanding of the gendering of the genre and of its central place in the daytime television schedules. Both programme and schedule are fragmented. Narrative lines are both endless and endlessly completed; story lines fragment and converge. The programmes themselves are interrupted by advertisements:

The formal properties of daytime television . . . accord closely with the

rhythms of women's work in the home. Individual programs like soap
operas as well as the flow of programs and commercials tend to make
repetition, interruption and distraction pleasurable ... Since the housewife's "leisure" time is not so strongly demarcated, her entertainment
must often be consumed on the job.

(Modleski, 1983, 73)

The programmes and the schedules are, in this argument, of a piece. The
domestic life of the housewife, but especially the suburban housewife, is a
product of the mobile privatisation that is the suburb: a domestic world that is
constructed through the particular relations of public and private spheres as
they are worked out in the constantly shifting balance of work and leisure
both within the home and outside it. The television schedule, and the soap
opera which expresses, in its fragmented flow, its own narrative structure,
together provide one of the coordinates of the temporal structuring of the
everyday. The soap operas themselves, in their constant mastication of
domestic and family relations, of neighbourhood and work, crisis and routine,
drama and tragedy, provide a backloth to, but also an expression of, the
gendered iteration of life in the suburb.

But what of that iteration? Does the relationship of soap opera to it stop
with the screen? Of course it does not. Perhaps one of the most important
dimensions of Dorothy Hobson's study of the British soap opera *Crossroads*
was her willingness to trace its significance for the lives of its viewers and
particularly in terms of its status as an object of talk, of gossip, both within the
home and outside it. As Geraghty (1990) argues, there is much more in the
relationship of the soap opera audience to its characters than can usefully be
described in terms of identification, yet in the 'tragic structure of feeling'
(Ang, 1986) or in the constant oscillation of identification and comparision
(Radway, 1984), but above all in talk, the life of the soap opera pervades life
in the home, life over the garden wall, on the street, in the pub, in the canteen
and in the factory (Hobson, 1989). This is true particularly, though not
exclusively, for women.[9] And it is, perhaps increasingly, the life-blood of the
fragmented sociability of the suburb.

Finally it is worth pointing out that the television text, the soap opera text
in this case, is only one aspect of the proliferation of meanings surrounding
television that circulate within everyday life. The gossip and the talk is
informed as much by the discussions about the actors and their roles, the
characters and their private lives, which are offered on a daily basis in the
newspapers and periodicals, as about the television programme itself. As
Hodge and Tripp (1986, 143) observe:

Discourse about television is itself a social force. It is a major site of the
mediation of television meanings, a site where television meanings fuse
with other meanings into a new text to form a major interface with the
world of action and belief.

This discourse is prompted both by television and by other parasitical, public discussions of television. I shall discuss the implications of this observation more fully in Chapter 6. Suffice it to say now, however, that daily life – suburban life in all its typicality – is multiply structured, in part, by the meanings that television generates and fosters. The soap opera, perhaps exceptionally, provides much of the fodder for that daily discourse, the discourse of suburban neighbourliness and peer-group interaction.

POLITICS OF THE SUBURB

Perhaps it is no accident that Jean Baudrillard (1983) opens his account of the particularity of television's significance in an age of simulation – an age in which signs and representations gain the status of reality in an endless play of mutual reference – with a discussion of American television's long running saga of the Loud family, broadcast in 1971. The subject of a television-verité experiment, the Louds were presented as a typical (or typically hyper-real) three-garage, five-children, well-to-do, Californian family whose everyday life would be faithfully reproduced on television: filmed by a camera which watches as if it were not there, and watched by an audience which is not there but which *is* there by virtue of that very camera (the knotted torture of the syntax here echoes the knotted torture of the simulation). 'Where is the reality in all of this?' Baudrillard asks. And the answer: everywhere and nowhere. It is absorbed, leached, in the eternal display of images, commodities, spectacles and representations, all of which owe their significance and insignificance to the insidious merging of medium and message in the mass media's new tyrannical hold on contemporary (and now post-modern) culture:

> Television, in the case of the Louds for example, is no longer a spectacular medium. We are no longer in the society of spectacle which the situationists talked about, nor in the specific types of alienation and repression which this implied. The medium itself is no longer identifiable as such, and the merging of the medium and the message is the first great formula of this new age. There is no longer any medium in the literal sense: it is now intangible, diffuse and diffracted in the real, and it can no longer be said that the latter is distorted by it.
>
> (Baudrillard, 1983, 54)

In the example of the Louds (and later in a similar series in the UK) a version of suburban life was reproduced, mirrored in the lens of the 'unlying' camera and the 'faithful' screen: more real than real. The family, in both the American and the British examples did not ('in fact') survive the experience. Yet the suburban family, Baudrillard seems to be saying, is the perfect fodder for a medium whose meaning is the denial of meaning; for a medium whose most powerful affect lies in its denial of the difference between public and private worlds (see Meyrowitz, 1985); and for a medium that, in its broadcast form, fundamentally hybridises culture.

Baudrillard's characterisation of the medium of television, and of the post-modern culture which he sees as having been created by it, involves the blurring of the essential (or essentially modern) distinctions that I have already noted as those that the suburb is also challenged with blurring. The culture which television, *inter alia*, creates is the culture of the suburb, already the site of an homogenised, depoliticised culture: a domestic culture that is no longer private; a public culture that is, through the media, domesticated; a politicised culture without power; an informed and informing culture without information.

Baudrillard has been justly criticised for the scale of his generalisations, his technocentrism, his pessimism and his lack of attention to the sociological, political and historical factors that would actually need to be applied to any adequate analysis of the relationship between media, culture and society (Kellner, 1989, 72). As Margaret Marsh (1990, 188–9) points out in her study of the rise of the American suburb:

> Americans have moved to the suburbs since the early nineteenth century, but living in the suburbs meant something different in each period of suburban growth . . . From the fringe communities of the early nineteenth century to the 'technoburbs' of the late twentieth, the relationship of the city and the suburb has been changing . . . The residential suburbs of the 1950's, which sheltered nuclear families with young children in racially homogeneous enclaves, were the culmination of more than a century of the creation of a set of political and cultural beliefs. That era is over.

Both suburbs and the media are changing. With respect to the first, Marsh points to yet another suburban paradox. Alongside the consolidation of suburbia within American society comes not only its increasing physical and cultural distance from the city, but also its 'urbanisation' as homogeneity has given way to heterogeneity, and as the family and community ideals of the predominantly middle class are breaking down. Running through these changes, and profoundly influencing them, has been the changing status of suburban women, who are increasingly involved in the workforce, and are increasingly unlikely to be part of a nuclear family.

With respect to the second, the media, it is possible to point to an equivalent fragmentation, at least at the level of technology and delivery systems. The coherence that broadcasting offered both to the suburban community and the community of suburbs, is also beginning to break down. Satellite, cable and video provide – at least superficially – an increasingly heterogeneous television culture, unconstrained by the schedule or over-arching reach of 'national' culture.

Yet these changes can easily be exaggerated. The forms of life that have sustained the suburb throughout its long and varied existence, as well as the cultural forms that have sustained television, are not simply going to disappear. Nor can they. For they are both of a piece with the suburbanisation of culture which provides an essential link, I believe, between modernity and post-modernity. This hybrid culture, paradoxically both sterile and creative, which no longer offers us the security of boundary and difference is, as Marilyn Strathern has argued, sustained and supported by technological developments and technologies' trespass on natural (p)reserves.

And politics in and of the suburb is still, mostly, a domestic politics of self-interest, conformity and exclusion undertaken within political structures which are, mostly, barely recognised, let alone challenged. It is a politics of anxiety. It is a politics of defence. The suburbanisation of the public sphere has produced a politics of invulnerable vulnerability, a fragile web of technologically mediated strands of information and illusion. Participation of a kind may have been substantially enhanced by the mediation of national and international agendas, by access to the public and private lives of those in power, by a constant critique and analysis of the issues of the day, but the terms of that participation and the possibilities for its realisation are very much in question, and very much the product of the essential tensions of media, culture and power in contemporary everyday life.

Equally, the choices that are made from the offerings of broadcast television, out of which individuals, to a greater or lesser degree, construct their own cultural identities and which become core components of their daily lives, are all cut from the same cloth. We are all, to some extent, *bricoleurs*, but our *bricolage*, even in a post-Fordist world of flexible specialisation, is the product of a standardised, if not standardising, material and symbolic environment.

The suburbanisation of the culture and society of the twentieth century is one which, in its fundamental structure, is sustained by the existing forms and content of television. It can be suggested that boundaries are denied in both; differences are conflated in both; public and private spheres are elided in both; nature and culture are merged in both; realities and fantasies are confused in both; and power is exercised (but also resisted) through both. In the next three chapters I will explore, in more detail, some of the dimensions of this: through an examination of television as technology, of television and consumption and of the present state of research on the television audience.

Chapter 4

The tele-technological system

The arrival of ice in certain fishing villages in Sri Linka bought new-found wealth to the traditional fishermen, now that their fish could be transported to inland markets. Yet their villages remained remote, boasting no electricity, no roads, no piped water. Despite the lack of what we would regard as some of the essential basics of everyday life, a number of the richer fishermen invested their new-found wealth in television sets, garages for their houses and water cisterns for their roofs. Why did they do it? Why did they, in particular, install television sets that could not be watched? There are many possible explanations. The anthropologist (Stirratt, 1989, 107) who reported this behaviour suggested that this was an example, exaggerated, absurd maybe, of something we all know about: a kind of conspicuous consumption, an aping of middle-class values. But another anthropologist (Gell, 1986, 113–15) offers a different view. He suggests that the television was certainly conspicuously consumed, but that this consumption spoke of their own lives and of the labour that went in to the earning of their new wealth. The television symbolised all that their own lives were not: opposed to the messy, precarious, smelly, technological and economic uncertainties of their daily routines, the television – 'a smooth dark cabinet of unidentifiable grainless wood, geometrically pure lines, an inscrutable gray face, and within, just visible through the rows of little holes and slots at the back, an intricate jungle of wire, plastic, and shining metal' (Gell, 1986, 114) – a television without sounds and pictures – became the embodiment both of modernity and of their own achievements.

Yet another version of life in a Sri Lankan fishing village is offered by Stephen Hill (1988). In this account it was not ice but the mechanisation of the fishing boats and the introduction of nylon nets which transformed the local economy, dragging it into a cash economy, bankrupting most of the poorer fishermen, undermining traditional social relations and creating a microcosm of the social structure of the capitalist society of which they had now become, unwittingly, a dependent part:

Originally within the Sri Lankan villages there was willing acceptance of the new technologies of mechanised boats and synthetic fishing nets. Both technologies appeared to provide greater ease of labour, greater wealth and greater power. But neither technology could be *integrated* into existing productive practices or stocks of knowledge ... behind the immediate artefacts stood the modern industrial production system that villagers had to depend upon for the new production practices to survive.

(Hill, 1988, 78)

Technology, it can be seen, does not come naked. It does not come neutral. Nor, indeed does it come simply or straightforwardly. For technology arrives, dramatically in the case of the Sri Lankans, stealthily perhaps in our own case, carrying on its back a burden of social, economic and political implications, and carrying in its baggage bundles of material and symbolic string which tie those who use it into systems of social relations and cultural meanings, which are as disguised and unwelcome sometimes as they are obvious and welcome.

And television is, certainly, technology. Watching it is not just a matter of watching a window on the world, as if somehow the glass of the screen provided an innocent vision of the world untarnished by the politics of representation. Nor is watching it necessarily a submission to the irresistible forces of dominant ideologies and political manipulation. Watching television draws the viewer into a world of ordered meanings, ordered by and within an increasingly global network of institutional and cultural systems: systems which include the increasingly sophisticated and converging technologies of information and communication – the screens, satellites, fibre-optics, computers of an emerging information age; systems which include the multinational institutions that increasingly control the production and distribution of the programmes and software on a global scale; and systems which include the internationalisation of programme content, wherein hybrid cultural products are produced through co-production deals for worldwide distribution or national products are simply and relentlessly exported to cultures that have few means of resisting them. But the systems also include the domestic, the suburban and the local, where the certainties of domination become the uncertainties of resistance, as audiences and consumers overlay their own meanings on the hardware and software of television technology in an always unequal, but constantly engaged, struggle for control.

I want, in this chapter, to explore the significance of television as technology in and for our everyday life. Television is no longer, if ever it was, isolated from other media of information and communication transmission, either at a global or at a domestic level. It is no longer possible to consider television as a cultural apparatus or as a cultural industry without considering it alongside the supporting and interweaving technologies and political and economic structures that integrate it, both in production and consumption, into a more complex cultural and industrial whole. Equally it is no longer possible to consider the texts of television without considering their status as technologies, potentially or actually transformative of social and cultural relations, any more than it is possible to consider the technology of television without considering its status as a text, inscribed by, and inscribing, the meanings of dominant and subordinate cultures alike.

In structural terms the arguments here will draw on, but also cut across, those offered in the first three chapters of the book. In those chapters I enquired into television as a dimension of the ontological, domestic and suburban environments of everyday life. Here the enquiry will be on television in all of those domains, but as technology; as what I want to call the tele-technological system.

THE QUESTION CONCERNING TECHNOLOGY

Technology is, of course, as problematic a term as television is. Recent work in the sociology and history of technology has, however, provided a framework for the analysis of the significance of technology in the modern world which leaves behind much of the crude theorising of a technological determinist cast. Instead, it favours a view of the production and consumption of technology which is firmly embedded in the social, cultural, political and economic matrices of industrial society. The effects of technology – which in many cases may appear to be determining other aspects of social life – are not of themselves simply, or only, technological. Technologies are themselves effects. They are the effects of social, economic and political circumstances and structures, decisions and actions. These in turn define, in their development, their implementation and their use, technologies' meaning and power.

Such a view of technology – and one that informs my own arguments – involves therefore a consideration of technology not simply as an object or as an artifact. It involves a consideration of technology as both social and political and as both material and symbolic. It involves a consideration of technology as being a part of, and not separated from, the social institutions that produce and consume it. It involves a consideration of technology both in its determinacy and its indeterminacy. And it involves a consideration of television in just these terms, as a technology which is also a medium, and as such doubly inscribed by, and inscribing, social and cultural meanings. The fishermen of Sri Lanka, in their embrace of television alongside the other technologies of the modern age, are not just embracing a series of objects which are in one sense or another seen as functionally or symbolically necessary or desirable, they are embracing a system: a system of values, practices, politics which will certainly change their lives but will do so in a way which is both general and generalisable, as well as unique to them. Technology, in this view, is the site of an (albeit often unequal) struggle for control: for the control of its meanings and for the control of its potency.

I have already noted that technology has to be seen as more than simply an artifact or a machine. In Martin Heideggar's (1977) formulation, which for all its obstruseness is nevertheless extremely suggestive, technology becomes *techne*, and techne becomes *poiesis*. Techne refers to all the arts and skills that go into the making of technology; and poeisis itself is seen as a bringing forth, a revealing and a challenging of reality. Technology becomes then not just a matter of hardware, but both a set of human activities and a set of knowledges. These knowledges are 'technical' in the sense that the techniques of which they consist are 'a roundabout means of securing some desired result' (Gell, 1988a, 6). The objects become processes, the hardware becomes software, the fixed meanings and the determining effects become subject to human vision and control. And technology becomes a matter of unlocking, transforming, storing, distributing, switching about and regulating knowledges and practices.[1]

Such a conceptualisation of technology runs the risk of becoming indistinguishable from knowledge as such, since thought itself can be seen as technical if this broad definition is rigorously adhered to. Yet it is this lack of boundary around the idea of technology that is, paradoxically, important; for it insists on seeing both technology and its various conceptualisations as being vulnerable to social and historical differentiation. It insists on not taking technology for granted. This way of understanding technology in general can also be applied to the media in particular, as Carolyn Marvin (1988, 8) points out:

Media are not fixed natural objects; they have no natural edges. They are constructed complexes of habits, beliefs and procedures embedded in elaborate cultural codes of communication. The history of media is never more or less than the history of their uses, which always lead us away from them to the social practices and conflicts they illuminate.

Technologies, then, and television is no exception – though it is, perhaps, exceptional – are both symbolic and material objects. But they are objects that are constructed through a whole range of socially defined activities, in production and consumption, in development and use, in thought and in practice, and cannot be understood outside their systematic embedding in the political, economic and cultural dimensions of modern (and pre-modern) societies. As Langdon Winner (1985, 30) also points out:

The things we call 'technologies' are ways of building order on our world. Many technical devices and systems important in everyday life contain possibilities for many different ways of ordering human activity. Consciously or not, deliberately or inadvertently, societies choose structures for technologies that influence how people are going to work, communicate, travel, consume, and so forth over a very long time. In the processes by which structuring decisions are made, different people are differently situated and possess unequal degrees of power as well as unequal levels of awareness.

Television is part of that project of building order in and on the world, as I have already pointed out in Chapter 1. But television has a number of qualities which (together with other communication and information technologies) make it a distinct kind of technology and create distinct problems when it comes to understanding its significance for everyday life.

Raymond Williams (1974), once again, provides a starting point, since he saw clearly how powerfully etched the technology of television was within the institutions of broadcasting, and how powerfully etched these institutions were within the political and economic structures and agendas of the modern State. They now, of course, transcend them. Perhaps the first thing to note is that television is neither a static nor an isolated technology. It is not static in that both the machine itself and the institutions which it embodies and in which it is embedded are constantly changing. Television has developed from a cumbersome, ugly box for the reception of flickering black and white pictures (but always useless without both a system of electrical power and of programme production and transmission), to a still developing receiver of colour and stereo, broadcast, narrowcast and information services. Soon it may well be transformed once again by digital compression, and high-definition and interactive technical innovations. It is not isolated either. Increasingly the television is becoming integrated into, becoming an essential part of, what is often (but perhaps mistakenly called) the 'information age': an age in which the various technologies defined by broadcasting, telecommunications and computing, are converging and offering the promise (or the threat) of an integrated information and communication environment in and through which McLuhan's vision of the global village may yet become a reality. This convergence, visible both in the structures of multi-national organisations (Golding and Murdock, 1991) as well as in the interconnections of technology, the social and technical relationships and discourses, in the household (Silverstone, 1990), provides an increasingly complex environment from within which to make sense of television in everyday life. Equally, though, this convergence as well as the consequent complexity, provide increasing challenges for the State when it comes to regulation. And Heideggar, as we have seen, considers regulation an essential aspect of techne.

The particularity of television, as technology, consists however in its status as a medium of information and communication. There is no need to accept the full force of McLuhan's other famous catchphrase – the medium is the message – to recognise that the mass media do have a particular claim on the technological culture of the modern world. This claim consists of what I want to call their double articulation, particularly in and through the moral economy of the household. I will have more to say about this later, but for the moment I want to use the notion as a way of identifying something of the uniqueness of television (together with the other media) as technologies. Put very simply, television is doubly articulated into a household because its significance as a technology depends on its appropriation by the household both as an object (the machine itself) and as a medium. As an object it is bought and incorporated into the culture of the household for its aesthetic and functional characteristics, and it is displayed (or hidden) in the public or private spaces of the household, and collectively or individually used. As an object the television becomes both an element in a national and international communication network and the symbol of its domestic appropriation. As a medium, through the structure and contents of its programming as well as through the mediation of public and private spheres more broadly, it draws the members of the household into a world of public and shared meanings as well as providing some of the raw material for the forging of their own private, domestic culture. In this sense, through its double articulation, the medium does become the message, though that message is not pre-given by the technology. It is worked and reworked within the social circumstances under which it is both produced and received (see below, and Ferguson, 1990).

That this double articulation requires the active involvement of the consumer of television (as well as other technologies) is evidenced by the need for such technologies to be domesticated by the household which receives them. By domestication I mean something quite akin to the domestication of the wild animal: that is a process by which such an animal is accustomed 'to live under the care and near the habitations of man', a process of taming or bringing under control, a process of making or settling as 'a member of the household; to cause to be at home; to naturalize' (OED). Technologies, and television and television programmes must be domesticated if they are to find a space or place for themselves in the home. That process of domestication starts, of course, in the production process ('user friendliness', giving audiences 'what they want' are common enough characterisations); it is continued in the marketing and advertising, but it is completed in consumption (see Chapter 5). Through these various stages both the object and services, hardware and software, become (or do not become) accepted and acceptable. The history of technologies is a history, in part, of this process of domestication (see Marvin, 1988 on the telephone). And the biography of a specific example of a technology is also a biography of its domestication (see Kopytoff, 1986). Once again I will have more to say on this both later on in this chapter and in the next.

Central, however, to my argument about television as technology is its status at the heart of a socio-technical system – a tele-technological system (or more precisely a series of overlapping and constantly changing tele-technological systems). And it is to this way of framing television that I now turn.

TELEVISION AS A SOCIO-TECHNICAL SYSTEM

In popular accounts of technology, inventions of the late nineteenth century, such as the incandescent light, the radio, the airplane, and the gasoline-driven automobile, occupy centre stage, but these inventions were embedded within technological systems. Such systems involve far more than the so-called hardware, devices, machines and processes, and the transportation, communication and information networks that interconnect them. Such systems consist also of people and organizations. An electric light and power system, for instance, may involve generators, motors, transmission lines, utility companies, manufacturing enterprises and banks.

(Hughes, 1989, 3)

Seeing technology as a system involves, above all, seeing technology as both a material and a social phenomenon. Relations between objects and artifacts; relations between people and institutions; the power of the State and the politics of organisations; the embeddedness of the systemic relations of technology in a constantly vulnerable environment of social, political and economic structures: all of these elements define a framework from which new technologies emerge, old technologies are discarded, and from which all technologies are produced and consumed.

Systems are not just analytic constructs. As Mackenzie (1987) points out, systems and networks should not be taken simply as given; they are not unproblematic features of the world. Nor should it be assumed that the term 'system'

be taken to imply stability and lack of conflict. Systems . . . hold together only so long as the correct conditions prevail. There is always the potential for their disastrous dissociation into their component parts. Actors create and maintain systems, and if they fail to do so, the systems in question cease to exist. The stability of systems is a frequently precarious achievement in the face of potentially hostile forces, both social and natural.

(Mackenzie, 1987, 197)

Pursuing this analogy, John Law (1987) talks of technology as being constituted by 'heterogeneous elements', themselves the product of the work of 'heterogeneous engineers'. There are a number of points to be made here. Law prefers the term 'network' to system. His argument relates both to Thomas Hughes' notion of system and to another perspective available within the sociology of technology which sees technology as being socially constructed in a similar way to science (see Woolgar, 1988 for a review). In relation to the systems metaphor, Law suggests that it tends to underestimate the fragility of the emerging system in the face of the conflictful environments and conditions in which it is embedded (though Mackenzie's formulation does seem to take this into account). In relation to the construction metaphor, he argues that the privileging of the social which it demands (and the dependence of all other elements on the social) mistakes the complexity of the relationships that need to be understood if the emergence of new technologies is to be explained: 'Other factors – natural, economic, or technical – may be more obdurate than the social and may resist the best efforts of the system builder to reshape them' (Law, 1987, 113). However, one can grant this and still privilege the social; indeed one must do so, since the natural, the economic, and the technical, in their obduracy or their malleability, have no significance except through social action. And it is possible to frame the problem of technology in these terms without resorting to constructivism (with its inevitable relativist corollaries). The socio-technical system is therefore just that: a more or less fragile, more or less secure, concatenation of human, social and material elements and relations, structured in, and structuring of, social action, and embedded in a context of political and economic (and physical) relationships. From this point of view the notion of network does not add much to that of system.[2] And indeed since many of the elements that one would need to include within the model of the socio-technical system are themselves systems or systematic (the family, the organisation, the knowledge and practices associated with the design and production of artifacts, etc.) I will stay with it in my own account.

Two interrelated points, however, need to be made. The first follows directly from an observation made by Law. It is that an explanation of technology rests on the study both of the conditions and tactics of system building. 'Tactics' are important. Technology emerges in these accounts as a result of the potential space created within a network for the actions of individuals. Tactics suggest a reactive–active mode of action undertaken within a superordinate structure, yet at the same time, potentially at least, also affecting and defining that structure. The military analogy is pertinent. But as Law points out in a footnote, 'we are all heterogeneous engineers, combining as we do, disparate elements into the "going concern" of our daily lives' (Law, 1987, 133). This opens up a number of fascinating and important questions, not least the awareness of the particular structures and systems of everyday life (see Chapter 7 below) but also the relevance of the systems model (and the actor network) both to the production of technology where it has been most consistently applied, and to its use or its consumption where it has not.[3]

This in turn suggests, quite properly, that in relation to even a single technology – the electric light, the telephone, or the television – it is possible, necessary even, to consider not a single system of socio-technical relations, but a number of such systems which are all, potentially, inter-related. One such attempt to do this is offered by Ruth Schwartz Cowan (1987) in her study of the history of the introduction of home heating in the United States.

Cowan takes as her focus the consumer, and in particular the potential consumer of the domestic stove, who failed to materialise in the eighteenth century in the United States, but who, despite little change in the 'technology', did materialise in the nineteenth and twentieth centuries.[4] She argues that what turned the stove into an acceptable and accepted technology was not so much to do with technical innovation *per se*, but with a change in the organisation of the industry which resulted in a major reduction in its cost. The success of the stove depended on, among other things, reductions in the price of coal, the emergence of both individual and multiple consumers, and the involvement (eventually) of the gas utility companies in their retail.

Her model of what she calls the 'consumption junction' consists of a number of more or less concentric (but also overlapping) circles with the consumer – an active decision-making, system-defined and system-defining, actor – at the centre. The particular character of the network system changes through time, of course, as the elements, the institutions and the practices themselves change through time. Together what they signify is a sense of the structured complexity of social, political, economic and technical relations, which must be understood in their interrelationship if the activity of the consumption of technology (no less than that of production) is itself to be understood.

Yet there is more to be said. Cowan's account is limited both in terms of the generalisability of her case-study technology, but more significantly because she fails to consider technology as a symbolic as well as a material good. It is this second aspect of technology as a social system that I want now briefly to address.

The symbolic aspect emerges quite clearly in a very differently oriented analysis of technology, that of Henri Lefebvre (1984). Lefebvre undertakes, within the framework of a critique of bourgeois culture and society, an excursion into the realm of the motor car: what he calls the epitome of 'objects': the Leading Object. He defines the motor car as an example, a subsystem, of the particular consumption oriented culture of bourgeois society.[5] The motor car is the focus of a whole range of material and symbolic communicative relations: with implications for, and effects on, everything from urban design to our sense of excitement. It fosters hierarchies and performance (we compete within and through the motor car); it is consumed as a sign, as a status object; it has its own code, the Highway Code:

> It is an unimposing technical object, depending on relatively simple functional requirements . . . , and structural requirements . . . , and [it] figures also in a simple, unimposing functional and structural social complex where it plays an increasingly important part; it gives rise to an attitude (economic, psychic, sociological, etc.), assumes the dimension of a complete object and has an (absurd) significance; in fact the motor-car has not conquered society so much as *everyday life* on which it imposes its laws and whose establishment it ensures by fixing it on a *level* (levelling it).
> (Lefebvre, 1984, 101, italics in original)

The motor car, as the leading object of modern civilisation has 'not only produced a system of communication but also organisms and institutions that use it and that it uses' (ibid., 103).

My argument is, of course, that television can be seen to have an equivalent status to the car as a Leading Object in high–modern or post-modern society, by virtue of just such a system of attributes: television is a relatively simple technical object defining in use, and being defined by, a whole network of communication channels, both formal and informal, institutionalised and quotidian; it can be seen (as Baudrillard, for example, sees it) as the centre of a system of substitutes (eroticism, adventure, reality, contact); it is consumed as a sign, as a status object both in itself and through its communications (the consumption of programmes to be shared and discussed); and it has its own code, in the broadcasting schedules, in the systems of moral and political regulation and in the various guidelines for media producers. Television too is a great leveller, providing in its programming and in the standardisation of its technologies (the micro-differences of packaging and latest gadgetry notwithstanding) a profound and basic substrate for the conduct of everyday life.[6]

The car and the television are both manifestations of the same socio-technical processes. Both provide a material and a symbolic expression of something quite specific: the uniqueness of their technical arrangements and functions. Both also provide something quite general: their status as the centre and articulating principle of a system of technical and cultural relations which are both historically defined and socially sustained. It is their systemic quality which is the key, a system which includes both objects and actions, actors and structures, artifacts and values, all of which together are both determined (by, and in relation to, other systems) and determining (we are bound by them to a greater or lesser extent). What the roads are to the motor car, broadcasting is to television. The networks of institutional dependencies supporting and being supported by both are equivalent. Yet television takes that systematicity one step further. It also transcends it. Whereas the car becomes the focus of mediation – cars are symbols and the objects of much symbolic and communicative work – television is constituted as a medium *sui generis*. And as such, and through recent technological developments, some aspects of its systematicity are being broken down. Narrowcasting provides a fragmentation of the experience of television (a kind of 'off-road' tech-nology) but it is still dependent on an extensive support structure of cultural as well as technical relations.

The tele-technological system consists, then, of a multiplex of relation-ships constructed and reconstructed psychodynamically and sociologically in domestic and suburban environments, each of which, in its own way, is systemic. It consists in (as I shall be describing in the next section) the interrelationships of artifacts (convergences), mediations (textualities), and regulations (controls) that define the conditions of its possibility as a communication technology in modern society. It consists in and through the dynamics of consumption as the operational process (see Chapter 5) of modernity. And it is created by, and incorporates, the television audience (Chapter 6) which is constituted at the interface of technology and everyday life (Chapter 7).

CONVERGENCES, TEXTUALITIES AND CONTROLS

I began this chapter by referring to the villagers of Sri Lanka, drafted into a world of capitalist social, economic and political relations as a result of their adoption of new fishing technologies. These same fishermen (or maybe they were some others) in addition found themselves on the edge of a cultural precipice with their adoption of new media technologies. Television, with or without electricity, provided a link to a world which was new, but at the same time it offered, in its materiality – in its objectification as well as in its symbolisation – a potential space for their own cultural work: work which could only be understood in the context (albeit rapidly changing) of their own locale, their own everyday lives. An account of the tele-technological system must include, therefore, not just the environments in which media are consumed but an account of the environments – the political, industrial and cultural environments – in which they are produced.

For the moment I want to focus on the first part of this equation: the emergent structures of the tele-technological system as they are manifested in and through three levels of convergence: the convergence expressed in the political economy of the medium; the convergence expressed in the techno-logical culture of the medium; and the convergence expressed in the content of the medium. Perhaps convergence is too strong a word. It certainly expresses something different in each of the contexts in which I will be discussing it. Likewise the various levels of convergence are not to be seen either as simply reinforcing one another, or as being themselves unprob-lematic or uncontested. The globalisation of culture and society which has become the byword for one of the, albeit major, dimensions of post-modernity is neither a homogeneous nor an uncontentious process.[7]

However, recent theories of cultural change and transformation have focused on what appears to be an entirely new aspect and dynamic of the world environment: the globalisation of culture (Featherstone, 1990; Harvey, 1989). This globalisation is not perceived as an homogenisation but is described in various ways: as a hybrid culture, as a cosmopolitan culture, as a culture of networked and mutually reflexive differences. The globalisation of culture follows (or precedes, or accompanies) the globalisation of econ-omic relations, which itself follows (or precedes or accompanies) the globalisation of the movement of information and communication – as commodities – which are in turn released by the new generation of electronic technologies. At stake in these discussions is the significance of the Nation

State as a focus for identity and cultural change; at issue are just those questions of individual and collective identity which are perceived to be threatened by the new heterogeneities and fragmentations of contemporary cultural forms and products.

Industrial societies have moved from a Fordist to a post-Fordist world: a move from the regimes of order, control and mass production both of commodities and of labour, towards what Harvey (1989, 127, following Piore and Sabel, 1984) calls a regime of flexible specialisation (but it is also called other things: for example, disorganised capitalism (Lash and Urry, 1987)). Such a regime is one in which industrial organisation and distribution adopts a much more flexible and responsive pattern of production and consumption (specialisation, sub-contracting, inter-firm cooperation; 'just-in-time' stock control), and work (flexible hours, flexible contracts, flexi-time). It also generates a much more 'flexible' product (the rapid changes of fashion and the increasing diversity of objects) and it results in a much more 'flexible' set of life-styles (local and neo-local cultures, gendered, aged and or ethnic, cross-cut by class, ideology and geography).

Within this overall, and highly generalised, scenario, a number of different things appear to be happening. Many of them are directly related to developments within the media industries themselves, and are both product and producer of the overall shifts in the organisation and regulation of national and international culture.

The two terms 'concentration' and 'globalisation', while indicating dramatically new dimensions in the development of media industries, have also provided, in many recent accounts, the basis for an analysis of a fundamental shift in the wider organisation and control of the cultural industries. Together with the breaking up of a Fordist regime of accumulation and the rise of flexible specialisation (Harvey, 1989) or flexible integration (Robins and Cornford, 1992), these industrial developments have led to a convergence of sorts within national and international media: a convergence of ownership, a convergence in the regulatory regimes, and a convergence, expressed in the internationalisation (Europeanisation or co-production) of the product.[8]

In relation to the first, the convergence of ownership, it has long been argued that the media industries have lent themselves to a steady concentration and conglomeration in their organisation (Murdock, 1982, 1990). The political economy of the industry in the UK and the US, and of course increasingly in Japan and worldwide, has been one of both horizontal and vertical integration, as companies have sought to control all aspects of their own market (as Sony have attempted to do in the purchase of CBS and Columbia pictures) as well as diversifying into a broad range of interlocking but not necessarily interdependent companies (Rupert Murdoch's News International being only one among many of such conglomerates).

These developments are not to be understood in isolation of course. They are part of an increasing internationalisation of the world economic order, an internationalisation that is itself predicated on, and facilitated by, changes in information and communication technologies, changes which enable, above all, the rapid transfer of information and capital around the globe (Schiller, 1989, 113). As David Harvey (1989, 161) notes:

> The formation of a global stock market, of global commodity (even debt) futures markets, of currency and interest rate swaps, together with an accelerated geographical mobility of funds, meant, for the first time, the formation of a single world market for money and credit supply.

And not just for money and credit supply, but increasingly also for information itself and for television, both for its hardware (the current battle over HDTV standards is a battle very much for the world market in the next generation of television) and programmes (within the 'satellitisation' of television news (CNN) or music video (MTV) or programming *tout court* (Europe's SuperChannel)).

Graham Murdock (1990) identifies four aspects of the formation process of the newly emerging and increasingly powerful media conglomerates. The new 'deregulation' is regulation in disguise: a re-regulation of media ownership and control vested in the interests not of the public but of the corporation, and having significant effects on the power of national governments as well as of the citizen (see Schiller, 1989). Murdock (1990, 9) describes this process as 'privatisation', by which he means all the 'forms of public intervention that increase the size of the market sector within the communication and information industries and give entrepreneurs operating within it increased freedom of manoeuvre'. Denationalisation, which despite its intention (at least in the UK) has led to further concentration of share ownership; liberalisation, which introduces competition into markets previously served only by public enterprise; commercialisation, in which public service broadcasters open up some or all of their airwaves to private and commercial use; and re-regulation itself which has released but not erased the restrictions on cross-media ownership: all of these elements of the privatisation process have dramatically favoured the large corporations.

Although the trend is not uniform (different strategies and paces of privatisation; the emergence of community television and the independent production sector), the overall direction and implications are clear. The commercialisation of the media and information industries is well nigh complete. As Murdock (1990, 15) concludes:

> The cumulative result of these shifts, and the other dimensions of the privatisation process . . . has been to strengthen and extend the power of the leading corporations and to pose more sharply than ever the dilemma that faces a liberal democratic society in which most key communications facilities are held in private hands.

Convergence of ownership and convergence in the regulative environment (the two are closely connected of course) tend to suggest a convergence of another kind: that within the product, the programmes and the content of the media. Here once again there are a number of dimensions. The spread of US-dominated material, particularly, but by no means exclusively into the Third World (Tunstall, 1977; Boyd-Barrett, 1977) – media imperialism – is perhaps only the tip of a cultural iceberg in which not just the specific programmes but the models of genre and the format of Western (principally US) television have equally wide currency. Television news, for example, is in some senses at least, the same *product* almost everywhere. The game-show is, equally, ubiquitous. The European response to *Dallas* was, in part, to create, in *Chateauvallon* and *Schwarzwaldklinik*, their own equivalents (Silj, 1988). Increasing budgetry pressure on, as well as the perceived demand for, and profits to be gained from, the big blockbuster documentary series, have led to an increased number of international co-production deals, generating, it is often claimed, a kind of a cultural anaesthesia: yet another hybrid in which cultural differences are elided in a homogenised text. And, finally, the creation of a network of products and texts – what Fiske describes as the intertextuality of the media – defines yet another converging environment, of which television programmes, the secondary newspaper and magazine discourses around the actors, the characters and the interweaving of their public and private lives (Meyrowitz, 1985), and the interconnections of trade-marked products, songs, videos and books are all expressions. Running through all of this, of course, is the ubiquity of 'commercial speech', the advertisements, which are the true delivery systems of the modern media.

There are many arguments, of course, that this media totalitarianism, this process of commercial and cultural globalisation, is leaky. The flexible specialisation – 'choice' – inscribed into the structure of post-Fordist regimes of media and information production, as into other commodity production, is one way of understanding a kind of cultural diversification. And in the context of the globalisation of media form and content we can recognise the 'reverse-flow' (Sreberny-Mohammadi, 1991; Boyd-Barrett and Thussu, 1992) and the indigenisation of cultural commodities (Miller, 1992), as individual cultures assert their own status and negotiate with the products of the multi-nationals, as well as providing, perhaps most significantly in music, alternative offerings which run counter to, and sometimes influence, the dominant trends in otherwise predominantly Western mass-produced culture. Both of these dimensions of the map of contemporary culture could be seen as high- or post-modernity's vulnerability, and in much recent cultural theory that is how it does appear. And it is central, too, to my own argument that this overweening system must itself be understood within a wider frame of cultural difference and more than token resistance.

In this the problem is stated but not resolved. The system itself is not without its contradictions, its weaknesses and its licence (Thompson, 1990). Equally, there are numerous opportunities to, and examples of, our capacity to counter, to work with, and to transform its products. Nevertheless any discussion of the tele-technological system as a whole must be prepared to acknowledge where the locus of its power lies, and any project which seeks to construct a theory of the place of television in everyday life must take this as central. The freedoms that we have to choose and construct our own media environment; the mechanisms that we adopt, the tactics that we pursue in integrating the products of mass communication into our own lives, at whatever level, are all crucial. But it should not be forgotten that in the processes of mass consumption we are swimming in a sea not of our own creation. Almost all of us can indeed swim. Most of us will swallow water. A few of us will drown.

TECHNOLOGICAL DETERMINATIONS

There is one final, but vital dimension of the globalisation of the media still to be considered. It concerns the technology itself. The development of satellite communication is, from one point of view, a radical innovation in terms of the speed at which huge quantities of information can be transmitted around the world. But from another, it is merely the latest development in the process of the electronic delivery of information that began with the telegraph.

Tracing the implications of these developments for social and cultural change has been, consistently, contentious. Many of the discussions are cast very much in technologically determinist terms, and many refuse to consider the social and cultural influences that lie behind the emergence of these new technologies and inform their reception. Yet, equally, many of these discussions are highly suggestive, above all because, paradoxically, they do insist on isolating or privileging media technologies, and in that isolation and privilege they raise important questions about their significance in a way that is relatively free from the determinations of the polity or economy.

I would like now, briefly, to follow this line of reasoning as a way of opening up, once again, the phenomenology, as well as pursuing the politics, of the tele-technological system.

There is a familiar line of theorising about the significance of electronic media stretching from Harold Innis, via Marshall McLuhan, Walter Ong and Joshua Meyrowitz, which insists, in a more or less unqualified fashion, on registering their transformative effects on human sensibilities and social structures. McLuhan's infamous (and actually often misunderstood) catch-all, 'the medium is the message', acts now more as a symptom of a misleading generalisation – of how not to think about the media – than as a statement which has any serious claims to empirical relevance. Yet the potential, a potential often, if not always evenly, realised, of media to reach down to the roots of social life and individual psychology is, as I have argued in Chapter 1, not so easily dismissed. Nor is this potential, even in these accounts, always pursued in isolation from a consideration of the political and economic context in which the technologies emerge and on which they are argued to have such a powerful effect.

Indeed, as James Carey (1989) points out, Harold Innis' pioneering discussion of media in terms of space and time was undertaken both within a concern for the political implications of changing media environments and within a framework exploring the interrelationship between technology and economic and social change. Originating in his study of the Canadian paper industry, an industry increasingly dependent on decisions being made in newspaper-producing cities all over the globe, Innis came to realise the extraordinary importance in changes in communications for the organisation of empires. For Innis however, the decisive boundary was not between mechanical and electronic means of communication, but between a pre- and post-print-based culture.[9] The emergence of printing marked the transition between time- and space-based societies:

> Media that emphasize time are those that are durable in character, such as parchment, clay and stone. The heavy materials are suited to the development of architecture and sculpture. Media that emphasize space are apt to be less durable and light in character, such as papyrus and paper. The latter are suited to wide areas in administration and trade . . . Materials that emphasize time favour decentralization and hierarchical types of institutions, while those that emphasise space favour centralization and systems of government less hierarchical in character.

> (Innis, 1972, 7)

Time-binding cultures stress history, continuity, permanence. Their symbols are based on and in trust: myths, rituals, tradition, religion. Their values and communities are rooted in place. Space-binding cultures stress land as real estate, voyage, discovery, movement, and expansion. Science, bureaucracy and reason provide both their structure and symbol. And in the realm of communities, space-binding cultures create 'communities of space: communities that were not in place but in space, mobile, connected over vast distances by appropriate symbols, forms, and interests' (Carey, 1989, 160).

But, Innis argues, it is through their ability to manage the biases of both time- and space-based media that empires survive. Radio has once again shifted the bias of communication towards time (Innis, 1972, 170), and once again posed huge management problems for empires and nations. And, it can be suggested, television has reinforced this, as recent events in which television seems to have been a central facilitator in the breaking down of communism (and the reassertion of national and regional identities) in Eastern Europe and the Soviet Union have demonstrated.

This shifting media-based phenomenology of time and space is not without its contradictions in Innis' account. For while it is clear that radio (and television) create a transforming environment for empires based on print, and appear to be providing something of a return to a time-based culture, it is a time-based culture paradoxically based on this occasion not on the durability of parchment, clay and stone, but on the dramatically enhanced ephemerality of the widely broadcast spoken word and visual image. This betokens a return to oral culture, and Innis values that as a potential counter to the bureau-cratising and centralising forces of the modern State, but it also suggests to him (and to Carey, 1989) a strain towards the reinforcement of the illiberal trends set in motion by print. This contradiction is not fully worked out.

Yet are radio and television different in their biases to print, as Innis and, following him, McLuhan (1964) and Meyrowitz (1985), seem to believe? Or are they, as Carey argues, (merely) an extension and reinforcement of existing power relations? Maybe one would need to see the emergence of electronic technologies as offering a new synthesis: operating within deeply entrenched political and economic systems, but acting in a number of different ways to shift the balances within contemporary culture away from the more or less clearly defined stabilities of a print-based society towards a new kind of orality, powerful in its implications, above all insofar as it affects the basic character of communication in the modern world.

This is a position taken by Walter Ong (1971) in his attempts to describe contemporary technologically defined culture in terms of what he calls secondary orality:

> This new orality has striking resemblances to the old in its participatory mystique, its fostering of a communal sense, its concentration on the present moment, and even in its use of formulas. But it is essentially a more deliberate and self-conscious orality, based permanently on the use of writing and print, which are essential for the manufacture and operation of the equipment and for its use as well.
>
> (Ong, 1971, 299)

Secondary orality is another hybrid. Ong insists that the new technologies have a transformative potential, but it is regressive, opening up by virtue of the spread of images and voices, forms of storytelling and forms of formulae, a new collective culture different in focus and effects from the individualising tendencies of print.

Yet another version of this thesis is that offered by Joshua Meyrowitz (1985). His argument is a relatively simple, and by now an unsurprising, one. Television, he suggests, not uniquely, but preeminently, has transformed our social and cultural environment. It has transformed the relationships between public and private spheres and between physical and social spaces. It has, in addition, profoundly affected the normally clear boundaries which separate the sexes, the generations, the powerful from the powerless. It has made the world visible and accessible in dramatically new ways. The changes that television has wrought continue. They have a dynamic all of their own, returning us to a form of social and cultural experience which Meyrowitz claims is akin to that of hunters and gatherers: politically egalitarian, discriminating little between play and work, living more and more of our lives in public, hunting and gathering information rather than food. What Meyrowitz misses, of course, is any sense of the other side of this techno-logical coin (its 'double life': de Sola Pool and see Thompson, 1990) or any indication of the possibility of negotiation or resistance. He is equally blind to questions of power and cultural difference.

As I have suggested, paradoxes abound in all these accounts. The forces for the institionalisation, the centralisation and consolidation of media power are expressed through the vertical and horizontal integration and international-isation of media industries. Their close alliance with national and inter-national interests; the capacity of these institutions to dominate technology's ability to extend its reach, to speed up the movement of information and to exercise control over time and especially space, are all important factors in this exercise of power. But they have to be set against what the media-centric theorists regard as the biases, the messages or the effects, of these changing media beneath or beyond the political structures; potentially transforming (or threatening to transform) sensibilities and social relations as a result.

Centralising or decentralising, conservative or radical, oral or literary, progressive or regressive; perhaps not surprisingly, media-centric accounts of social and cultural change continue to be tantalisingly inconclusive. The texts of technology remain, at least in part, open. Television quite clearly offers new horizons and new opportunities, and as one component of an electronic network of information and communication technologies, provides the means for, and emerges as the result of, fundamental transformations in our relation-ships to time and space. Yet these media biases are ambiguous and open precisely because, for the most part, they are still (albeit unevenly) framed by the political and economic strategies of the powerful, and are vulnerable to the tactics of everyday life – vulnerable to the dynamics of their appropriation into domestic, local and regional cultures (see de Certeau, 1984).[10]

Ambiguous and uncertain or not, and the ambiguities and uncertainties do not lie only in the regimes of production or in the institutionalisation of power within nation states, television and other media embody both socially systemic and technologically systemic dimensions which interact with each other, and with other dimensions of social and technical reality. As Marjorie Ferguson (1990, 155) points out:

> Clearly changes in the public use and private consumption of new com-munication systems and services have implications for how we comprehend time-space relations and priorities. Despite the technological ease with which electronic media seemingly render time transparent through instan-taneity or culture opaque through quasi-universality, such mediations do not necessarily provide new sets of categorical certainties or universal meanings about duration or distance.

What seems more probable is that increased internationalism in all forms of communication overlays both the current, local ideas about time and space, and the earlier, sensory-based epistemologies where what was directly experienced . . . defined the world with alternative definitions and meanings.

This is an important point. It opens up for examination, once again, the complex nature of the tele-technological system. The system has a separately identifiable technological component and *qua* technology (as a system and as a service) television offers, at every level of its incorporation into everyday life, a potential for the systematic reorientation of time and space relations and perceptions. But this has to be set against an understanding of that capacity in relation to the significance of other technologies and in relation to the specific, and often determining, contexts of both production and consumption. These contexts are, together, international, national, local and domestic.

Let me return, for the last time, to the Sri Lankan villagers. In buying their fishing nets, their motor boats and their televisions, they were buying not just objects but a whole slew of economic, political and cultural relationships and values – a technological system. This initial example is an extreme but a very clear one. The consequences of their purchase of new boats and new nets included the emergence of hierarchy and an exploitative structure within village life; and above all they included dependence: dependence on machines, involving the loss of traditional skills. Down the route created by technology, literally sometimes the road or the communication channel (television much more dramatically than radio or the newspaper), modernity thunders in all its chameleon colours (see Betteridge, 1992). Inscribed within the texts of technology are all the hieroglyphs of State and commercial power, all the more visible in the confrontation between First and Third World countries, but no less significant in our own. As Stephen Hill (1988, 65 and 75) observes:

The text that is presented to us in machines is 'written' in the sense that it is embodied, autonomous, not derived from immediate life-world cultural participation, but from sedimented meanings and stocks of knowledge that are 'objectified' in the machine.

(p. 65)

technologies introduced from a more instrumentally powerful culture into traditional society 'burn like a cigarette on a silken fabric' into the wholeness of the cultural patterns that existed before.

(p. 75)

Arguments derived from the study of Third World cultures as well as, principally, from the study of basic industrial or mechanical technologies, should be treated with caution when applied to our own culture and to communication and information technologies. Hill argues a strong case. It is dramatic and persuasive but it can be qualified in a number of ways. First, the arrival of new technologies does not always nor does it immediately involve substantial change in the social structure or cultural values of those receiving it. This has been shown to be the case in both pre-literate (Sahlins, 1974) as well as modern societies (Thrall, 1982). Indeed, arguments about the emergence of new household technologies in the First World have focused on how they have reinforced, for example, the domestic division of labour (Cowan, 1989). Second, the use of new technologies, even something as taken for granted now as television, has to be learnt, and in the learning both technology and culture may change. Third, information and communication technologies have, as de Sola Pool points out, a double life; and they are, in my terms, doubly articulated. Both medium and message are open to appropriation differently and in multiple ways. Televisions may all look more or less alike, but they will be placed in different domestic and other spaces, accorded different significance, and above all will be watched or used differently: each member of an audience, each user, taking away something that is both general and particular from what they see and hear (Lieber and Katz, 1991).

It is to this last but crucial aspect of the tele-technological system – its domestication – that I now want to turn.

THE DOMESTICATION OF THE SAVAGE MEDIUM

The globalisation of the media – its political, economic and technical reach and implications – is only part of the story of the tele-technological system. To focus on it alone engenders the risk of producing a kind of seamless robe, whose train is unruffled and unsnarled by the unevenness and friction of a complex, diverse and contrary world of lived relations. Many versions of innovation theory, political economy and cultural analysis have this quality. They are seductive, of course, but the seduction should be resisted. Why?

Principally because we need to know about cultural difference and cultural variation, and because we can recognise, historically and contemporarily, the capacity of societies and social groups, both large and small, to work with the products of an over-arching colonial, religious or media-based system, and through that work to transform and domesticate it. Not always of course, and not always necessarily very successfully. But the world is full of examples of the ways in which both nations and households do produce something other, something novel, at the conjunction of, and in their transactions with, the products of an imposing system.[11] This will be my theme for the remainder of this chapter and the next.

At this point, taking a focus both on technology – as object and as text – and on our capacity to tame those objects and meanings, to make them our own, I want to explore the notion of domestication, through a concern with what I will call (following Kopytoff, 1986) the various biographies of television, and through a concern with issues of gender and control.

Marilyn Strathern (1987) understands domestication as being a matter of subordinating objects to ends of one's own and thus to one's subjectivity.

Domestication is, indeed, about bringing things under control, but as Eric Hirsch (1989) points out it is also about the expression of the subjectivity of those who are involved. Domestication does, perhaps literally, involve bringing objects in from the wild: from the public spaces of shops, arcades and working environments; from factories, farms and quarries. The transition, which is also a translation, of objects across the boundary that separates public and private spaces is at the heart of what I mean by domestication. Through it, objects and meanings are, potentially, formed and transformed. Some objects, some technologies, some meanings, are more amenable to domestication than others. All are in a state of alienation until that boundary is crossed and the claim associated with their appropriation made. Some of us will have more resources: more patience, more money, greater skill, for this task than others. We will not always be untouched by the effort. Yet the end point of any work of social production and reproduction is this transaction between the private and the public sphere (Appadurai, 1986; Parry and Bloch, 1989). I have already discussed this in terms of the moral economy of the household, and I will develop the position embodied in that notion in more detail in the next chapter.

However, in the context of the present discussion, the domestication of technology refers to the capacity of a social group (a household, a family, but also an organisation) to appropriate technological artifacts and delivery systems into its own culture – its own spaces and times, its own aesthetic and its own functioning – to control them, and to render them more or less 'invisible' within the daily routines of daily life. Both the potential inscribed within the technology as object (and the meanings of the texts that are conveyed), as well as the resources available to the group, are material for understanding how any given transaction or set of transactions takes place. As Daniel Miller (1987, 175) suggests:

> All ... objects ... are the direct product of commercial concerns and industrial processes. Taken together they appear to imply that in certain circumstances segments of the population are able to appropriate such industrial objects and utilize them in the creation of their own image. In other cases, people are forced to live in and through the images held of them by a different and dominant section of the population. The possibilities of recontextualisation may vary for any given object according to its historical power or for one particular individual according to his or her changing social environment.

Domestication, as Daniel Miller implies, is an elastic processs. It stretches all the way from complete transformation and incorporation to a kind of begrudging acceptance, and from total integration to marginalisation. But what links both extremes is the quality of the work involved, the effort and the activity which people bring to their consumption of objects and their incorporation into the structure of their everyday lives.

Objects and meanings – television and its texts – have their own lives. Their individual histories: the histories of the technologies, of the products or commodities, of the individual objects and of the transmitted meanings, all contribute to the particularity of a technology as object and to its changing status within public and private spheres. Once across the threshold of the domestic spaces, of course, those lives continue, played out in the micro-social and cultural environments of the home. And, equally, they are prepared for in their production and marketing. The particular route that each object follows as it runs its life-history from inception to obsolescence (an obsolescence no longer only defined by the emergence of a replacement product, but also by its altogether more unpredictable death in individual use) not only illuminates its own biography but also throws a light onto the culture and cultures through which it moves.

Things, objects, technologies, texts, have biographies, therefore, in the same way that individuals do. However their lives are not just a matter of change and transformation. Through those changes and transformations, in their birth, maturity and decline, they reveal the changing qualities of the shaping environments through which they pass. As Igor Kopytoff (1986, 67) suggests:

> The biography of a car in Africa would reveal a wealth of cultural data: the way it was acquired, how and from whom the money was assembled to pay for it, the relationship of the seller to the buyer, the uses to which the car is regularly put, the identity of its most frequent passengers and of those who borrow it, the frequency of borrowing, the garages to which it is taken and the owner's relation to the mechanics, the movement of the car from hand to hand and over the years, and in the end, when the car collapses, the final disposition of its remains. All of these details would reveal an entirely different biography from that of a middle-class American, or Navajo, or French peasant car.

In a sense, of course, Kopytoff is only telling half of the story. For crucial to the biography of this car in Africa is also the narrative of how it was produced, and for whom, how it was marketed and sold, and how those processes illuminate the relationship between producing and consuming cultures.

Some of these issues emerge in recent work on the early years of communication and information technologies, particularly the television (Spigel, 1989, 1990, 1992; Haralovich, 1988; Boddy, 1986), but also the radio (Moores, 1988), the telephone (Marvin, 1988; de Sola Pool, 1977), the VCR (Keen, 1987) and the home computer (Haddon, 1988). Much of the more detailed work, particularly of the biography of these technologies once they have crossed the threshold of individual homes and households remains to be done (but see Silverstone and Hirsch, 1992).

Lynn Spigel (1992), in the study (from which I have already drawn) of the emergence of television in the US during the immediate post-war years, charts its representation through an analysis of advertisements and articles appearing in women's home magazines. Television's appearance was by no means trouble-free nor without anxiety. Prompted, as it was, by the rapid expansion of suburban development during the ten or so years after 1945, it provided a focus for the expression (and the attempted resolution) of the new contradictions of public and private worlds, of gender roles and domestic space that became increasingly visible in the dispersed and hybrid world of Levittown.

The placing and watching of television in the new ranch-style and open-plan homes of those years became a central preoccupation. The significance of television in the family, and its capacity to bring families together or to tear them apart: its effect on gender roles, reinforcing in its imagery and in its marketing the domesticity of the stay-at-home housewife, and threatening to undermine the authority of the father, these were constant themes in the popular literature of the time. Television spawned supporting technologies and created new spaces: TV dinners, the TV lounge, the open plan itself, labour-saving household technologies, all were designed in one way or another to integrate television into the spaces and times of the household and above all to legitimate its presence, to make it invisible, to make it safe for children and families to watch, and to turn it into a decorative object – in short to domesticate it.

Along the way various still-born technologies were tried to make the whole process more manageable. Spigel reports two of the more bizarre: the TV oven in which a screen was incorporated into the cooker so that television could be watched without disturbing the meal-times or women's domestic chores; the 'Duoscope', a television with two screens set at right angles designed to enable two different programmes to be watched simultaneously, thus relieving the tensions surrounding programme choice. Yet these technologies were merely premature. The multiple-set household, the television on the kitchen table (the old black and white displaced by the more recent colour, stereo, or satellite-connected set from its central place in the sitting room), the video recorder, have all provided the means whereby many of those early anxieties and preoccupations have been resolved. As Spigel (1990, 93) herself remarks:

While the Duoscope never caught on, the basic problematic of unity and division continued. The attempt to balance ideals of family harmony and social difference often led to bizarre solutions, but it also resulted in everyday viewing patterns which were presented as functional and normal procedures for using television. Popular discourses tried to tame the beast, suggesting ways to maintain traditional modes of family behaviour and still allow for social change. They devised intricate plans for resistance and accommodation to the new machine, and in so doing they helped construct a new cultural form.

Spigel is telling the story of a new medium, a medium which, from the very beginning was also a commodity, and in its double articulation into the households of post-war America became also a means for the further commodification of everyday life. The biography of television begins here (of course it actually begins much earlier, in the development of the technology and the development of the broadcasting system created to provide radio), and it is sustained, at so many different levels, in the continuous production and reproduction of objects and meanings: internationally, nationally; in public and in both commercial broadcast and narrowcast distribution systems; in homes and in everyday talk and gossip. It is interesting to note, in Spigel's account, that it was the object – the television itself – which was the site of so much concern, as if it were believed that it was enough to 'place' it in the spaces and times of the home for it to be made safe. Perhaps this is a little misleading, for as Spigel herself analyses, the moral panics around the content of television were also much in evidence. They too had to be resolved, and the challenges they appeared to present to public and private morality firmly dealt with. Yet the dependence of anxieties over content (the 'message') on anxieties over the object (the 'medium') is clear; so much so that much of the content itself, particularly in situation comedies and soap operas, as well as of course, in the advertisements, was designed to provide a set of cultural tools for the accommodation of the new medium.

These aspects of television: the medium's integration into the emerging post-war economy of commodification and suburbanisation; the role of programme planning and scheduling; and the particular characteristics of situation comedy as a domestic genre, together provide a kind of ideological template for the definition of gender roles and a particular – middling-class – model of family life. This has been analysed by Haralovich (1988), Boddy (1986) and Modleski (1984). I have already discussed certain aspects of these arguments in Chapters 2 and 3. Each of these accounts stresses, as does Spigel, how crucial the construction of gender was to the domestication of television. Women returning to the home after their war-time draft into male working environments had to be resocialised into a family role and a family structure that seemed to have changed little from at least the idealisation of the Victorian middle class. The woman at home was the key to the success of the household as a consuming unit, but also of its viability as a component of the system of production. She had to stay at home and provide the material and moral wherewithal for the support of her husband, the producer in the formal economy. Television was potentially a distracting threat, but also potentially an opportunity for education and socialisation.

But television was only one element in a system of political, architectural and commercial relations which separately and together imposed a version of highly gendered social life, which is now taken so much for granted. The suburban family sit-com during the 1950s and on into the 1960s made a significant contribution to 'the construction and distribution of social knowledge about the place of women' in society (Haralovich, 1988, 39).[12]

These various accounts of the gendering of television as technology and its embeddedness in a system of overweening cultural and material relations beg, however, some important questions. These questions do not necessarily undermine the force of the analysis but do require a consideration of the empirical dynamics of television, as technology and as medium, as it is incorporated into the daily lives of families and households. The biography of television, just as much as the biography of other technologies, is marked by a degree of uncertainty and openness that these accounts tend to gloss over. Its place in the home, its domestication, just as much as the construction of individual identity, of which gender is a crucial but not the only element, is something that cannot be understood exclusively from the analysis of public texts, be they the television programmes themselves or the marketing strategies designed to order the world in such a way as to make television acceptable. There is an indeterminacy in the tele-technological system just at the point where television crosses the threshold of the public and the private spheres. And this indeterminacy is registered as much in the litter, and litany, of failed or transformed technologies as it is in the conflicts within the negotiation and renegotiation of domestic gender relations in the daily lives of family members (Silverstone, 1991).

The gendering of the tele-technological system is, therefore, a dialogical process, built out of a dialogue between publicly defined relations inscribed into the design and marketing of all technologies, television included, and privately negotiated relations inscribed in and through the patterns and discourses of everyday life. There is little doubt that the gender relations constructed around the television, in the control of the remote (Morley, 1986) or in the competence around the video recorder (Gray, 1987, 1992), or indeed in the ownership and use of the computer (Haddon, 1988) or the telephone (Moyal, 1989), express a gendered division of labour in turn expressive of the dominant gendered structures of modern society (Cockburn, 1985). But there is equally little doubt that the gendering of technologies is not irrevocably fixed within the technologies themselves, nor does it determine how or by whom they will be used (see Livingstone, 1992). A woman's (and also a man's) relationship to the television (Hobson, 1982) or to the telephone (Rakow, 1988; Mayer, 1977; Moyal, 1992) is a function of woman's status and role in the household, certainly, but that itself can only be understood both with regard to the dominant structures in which masculinity and femininity are defined in the public sphere and their particular character within, from the point of view of the household, its moral economy. It is also important to note that the gendered nature of the tele-technological system must also be understood through the mesh of class and ethnicity and through the dynamics of age and stage in an individual's or household's life-cycle.

The domestication of television is therefore itself a complex process that can be understood both phylogenetically and ontogenetically. In phylogenetic terms the story of television's domestication is the story of the emergence of a technology and a medium within a particular set of historically defined social, political and economic conditions. That emergence required the interplay of a number of different discourses operating within a number of different fields: the design of the equipment, its marketing, the scheduling and the content of the programmes, the coincidence of urban, architectural and domestic design, changes in the division of labour, and something I have hitherto taken quite for granted: an increase in disposable income. In ontogenetic terms the story of television's domestication is the story of the changes and persistences in domestic relations: the suburbanisation of social life, but also the particular character of a household's own domesticity in which distinctions of class, ethnicity, location, religious identity and so on inform and define the conditions for any and every technology's appropriation into the home. These two dimensions of the domestication of television operate together, as I have suggested, dialogically. Insofar as television is appropriated into a given household or other environment it is involved in a struggle for control and identity, both by the household itself in its involvement with the world beyond its front door and by the individuals within it. For television to find its place, and for television programmes to find their place, in the home, literally to be accommodated, then the interrelationship of these two levels needs to be understood.

I began this chapter by implying that the tele-technological system was in reality a number of overlapping and interweaving systems, drawing its coherence and its strength from the tension between technological, political-economic and domestic environments and pressures. This is now how I hope it appears. Television is not simply an open window, nor is it an open sluice; it is not innocent and it bears the scars of its production and its position in the modern world system. We who receive it, who buy the latest technologies as well as making do with the old, who watch the latest programmes as well as the reruns; we confront a medium with a history and biography. We have little control over the first but some considerable control over the second. The tele-technological system is therefore the product of the relations and determinations of both production and consumption.

The challenge for media research in general and television research in particular now is to try and make sense of the interweaving of the political economy of the media with their cultural appropriation. I have tried in this chapter to offer a framework for beginning to meet that challenge. In the next chapter, in a discussion of consumption, I will develop the argument by considering the dynamics of the process.

Chapter 5

Television and consumption

There is a paradox lying at the heart of the term, and the activity of, consumption. To consume is to destroy. Consumption is associated with waste, with wanton dissipation, with decay (see Williams, 1974). Consumptive bodies are those eaten away by disease. Fires consume. Conspicuous consumption – from the potlach to the Polo shirt – is a waste: a public, visible, dramatic waste (Veblen, 1925). We consume and are consumed.[1] Yet recent and not-so-recent theorists searching for the key to understanding the particular character of middle and late capitalism have found it in consumption. And some of the most recent critics of contemporary culture have found in consumption the basis for a defining critique of modern and post-modern culture – a cause for celebration and a definition of culture not as destructive but, on the contrary, as the source of much (if not all) that is creative both in the pointillism of everyday life and in the surrealism and hyperrealism of the mass media.

There is another paradox. Consumption depends on production. We can not consume what we do not produce. Consumption stimulates production. Without destruction we cannot create. And furthermore it is in the stimulation of consumption that we forget about production. In advertising's encouragements very little is displayed about the conditions under which our goods are produced, as if that recognition might somehow tarnish the glow or dampen the flames of desire.

In this chapter I want to consider television and consumption. I want to do it as a way of approaching something of the dynamics of contemporary culture, the mechanisms by and through which we engage in, and are engaged by, the systems and structures of life under late capitalism. Television is only one element in all of this. Yet arguably it is crucial. It provides most of the core images, the concerted blandishments, the musical accompaniments, of this so vital an activity. And I want, if I can, to hold on to these paradoxes, for they express yet another of the essential tensions in contemporary society that this book seems to be identifying and which any discussion of television must inevitably reveal. This time the tension is between the claiming power of an increasingly international cultural–industrial complex and the possibilities released by those powers for self-expression, through denial, transcendence or transformation. And it is a tension articulated through, as well as ameliorated by, television and the other mass media. In consumption we express at the same time and in the same actions, both our irredeemable dependence and our creative freedoms as participants in contemporary culture. Television (and of course the other mass media), I want to suggest, provides both the models and the means for this participation.

THEMES AND TENSIONS

There are a number of identifiable but obviously interrelated themes running through what I have to say on the following pages. I identify them now as a sensitising signal in the certain knowledge that they will only intermittently be the direct focus of the ensuing discussion, but also in the certain knowledge that they will always be not far below the surface. They are themes that run through the literature on consumption as it emerges from the Marxian and post-Marxian critique of twentieth-century capitalism and in particular the emergence of a concern with culture as an object of critical attention. And they run through more recent discussions which have adopted a focus on, and a language of, the semiotic as a way of understanding the particular dynamics of technology, political economy and public images as they have emerged in modern and post-modern society.

The first theme is that of commodification. Commodification involves exchange. Objects acquire a value not according to their usefulness but according to their capacity, within a market, to be exchanged. Marx traced the emergence of the commodity form as the dominant expression of economic rationality as coexistent with capitalism, and closely tied to production, and the relations of production. Indeed the history of capitalism can be traced through the increasing significance of the commodity not just in relation to produced goods or objects but in relation to culture, leisure and consumption. The critique that was associated with this analysis of commodification was, of course, that of alienation (Meszaros, 1970). This involved the separation of the worker from his or her product, and workers from each other, as the atomisation associated with exchange value (not social or use value) replaced the moral economy (Thompson, 1971) of pre-industrial society. This doomed, moral, economy was articulated to other forms of social and economic rationality: more sensitive to the individual and to the support of community.

While some (e.g. Kopytoff, 1986) have suggested that commodification is antagonistic to culture, so that culture ensures that some things remain outside commoditisation: sacred, singular, unexchangeable; others (e.g. Haug, 1986) suggest that culture cannot resist (does not, under capitalism, resist) the process of commodification. Culture, by implication, disappears beneath it. The critics of the Frankfurt School (see below) take this as their starting point. The insidious commodification, and reification, which they saw as the work of the cultural industries, stamps an alien rationality and an alien aesthetics on the images, objects and pleasures of contemporary culture. The result is an atomisation and an homogenisation of everyday life – atomised because value lies in the individual objects of exchange – homogenised because everything is exchangeable and in some sense, therefore, equivalent.

Yet others see in commodification not an antagonism to culture, nor even a repression of culture, but an embodiment of culture (Appadurai, 1986). No exchange without meaning. No economy without value. No culture without exchange. In this dialectical approach in which commodification is to be understood as a social process, some of the arguments about commodification and consumption became more complex and more challenging. The histories of consumption (e.g. McKracken, 1988) which incorporate such a view depend less on a version of commodification that demands an analysis of its iron-fisted imposition, or on the malleability and vulnerability of the new consumer, and more on the constructive logics embodied in commodity exchange and their openness to creative attention in and through consumption itself.

To see commodification and consumption in this way involves the second of the themes of this chapter: goods as symbols, and it might be said, symbols as goods.

Once goods enter a system of exchange they enter a system of differences, of differential values and meanings which provide the basis not only for their position in a hierarchy of value, but increasingly in a society constructed around and through consumption, the basis for a classification of consumers and owners, tastes and styles. And these public meanings have to be visible meanings if they are to have any weight and significance, and if any power is to be exercised through their expression. Consumption has to be conspicuous. And the needs which it expresses, and to some extent must fulfil, are social. As Appadurai notes (1986, 31) consumption (and the demand that makes it possible) is 'a focus not only for *sending* messages ... but for *receiving* them as well'.

Goods and commodities become symbolic objects within a system of meanings. But that system can be understood in a number of overlapping ways. It can be seen as oppressive, the motor and motivation of a society of the spectacle, the spectator, the spectacular. It can be seen as a system of classification, a code. Or it can be seen as the basis for a complex web of creative possibilities. In the first, consumption, fashion and style are all seen to be expressions of a false reality, in which objects are no longer meaningful because they are useful but are only deemed useful because they are meaningful; and in which the image replaces reality as the basis for their, and all, value (see Debord, 1977, 1990). The result is an imposed and reifying system: a tyranny of appearance.

In the second, consumption is a dynamic but still containing a code in which:

the virtual totality of all objects and messages [is] presently constituted in a more or less coherent discourse. Consumption, insofar as it is meaningful, is a systematic act of the manipulation of signs.

(Baudrillard, 1988, 22)

In this too we are deceived by the sign, seduced into believing that the image is the reality. But in that seduction we are also willing participants. We collude with it.

And the third, still within the linguistic metaphor, finds in the consumption and exchange of goods a language in a stricter sense, creating the possibilities for speech and communication in the manipulation of their meanings (see Bourdieu, 1984; Douglas and Isherwood, 1979). Here personal and social identities are formed on the web of consumer possibilities and in the choice and display of objects to hang on it. We speak through our commodities, about ourselves and to each other, making claims for status and for difference, and actively and creatively marking out a map for the negotiation of everyday life.

In consumption the sign is indeed the arena of struggle – though not exclusively class struggle (Voloshinov, 1973). But how much struggle and how consequential? How we come to adjudicate between competing definitions of power within the discourses of consumption, between the possibilities for freedom and the degrees of freedom, as well as the meaningfulness of those freedoms, is very much the issue. The analysis of television's role in this is once again arguably quite crucial, for as Robert Dunn (1986) suggests: 'it is primarily the visual form of television which exemplifies the commodification of culture . . . As a sign system within a sign system, television mirrors consumerism's master code only to reinforce it at a deeper logical and psychological level' (Dunn, 1986, 53 and 55).

This observation (and challenge) leads to a consideration of the third underlying theme of this chapter, that of articulation. This concerns the various levels at which it is possible to consider television as being locked into the consumptive discourses of contemporary society. Leo Lowenthal (cited in Adorno, 1957, 480) talked of television in terms of 'psychoanalysis in reverse', implying that the psychoanalytic notion of the personality has been taken up within the cultural industry as a discursive mechanism to entrap and seduce the viewers of television. Programmes would be layered in a kind of homologous way to the layers of the personality and, through this coincidence of structure, the trap – the latent and ideological messages – would be set.

More recent and more focused psychoanalytic work makes parallel claims (e.g. the journal *Screen*, Mellencamp, 1990). One can certainly argue that television does indeed provide in its programmes, through its narratives, its genres, and its rhetorics, one way in which the logics of commodity culture are articulated with the concerns, values and meanings of everyday life.

Programmes and advertisements can hardly fail to provide an expression and a reinforcement of the dominant and dominating ideologies of consumer society – Jerry Mander (1978, 132) calls it 'a delivery system for commodity life'. And equally it is clear how in the forms of television, in the structures of its schedules, in the patterns of the media calendar and in the array of channel choice, the medium provides yet another route into consumer culture, offering itself as an object of choice to a more or less active/passive spectator. And finally, it can also be argued that television as technology is articulated into contemporary culture – domestic culture and the culture of consumption – through producing and reproducing the very forms of the relationship between consumer and object that define the system as a whole. We consume television, and we consume through television.[2] And as Lynne Spigel (1992) has argued, we have had to learn how to do both.

Even in this brief discussion of articulation it is important to recognise its limits. Such arguments raise the spectre of total passivity, of views of the audiences as rats in a maze, making artificial and meaningless choices under the illusion (if rats have illusions) that they are meaningful. To talk of articulation as if that was the end of the story, as if there was no room for difference, no room for transformation, negotiation or denial, obviously mistakes things. Here too there is an essential tension: a tension between structure and the possibilities for action; between representation and reading; between public commodities and private objects. I shall return to this theme throughout this chapter.

The last of the themes can also be posed as a tension. Arguments within contemporary cultural theory, and particularly those that have emerged under the banner of post-modernism have focused on the two quite opposite tendencies within consumption towards, on the one hand, the homogenisation, and on the other, the fragmentation and disintegration, of cultures and tastes (Featherstone, 1991). I have already referred to them. The critique of the increasing internationalisation of industrial cultural production, which has its origins in the work of the Frankfurt School, sees the results as being a global culture, the product of American cultural and media imperialism and generating, both in form and content, a universal cultural framework from which there is very little escape (see Schiller, 1989). The post-modern critique, in identifying the same tendencies, nevertheless makes a different case. Globalisation both recognises and releases the national, the ethnic and the individual. Incorporation into global culture (which may or may not be bad thing) also creates a space for, and to some extent also legitimises, the assertion of difference.

This tension plays out at the national and regional levels, and also at the local and the individual level. The breakdown of the Communist bloc (arguably itself in part the result of the attractions of consumption) has both opened up a new market for capitalism's commodities (a force for integration and homogenisation) and at the same time released huge pressures for cultural autonomy and the assertion of national and regional identity. Similiarly it can, and will, be argued that the commodities produced within an increasingly consolidated cultural industry, are no longer mass produced but emerge within a regime of flexible accumulation (Harvey, 1989), produced both for intensely fragmented and highly differentiated markets (both in time and space), and subject to further fragmentation and differentiation in use.

These four themes: of commodification, symbolisation, articulation and globalisation/fragmentation make up a ground base for many of the arguments in and around the study of consumption in contemporary society, and they will continue to do so in what follows. And in what follows I will attempt to sketch a model for the dynamics of consumption, particularly insofar as it affects the consumer – in the domestic or the private sphere.

The model-building begins with the identification of the key elements, and through the key elements some of the key theoretical ideas that inform any discussion of consumption. My intention is to suggest that consumption be seen, both literally and metaphorically, as one of the main processes by and through which individuals are incorporated into the structures of contemporary society – but that this incorporation is neither a simple nor an unambiguous process. It involves both activity and passivity, competence and incompetence, expertise and ignorance. But it also throws into some relief, and gives some expression to, the particular dynamics of structure and agency (Archer, 1988) – and especially the role of the media in articulating those dynamics – which provide one of the central problematics of social and cultural theory.

In providing an account of consumption in this way I draw on, but also extend, some of the discussions that have taken place in earlier chapters. I want to identify consumption through the interweaving of the following: industry, 'technologies', taste, identities, recontextualisations, and power, and in doing so I hope to introduce a number of different but complementary theoretical perspectives which will inform the model as it emerges in the last section of the chapter.

INDUSTRY

The culture industry fuses the old and familiar into a new quality. In all its branches, products which are tailored for consumption by masses, and which to a great extent determine the nature of that consumption, are manufactured more or less according to plan. The individual branches are similiar in structure or at least fit into each other, ordering themselves into a system almost without a gap. This is made possible by contemporary technical capabilities as well as by economic and administrative concentration. The culture industry intentionally integrates its consumers from above.

(Adorno, 1991, 85)

The might of industrial society is lodged in men's minds.

(Horkheimer and Adorno, 1972, 127)

Horkheimer and Adorno, fresh from the political and economic totalitarianism of Nazi Germany, discovered a new form of tyranny in the United States in the form of Hollywood and the cultural industry. Their analysis and critique of this industry, an element in their forlorn interrogation of the punishing success of advancing capitalism, provides, for all its imperfections, a starting point. It does so because it plausibly, and remarkably presciently, identifies that industry as the source of what they saw as the profound and pernicious remystification of contemporary culture. And it does so because their critique, which insists on the integration of political-economic and cultural analysis, provides (despite its pessimism, or even because of it) a significant influence on a whole slew of recent critics who similarly take changes in the industrial and technological complexes of late capitalism as the key to an understanding of the contradictions of post-modernity (Baudrillard, 1988; Harvey, 1989; Lash, 1990, and see Adorno, 1991, 23).

In fact, of course, Horkheimer and Adorno do not engage in a detailed analysis of the ownership and control of the cultural industry. Instead they develop a post-Weberian analysis of the forms of rationality that are expressed simultaneously within industrial organisation, technology and cultural forms. That rationality is the punishing rationality of Weber's iron cage and, in its other expression, of Marcuse's one-dimensional man. That rationality is expressive and reinforcive of economic power (Horkheimer and Adorno, 1972, 121) and of the structures of industrial production which define the logics and the values of society under capitalism.

The cultural industry produces a standardised, homogenised mass culture in which the market, like a lava flow, consumes everything of value in its path. Citizens are turned into consumers. Culture and entertainment are fused. Negation, the possibility of denying the seductions of affirmative bourgeois culture, is rendered impossible. Consumers are classified and labelled in the same way as, and in order to sell, commodities. The media, and especially the new medium of television (they were writing originally on these matters in 1944) provide a constant and de-differentiating flow: of repetitive, pre-dictable, smug and superficial programming. Real life is becoming indistinguishable from its mediation in film and television. All is false: pleasure, happiness, spectacle, laughter, sexuality, individuality. Amusement is structured according to the rhythms demanded by the factory. And advertising is the litmus, both source and symbol of the cultural industry's triumph. Advertising offers signs without meaning within an assembly line repetition of constant appearance, and appearance without which commodities and objects themselves have no meaning:

The most intimate reactions of human beings have been so thoroughly reified that the idea of anything specific to themselves now persists only as an utterly abstract notion: personality scarcely signifies anything more than shining white teeth and freedom from body odour and emotions. The triumph of advertising in the culture industry is that consumers feel compelled to buy and use its products even though they see through them.

(Horkheimer and Adorno, 1972, 167)

There is much still of value in these observations and in the trenchant savagery of their critique. It provides, still, a significant obstacle for contemporary theorists who find in popular cultural forms expressions of authentic pleasures and fulfilled desires (see Caughie, 1991; Born, 1993). In the present context it is of value in other respects, for it provides, even in its exaggerated and elitist pessimism, an account of the media which does not depend on analysis only of the media and, similarly, an account of consumption which does not depend on analysis only of the consumer. The power of television is to be understood, as Conrad Lodziak (1986, 3) later recognises, not in any analysis of its decontextualised effects, but in its proper location within a political and economic framework.

Their analysis is also of value because it identifies, from the point of view of its particular rationality, commodification and consumption as keys to understanding the dynamics and the logic of late capitalism. Within consumption, its reifications and its repressive desublimations, the masses are constructed, denied their freedom, denied their truths and denied their authentic pleasures. Within the cultural industry's hegemony the rhythms and routines of everyday life are moulded to an industrial timekeeping. Consumption replaces production as the visible marker of social life without, it should be added, denying production's fundamental, material, importance. Consumption is therefore doubly significant: it is both the signifier and signified of the order of later capitalism. But it is, at least in Horkheimer and Adorno's view, still a second-order reality.

I have already argued (Chapter 4) for a view of television which requires that it be seen as an element within a wider technological and political-economic rationality. And I have already suggested that at least one major component of its relationship to time and space is that defined by the schedules and their expression and imposition of a public, industrial timekeeping in the private sphere. Others have provided analyses of the current patterns of industrial order: of transnationalism, vertical and horizontal integration, media imperialism, information flow and flexible specialisation which mark the present character of the cultural industry (Murdock, 1982, 1990; Garnham 1991). Implicitly those analyses endorse the main direction of the Frankfurt School's critique, by providing extensive empirical evidence of the trends and consequences that they identified. Not all, of course, endorse their conclusions or their lack of subtlety.

But they do sometimes betray the same absences and the same blindness: the absence of actors and the blindness to the active participation of consumer-citizens in the creation, and recreation, modification and trans-formation, of culture. They tend to presume that a cultural logic can be read off from the analysis of industrial logic; to presume a homogeneity of culture which is often more an expression of their own homogenising theories; and they generally fail to acknowledge that culture is plural, that cultures are the products of individual and collective actions, more or less distinctive, more or less authentic, more or less removed from the tentacles of the cultural industry.

'TECHNOLOGIES'

> We have reached the point where 'consumption' has grasped the whole of life; where all activities are sequenced in the same combinatorial mode; where the schedule of gratification is outlined in advance, one hour at a time; and where the 'environment' is complete, completely climatized, furnished, and culturalized. In the phenomenology of consumption, the general climatiz-ation of life, of goods, objects, services, behaviours, and social relations, represents the perfected, 'consummated',[3] stage of evolution which, through articulated networks of objects, ascends from pure and simple abundance to a complete conditioning of action and time, and finally to the systematic organization of ambiance, which is characteristic of the drug-stores, the shopping malls, or the modern airports in our futuristic cities.
>
> (Baudrillard, 1988, 33)

Technology has a double reference in the work of Jean Baudrillard. The first is its literal appearance in the post-McLuhan critique of the effect of electronic technologies on culture. And the second is metaphorical, for it can be suggested, as the above quotation indicates, that consumption is seen by Baudrillard as some form of technology (see Douglas and Isherwood, 1979 and below, who also talk of the technology of consumption): as a totalising machine at work in the transformation of society. Media and consumption are crucially interrelated in Baudrillard's early writings (I leave to one side much of his later work). The phenomenology of consumption is expressed through an equivalent phenomenology of the media, a phenomenology dominated and subsumed by the sign, its proliferation, the merging of reality and fantasy, and the resurrection of the real in the symbolic.

There are three elements within Baudrillard's analyses of technology and consumption on which I want to focus, knowing that in doing so I do injustice to the expansiveness of his critique (as well as glossing over its contradictions and exaggerations)[4]. The first is his consideration of the television as an object. The second is his reformulation of the slogan that the medium is the message. And the third is his characterisation of consumption itself as an operating and defining characteristic of (post-)modern society.

As part of an analysis originally published in 1969 in which he attempts to relate the social function of objects to a class-based analysis of practices, which is in turn a way of opening up the question of consumption, Baudrillard draws attention to the significance of television as an object. He remarks that a television can be bought for two different reasons: as an object itself, and, as such, a claim for status or membership in which possession is an indication of 'recognition, of integration, of social legitimacy'. This, he suggests, is its status in lower-class households, which are to be contrasted to middle- and upper-class households in which the television is bought not for what it is but what it can do. The extremes are those of television as the site of a ritual practice, an object whose value is defined by its exchange value; and those of television as the site of a rational cultural practice, a medium whose value is defined according to its usefulness:

> There are those for whom TV is an object, there are those for whom it is a cultural exercise: on this radical opposition a cultural class privilege is established that is registered in an essential social privilege.
>
> (Baudrillard, 1981, 57)

Of course these two discrete marks of social status are never present in their pure state (though Baudrillard implies that the classes are). What is interesting however is his recognition both of the significance of objects as indicators of class position (see Bourdieu, 1984 and below) and that significance, in turn, as a function of the particular dynamics of consumption in contemporary society. Television can, indeed, mean different things to different people. But what is also interesting is his recognition of what I have elsewhere referred to as television's double articulation: that is to the separate dimensions of its cultural meaning, both as object and as medium. I shall return to this towards the end of this chapter.

Second, and what appears to be quite a distinct and separate excursion, is Baudrillard's reformulation of McLuhan's characterisation of the consequences of electronic mediation on social and psychic life – a reformulation that Baudrillard continually returns to throughout his work. The rise of the broadcast media was, for Baudrillard, an important element in the coming of post-modernity, for through them, and particularly through television, a fundamental (and fundamentally new) form of reproduction, which he defines as simulation, emerges as the predominant characteristic of culture.[5]

> By the late 1970's Baudrillard was interpreting the media as key simulation machines which reproduce images, signs and codes which in turn come to constitute an autonomous realm of (hyper)reality and also to play a key role in everyday life and the obliteration of the social . . . Baudrillard claims that the proliferation of signs and information in the media obliterates meaning through neutralizing and dissolving all content, a process which leads to both a collapse of meaning and the destruction of distinctions between media and reality.
>
> (Kellner, 1989, 68)

This is a position which shares an analysis (though not an evaluation) with McLuhan. It also shares both an analysis and an evaluation with the theorists of the Frankfurt School. However, whereas in his discussion of television as object he preserves a role for discrimination, for distinction, here, in media's banishment of meaning, all is bleached and leached: and all that remains is a technologically driven and interiorised mass culture of homogenised experiences and ideas. (See Horkheimer and Adorno's (1972) 'The might of industrial society is lodged in men's minds.')

There seems to be a problem in reconciling the force of these two discussions; the one acknowledging, as Bourdieu does, the class-based practices of discrimination in consumption, the other denying any significance to such activity. There is a problem, that is, until one recognises that Baudrillard's analysis of consumption itself depends on their integration. Consumption, for Baudrillard, seems to be an activity that takes place within the space of simulation; discriminations and choices are made, expressive and reinforcive of identity but in a world of objects and meanings that are removed from any experential reality. The choices are real choices (and ultimately unsatisfying choices) in a phoney world of simulations and unrealities. Consumption has to do therefore 'merely' with the manipulation of signs:

> If consumption appears to be irrepressible, this is precisely because it is a total idealist practice which has no longer anything to do (beyond a certain point) with the satisfaction of needs, nor with the reality principle.
>
> (Baudrillard, 1988, 25)

It is not just television therefore which is a technology. Consumption itself is a transforming activity, magically effective and operating as a kind of cultural machine, constantly providing a new range of identical symbols and representations, refined, recycled and mass produced from the discarded and obsolescent products of an earlier time. Television is central to this. Baudrillard may change his evaluation of its influence, but not his view of what that influence is. Television is both object and promoter of consumption, and as promoter it provides the currency – the eternally implosive, lavish sterility of simulation after simulation which defines both the limits and the possibilities of consumption behaviour, and from which there is no escape.

TASTES

> Consumption is, in this case, a stage in a process of communication, that is, an act of deciphering, decoding, which presupposes practical or explicit mastery of a cipher or code . . . A work of art has meaning and interest only for someone who possesses the cultural competence, that is, the code, into which it is encoded . . . Taste classifies the classifier. Social subjects,

classified by their classifications, distinguish themselves by the distinctions they make, between the beautiful and the ugly, the distinguished and the vulgar, in which their position in the objective classifications is expressed or betrayed.

(Bourdieu, 1984, 2 and 6)

Consumption, for Bourdieu, is a material activity which is real in its consequences. It involves active discrimination through the purchase, use and evaluation, and therefore the 'construction' of objects. Objects present themselves for consumption both as material and symbolic goods. Our capacities to consume are constrained both by our social positions and availability of resources, as well as by the materiality of the objects themselves. But consumption is also a symbolic activity, and Bourdieu's perception of contemporary culture is neither the homogeneous one of the Frankfurt School nor the fragmented (but equally reductive) one of Baudrillard. Culture is a patchwork, a constantly changing patchwork, of difference. These differences are ultimately expressive of class position, but of class position precisely constructed in consumption rather than simply by its position in the relations of production.[6]

Consumption expresses taste, and taste, life-style. All are in turn expressions of the habitus. The habitus – 'the durably installed generative principle of regulated improvisation' (Bourdieu, 1977, 78) – is defined by a set of discriminating values and practices by and through which one's own culture can be distinguished and defended from those above or below one socially. It is also a set of absorbing values and practices by which the new and the unfamiliar can be incorporated and accepted as part of the familiar and taken for granted. We buy and display what we value; and we value according to our social position. Our social position is the product not just of income or wealth, but also of the relatively independent influence of education and family culture. The habitus is the cultural residue of historical changes as they affect an individual's or a family's class, status and power. But it is a residue which is also generative of identity and difference through the application in practice of structuring (and structured) systems of perception and taste. The habitus itself is an expression of the various forms of capital – cultural and economic – which define the conditions of its possibility. It intervenes between the determinations of income and the displays of taste.

So for Bourdieu consumption is about distinction. It is about status, our claims for it and our denial of it to others. Consumption is an expression of competence, and of competence amongst the codes and conventions, the knowledges, skills and differences (real and imagined) which make up the mosaic of contemporary culture. The distinctions between classes, and within classes, are articulated through displays of competence. Objects, works of art, all are marked and arranged in a clearly defined though constantly interacting and changing matrix of difference. Those differences are not essential but socially defined. They are subject to claim and counter-claim. Their values change, but they change, always, within an established and insistent hierarchy of judgements and of class. Working-class and middle-class cultures are distinguished by the differences of cultural power, and the absence or presence of necessity. They are expressed in the differences between the 'authentic' and the 'imitation' – for example the insistently claimed and defended difference between champagne and sparkling white wine. Meanwhile, in Bourdieu's account of the French petit-bourgeoisie, there is another relationship to be seen, not of imitation but of reverence, not of copy but of a kind of simulation (not his term for it) in which the petit-bourgeoisie, in their eternal and suburban dependence, reduce, hybridise, delegitimate all that was once legitimate through their very touch – a freezing touch applied of necessity by virtue of their social position.

I have, of course, savagely condensed the arguments of perhaps the most significant anthropological contribution to the study of consumption in contemporary society. Nevertheless the burden of his position I hope is clear. The value of objects is neither pre-given nor inherent in them. It is granted through practice, and through the practices of informed consumption. All consumption, even that of the repressed, is informed: informed by the demands and statuses, the socially defined needs and desires of those who consume. In consumption, we communicate. And as I have already suggested for Bourdieu, as opposed to Baudrillard, that communication is real in its consequences. It provides the fundamental matrix for the conduct of our everyday lives, and for a politics of difference which maintains bourgeois culture as arbiter of taste and distinction, guaranteeing its place in the hierarchy by virtue of education, tradition and wealth.

There are a number of observations which might be made, and absences to note. For Bourdieu class remains the single most powerful determinant of consumption behaviour and status. And Bourdieu's perception of class, as something given, and in the last instance still explicable in terms of the relations of production, imposes an altogether too rigid and restricting framework on the analysis. For all its subtlety and sensitivity, *Distinction* has little to say about variations, transformations and oppositions within, especially, working-class culture; little to say about other dimensions of social differentiation which can be and are articulated in consumption (differences of religion, ethnicity, gender); little to say about the prior coding of objects in and through production; and little to say, in Daniel Miller's (1987, 155) terms, of 'the actual brilliance often displayed in the art of living in modern society by people of all classes [with the consequence that] the use of ambiguities, inconsistencies, resistance, framing, and such devices in individual and social strategies are thereby lost'. Daniel Miller (see below) articulates his own romantic vision of consumption at the same time as he chastises Bourdieu for his. But nevertheless while Bourdieu uses the analysis of consumption to display the structuring of patterns of everyday life in contemporary society, and does so to convincing effect, he understresses the dynamics: the shifts and turns, the squirming and the resistances which in their significance or lack of significance, do indeed make consumption an active, sometimes creative, process in which individual and social statuses and identities are claimed, reclaimed and constantly being negotiated. He also understresses, to the point almost of invisibility, the significance of the media in general, and television in particular, in articulating taste, style and culture.

IDENTITIES

consumption decisions become the vital source of the culture of the moment . . . Consumption is the very arena in which culture is fought over and licked into shape.

(Douglas and Isherwood, 1979, 57)

The possibility of finding in the practices of consumption a mechanism for the creation and expression of more finely tuned identities is one which emerges in another seminal work on consumption, that of Mary Douglas and Baron Isherwood (1979). Their work shares with Bourdieu and Baudrillard a concern with the languages of consumption, with goods and objects as markers in a complex communicative network in which statuses are claimed and denied and memberships of groups articulated and displayed in each and every consuming action. Consumption, Douglas and Isherwood suggest, is like Lévi-Strauss' myths, good to think with.[7] Their focus is however on the individual:

Within the available time and space the individual uses consumption to say something about himself, his family, his locality, whether in town or country, on vacation or at home . . . Consumption is an active process in which all the social categories are being continually redefined.

(Douglas and Isherwood, 1979, 68)

Consumption goods are not, in their view, the messages; they are the system of meanings themselves. Take them away and the system disappears. They are both the hardware and software of the information system, which is consumption. Consumption is therefore, principally a symbolic activity. It is important for what it says and does not say, for its reinforcement or its undermining of cultural boundaries. It is also a daily activity. It provides a mechanism (a rhetoric) for social classification. It is rational. And media technologies are an essential element of consumption not only (*pace* Baudrillard) as objects to be classified but also as links to a wider network of consumption activities and opportunities.

Consumption, for Douglas and Isherwood, is very much an activity taking place at one remove from the material conditions of production and existence. Objects and goods have no engrained utility, nor do they appear to offer resistance to the cognitive, affective and symbolic activities of the consumer. Obviously, as they recognise, one's capacity to consume, and the way in which one consumes (access to information about consumption and through consumption, for example) is class-based and dependent on available resources. Obviously too, as they also recognise, consumption is about access and as such about the structures and exercise of power and the denial of access (Douglas and Isherwood, 1979, 89). But as Daniel Miller (1987, 146) points out in his discussion of their work and the similarly oriented analysis of Marshall Sahlins (1976) they 'tend to assert the overwhelming desire for cognitive order, and thus offer an unrealistically cohesive model of cognition itself which ignores the problems of ideology and framing'. Identities may be formed or reinforced within a predominantly cognitive – information – system of consumption, and one can acknowledge the varied rationalities that might be involved, yet Douglas and Isherwood offer a version of that system which lacks conflict, ambiguity and struggle. They find in the system of objects an expression of prior social divisions. But the use of objects may have a wider relevance and reference than that, as Daniel Miller himself argues. It is to his discussion of consumption that I now briefly turn.

RECONTEXTUALISATIONS

> Mass goods represent culture, not because they are merely there as the environment within which we operate, but because they are an integral part of that process of objectification by which we create ourselves as an industrial society: our identities, our social affiliations, our lived everyday practices. The authenticity of artifacts as culture derives, not from their relationship to some historical style or manufacturing process ... but rather from their active participation in a process of social self-creation of ourselves and others. The key criteria for judging the utility of contemporary objects is the degree to which they may or may not be appropriated from the forces which created them, which are mainly, of necessity, alienating.
>
> (Miller, 1987, 215)

Daniel Miller builds his model of consumption on an analysis of the object in the work of Hegel, Munn and Simmel, and on a consideration of contemporary theoretical and empirical work on consumption practices in modern society. At the heart of his position lies a perception of consumption as negation, seeing in it a liberationary potential quite at odds, for example, with that of the Frankfurt School. Commodities are (or are not) transformed as they leave the world of public meanings and are appropriated into a more private (or less public) world: domestic, sub-cultural, gender- or age-based. Consumption, from this point of view, is work. Alienating commodities (alienating because they are the product of mass production) become inalienable objects as a result of a process of recontextualisation. The work of consumption is not necessarily physical work (it can merely involve long-term ownership, for example) nor is it only the visible work on the commodity/object. The work of consumption includes the 'more general construction of cultural milieux which give such objects their social meaning'. Miller (1987, 191) reworks a Bourdieuian (1984, 183) example to illustrate what he means. The work done on a pint of a beer in a pub includes the whole culture of pub behaviour; just as a visit to a cafe is not just for the drink, but a place to drink in company and to assert and display a distinct form of sociability and cognitive order.

Advertisers know this of course, and orient their campaigns in such a way as to make their products appear and appeal to socially defined and located groups and individuals. And the whole consumer movement operates on a set of shared, though not often articulated, assumptions that commodities are of necessity to be associated with, and increasingly constitutive of, life-styles and, indeed, distinct forms of sociability. The point however is that there is an indeterminacy at the heart of the process of consumption. Consumption is indeterminate because of the different kinds of potential for recontextualisation available in different commodities. And it is also indeterminate because individuals and groups in society have different economic and cultural resources at their disposal with which to undertake the work of recontextualisation. In many cases people are forced to accept the full weight of the public meanings inscribed in the commodity; in others these commodities can be domesticated, and turned into things with private meanings as well as, or in defiance of, their public ones.

However hard he tries to avoid it there is a romantic streak running through Miller's analysis; a romanticism of the popular, which arises from the failure to acknowledge the contradictions and frustrations necessarily associated with consumption, particularly with failed or compromised consumption. Full realisation through consumption is almost certainly an ideal (indeed it is in capitalism's interests that it should remain an ideal). As Alfred Gell (1988b) points out in a review of Miller's book, every consumption decision is at the same time an acceptance of its limitations. An understanding of consumption as a satisfactory form of objectification can only be realised if the parallel work of the imagination and fantasy – that is of the symbolic – is added to the first. Without some sense of these frustrations and limitations, as well as a sense of the inequalities of power which they express, analyses of consumption do have a tendency to romanticise consumer freedoms (and, as I shall suggest in the next chapter, the freedoms of television audiences as well).

POWER

In reality a rationalized, expansionist, centralized, spectacular and clamorous production is confronted by an entirely different kind of production, called 'consumption' and characterized by its ruses, its fragmentation (the result of circumstances), its poaching, its clandestine nature, its tireless but quiet activity, in short by quasi-invisibility, since it shows itself not in its products . . . , but in an art of using those imposed on it.

(de Certeau, 1984, 31)

De Certeau sees consumption as being at the heart of the politics of everyday life. And consumption is, in a number of senses, inscrutable. He talks of the 'consumer-sphinx', and in doing so he is making a number of linked but separable points. The first is that most acts of consumption are invisible. The second is that these same acts are essentially indeterminate. And the third is that they are, potentially and actually, transformative. Consumption and everyday life are coterminous: the one equals the other. This is so because consumption includes, has to be understood as, productive. Buying, using, reading, watching – none of these activities leaves the subject, the object or even the system untouched. To assume that it does (as he suggests Bourdieu does) misunderstands consumption's essentially dynamic, not to say creative, nature.[8]

His analysis is conducted through metaphor and his metaphors are geographical and military. Culture is perceived to be a battleground, but the battleground is unevenly occupied and treacherous. The mighty are never invulnerable. The weak are never without hope. Minor triumphs may sometimes lead to major victories. Daily life is a kind of guerilla war in which we find the cracks or blow open the weak spots of, attack and retire from, or provide occasional and ephemeral sniper fire against, the rationalities, technologies and productive forces of contemporary society.

De Certeau offers a view of an, albeit unequal, dialectic of culture: that between the dominating and the dominated, in which the latter is not condemned to the prison house but is offered (or more likely steals) the opportunities for the pleasures of utopian thought and expression, in both the procedures and the narratives of the everyday. In this sense the culture of everyday life is defensive, not just against the threat of chaos and the unknown, but against the threats of domination by science, reason and economic necessity. But at the same time that defensiveness is also (is it not always?) aggressive. It is creative. It resists. It traces what he calls *lignes d'erres*, indeterminate trajectories, through the structures, 'the rocks and defiles', of an established order (de Certeau, 1984, 34). His operative distinctions are between place and space, and between strategy and tactics; and the operative articulation is a political one.

Strategies are the games of the powerful, occupying theoretical and material places: a place for everything and everything in its place, physically, bureaucratically, scientifically, panoptically, politically. The powerful turn time into space (there can be no control of time without control of the spaces through which activities can take place), and space into place. De Certeau sees the strategic as an occupied territory, whose successful maintenance consists in its ability to transform and restrict temporal freedoms, the freedom of occasion and opportunity. Tactics seize the time; they are the expression of an opportunist logic: the rhetoric, the conceits and the tricks of the everyday:

> strategies pin their hopes on the resistance that *the establishment of a place* offers to the erosion of time; tactics on a *clever utilization of time*, of the opportunities it presents and also of the play that it introduces into the foundations of power.
>
> (de Certeau, 1984, 38–9, italics in original)

Tactics are, or can be, both self-consciously political and unself-consciously apolitical. However culture is fundamentally political. And politics are cultural. His primary interests are in the practices and procedures of the management of daily life: living, moving about, speaking, reading, shopping, cooking, dressing, watching television; in other words, in all aspects of consumption, where public and private culture meet and where commodities become objects. These tactics of the weak are not to be considered as somehow apart from social life, as somehow irrelevant to the exercise of power or to the shifts of social structure. They *are* social life and as such cannot be ignored.

There are at least two ways of reading de Certeau. One can find in his theories an opportunity to explore, and in exploring celebrate, the private, oral, poetic acts: the minutiae, the stubborn creativities, the potential trans-formations of public cultures, which mark and sustain our identities and our places in an overweening, increasingly imposing, contemporary society. Or we can recognise the scale and extent of that imposition, and see in the same activities a kind of superficial scratching, the equivalent to doodles on the backs of school exercise books, making marks but not affecting the struc-tures, and intermittently (when our doodles are discovered) being punished for a lack of respect for the projects and structures, and above all for the authority, of legitimate institutions and values.

Despite the deliberate ambiguities of his arguments and his judgements, de Certeau offers an approach both to consumption and television's role in the articulation of daily culture which is relevantly suggestive. In acknowledging the tensions between industry, technologies, objects, tastes and identity formations which I have just addressed, he opens up his own discursive space for a consideration of the dynamics of appropriation and resistance (unstable, uncertain, skewed, creative but also quite often sterile) which drive the mechanics of daily life.

Not only do his arguments allow us to think more critically about the role of television in the mediation between everyday life and the places occupied by the Other (that is in science, politics and the other expression of public and dominant culture), but they also offer a plausible route for the exploration of the relationship between television, as medium, as institution and technology, with its audience. They above all offer a plausible framework for rethinking the problem of the television audience as one of consumption, mediation and 'action' – for defining the problem of the audience as a sociological and anthropological problem – and they hint at possible methodologies for dealing with it.

I am going to approach the problem of the audience head on in the next chapter. For the moment I want to present the outline of a model of consumption, drawing on the arguments of the chapter so far, and paying particular attention to television's role in this so central an activity.

THE DYNAMICS OF CONSUMPTION[9]

In presenting the arguments in this section I refer back to my discussion of the moral economy of the household at the end of Chapters 2 and 4. There I argued for a view of the household as a transactional system, actively engaged both economically and culturally, with the products of the public, formal economy, and I suggested that in that interaction, and in the correlative dynamics of the appropriation of goods and meanings, something of the place of the household in relation to public space and public discourses could be understood. Now I want to develop those arguments by specifying the elements within the process that seem to be significant. In doing so I want to make clear that I am not attempting a reification of the household. On the contrary. The household as a particular expression of the domestic is the site in which much of our consumption takes place, but as I argued, also in Chapter 3, the household is not a fixed or necessarily simply a material entity. It has a phenomenological reality and the domestic as such extends beyond its literal boundaries. In the following discussion therefore I privilege the household, but do not insist on it as the necessary or only location for consumption (on other sites of consumption, see Shields, 1992; Fiske, 1989a). Indeed I want to suggest (though mostly by implication) that this model has a wider range of reference, revealing as I hope it does, something of the larger-scale processes of consumption and the role of the media, especially television, in those processes.

The second set of introductory remarks concerns the status of television (and other information and communication technologies) as doubly articulated in domestic culture. I have cited Baudrillard's discussion of the television as object, and without necessarily endorsing the full force of his analysis, I want to pay attention to the specific aspects of television and other media which distinguish them from other technologies and objects in the domestic sphere (see also my discussion in Chapter 4).

The notion of double articulation is derived from the work of André Martinet (1969), who understood the unique capacity of natural language to convey complex meanings to be the result of the articulation of both its phonemic and morphological levels. Sounds (without meaning) were a precondition for words or signs (with meaning). The meaningfulness of natural language is made possible by, and requires, both. The meanings of all objects and technologies are articulated through the practices and discourses of their production, marketing and use. The technical dimensions of the machine, its design, its image constructed through advertising and its final appropriation into domestic cultures (see the papers in Silverstone and Hirsch, 1992) are of a piece: what is being communicated is the meaning of the commodity as object, and while this meaning is significant, compared to that generated through the communication of words and images, it is invisible and relatively meaningless.

Television, and other information and communication technologies, carry, however, a second level of meaning, whose communication depends on its prior status and meaning as an object. Television is a medium and its communications – its programmes, narratives, rhetorics and genres provide the basis for its second articulation. They only become available as a result of the prior appropriation of the technologies themselves (see Haralovich, 1988; Spigel, 1992).

What I am suggesting here is that the cultural value of such a machine as a television lies both in its meaning as an object – embedded as it is in the public discourses of modern capitalism, but that meaning is still open to negotiation in the private discourses of the household (see Miller, 1987) – and in its content, which is similarly embedded (Morley and Silverstone, 1990). The consumption of both, the technology and its content, define the significance of television as an object of consumption. And it is in this sense that I refer to television as being doubly articulated.

It is worth pointing out that Baudrillard sees these two articulations as separable and as the basis for different, class-related, relationships to television. I am suggesting that they are not separable (though there is a class inflection), and that individuals and households will relate to television through both articulations, though with different degrees of emphasis, and subject to change. New technologies (or technologies that are claiming novelty) are likely to be bought, by some, for their status as objects (and by those for whom such status displays are important). Others will buy them for their functionality and for what they provide by virtue of their distinctive mediation. Television is a paradigmatic example of what I mean here. Through its double articulation into culture its significance is extended beyond its status 'simply' as object or medium, for in its status as medium, and through the provision of information and entertainment, television provides the basis for an 'education', a competence, in all aspects of contemporary culture (Haralovich, 1988).

There are six moments in the process of consumption which I now want to distinguish. They are identified as: commodification; imagination; appropriation; objectification; incorporation; conversion, and I shall consider each in turn, acknowledging now that they can be considered as neither discrete, nor necessarily as evenly present, in all acts of consumption. This 'model' of the consumption process is very much a sketch.

COMMODIFICATION

I have already referred to commodification as a core process in the establishment and maintenance of capitalism, and to the more or less constructive logics which are embodied in commodity exchange, constructive in the sense that they are, or can be, open to the creative work of the consumer. Such a view involves seeing commodification not just as linear or imposed, but as cyclical and dialectical.

Commodification, then, refers to the industrial and commercial processes which create both material and symbolic artifacts and which turn them into commodities for sale in the formal market economy. It also refers to the ideological processes at work within those material and symbolic artifacts, work which defines them as the products and, in varying degrees, the expressions, of the dominant values and ideas of the societies that produce them.

One might consider commodification as the beginning of a trajectory which ends (see below) in conversion. But that would be a mistake, for although it is easy to exaggerate the situation, it is nevertheless clear that consumption must be seen as a cycle, in which the dependent moments of consumption (imagination, appropriation, objectification, incorporation and conversion) themselves feed back, especially the last, to influence, and some would argue particularly in a post-modern context, to define the structure and the pattern of commodification itself (Featherstone, 1991; Lash, 1990).

To see consumption as cyclical in this way is both to challenge the overdetermination of the cultural industry which members of the Frankfurt School insist upon, and at the same time to qualify the kind of romanticism embodied in Miller's phrase 'the actual brilliance' of the consumer. It also involves a rejection of many of the dichotomies that mark discussions of consumption, and in particular that dichotomy which expresses the opposition between alienation (in the commodity) and its negation (through appropriation). The consumption cycle, perhaps more of a spiral in its dialectical movement, acknowledges that objects not only move in and and out of commodification as such (see Kopytoff, 1986) but that their status as commodities (and their meaning as a commodity) is constantly in flux. Objects can be, and are, simultaneously commodities and non-commodities. The de-alienating work of the consumer feeds back into the commodification process and informs it, while that process of commodification itself facilitates the activities of consumption (see Hebdidge (1988) for an analysis of some aspects of this process).

The cycle requires, therefore, a consideration of the dynamics of, and inter-relationships between, the various elements of the consumption process. And it also provides a focus on the particular role of television – object of production as technology and as medium – as a primary facilitator (principally but not exclusively through advertising) of consumption.

IMAGINATION

The work of imagination is contradictory work. Commodities are constructed as objects of desire within an advertising and market system which depends for its effectiveness on the elaboration of a rhetoric of metaphor and myth: a seduction of and through the image (Ewan and Ewan, 1982; Ewan, 1984; Leiss *et al.*, 1990). But the work of advertising and of consumers' participation in the imaginary which is its result, is necessarily and inevitably, as I have already observed, a frustrating experience (Gell, 1988a). It is frustrating because of the limits imposed by consumption itself: for every act of successful consumption, suggests Alfred Gell, there are many failures, failures defined by economic limits, inadequate resources and limited objects and products. But failure is endemic to the system of consumption itself. Baudrillard identifies consumption as a kind of general hysteria, based upon an insatiable desire for objects, a desire which can never be satisfied. Needs can not therefore be defined since consumption is based not on a desire for objects to fulfil specific functions, but on a desire for difference, a desire 'for social meaning' (1988a, 45).

Grant McKracken (1988) writes of 'displaced meaning' and consumption's role in creating it. The displacement is that between the real and the ideal. In our culture such displacement is mediated through the objects and commodities of mass consumption: 'Consumer goods are bridges to . . . hopes and ideals. We use them to recover this displaced cultural meaning, to cultivate what is otherwise beyond our grasp' (ibid., 104). Displaced meaning is a culture's resolution of the problem of the imperviousness of reality to cultural ideals. The ideals are removed from daily life into another cultural universe, in our own case the cultural system created by advertising and expressed in goods.

It is this desire for social meaning that advertising creates and sustains. The goods that are offered through it, that are represented through its images, tropes and metaphors, create a utopian discourse into which potential and actual purchasers buy. Goods are imagined, dreamed about, in their coveting. The focus of those dreams is both the ideal world that they come to signify, and the real world that they will enhance with new meaning. Whereas the first can be, and is, protected within the world of goods (the infinity of goods as well as the infinity of dreams), the second is entirely vulnerable to the erosion of everyday life. McKracken suggests too that goods offer a means of fixing our identities in fantasy (this is how we would like to be) rather than in reality (this is how we are). He notes the contradiction between these two kinds of meanings, without clearly suggesting that it is precisely in the contradiction that the motor for consumption is fuelled.

Yet it is in the mobilisation of fantasy in the pursuit of identity, and in our goods' capacity to fix identity within a more or less systemic discourse of commodity meanings that many analysts have seen advertising functioning. Stuart Ewan sees its apotheosis in style, and style is, of its essence, constantly changing. He cites the classic work of Sheldon and Arens (1932), who discovered in psychoanalysis the key to the creation of the endlessly mutating surfaces of fashion. The appeal to, and the enhancement of, desire is the stock-in-trade of advertising and marketing.

But the construction of desire is not only advertising's prerogative. As Leiss *et al.* (1990, 290) note, some 80 per cent of new products fail to reach their profit objectives. Consumers selectively create symbolic associations in recognising new wants and in constructing new life-styles. In other words the process of imagination, is, once again, a dialectical one: driven by stimulation and desire, stalled by frustration and indifference, transformed by the active engagement of consumers in the very process of commodification.

As commentators (e.g. Schwach, 1992) have noted, therefore, in the actual practice of consumption, goods are imagined before they are purchased, prior to any loss of illusion that comes with ownership. Purchase is in this sense, potentially, a transformative activity, marking a boundary between fantasy and reality, opening up a space (or not) for imaginative and practical work (de Certeau's tactics) on the meaning of the object, either as a compensation for disappointed desire or as a celebration of its fulfilment.

APPROPRIATION

As Daniel Miller (1987, 215 and above; 1992) has suggested, an object – be it a technology or a message – is appropriated at the point at which it is sold, at the point at which it leaves the world of the commodity and the generalised system of equivalence and exchange, and is taken possession of by an individual or household and *owned*. It is through their appropriation that artifacts become authentic (commodities become objects) and achieve significance:

> consumption as work may be defined as that which translates the object from an alienable to an inalienable condition; that is, from being a symbol of estrangement and price value to being an artefact invested with particular inseparable connotations. Commerce obviously attempts to pre-empt this process through practices such as advertising which most often relate to objects in terms of general lifestyle, but this does not mean that advertising creates the demand that goods should be subsumed in this way.
>
> (Miller, 1987, 190)

From this perspective appropriation stands for the whole process of consumption as well as for that moment at which an object crosses the threshold between the formal and the moral economies. It also embodies the particular tension at the heart of consumption, to which I referred at the beginning of this chapter: that in our daily acts of consumption we express our irredeemable dependence on the material and symbolic objects of mass production, and at the same time and in the same actions, express our freedoms as creative participants in mass culture.

But as Miller (1988) acknowledges, and Carrier (1990) also acknowledges, the meanings associated with the acts and objects of possession, the withdrawal of objects from public to private space, are often anticipated in the discourses of advertising and marketing, so that, for example in the mail-order catalogues analysed by Carrier, we are being presented with objects (or images of objects) which are already constructed as posessions. Mail-order catalogues can do this by making production as well as sale a personal matter. Commodity exchange is overlain by the symbolism of the gift, and the anonymity of production is displaced by the personality of the imaginary producer. Even here, therefore, the freedoms associated with, and necessary to, the acts of appropriation, the freedoms for symbolic manipulation and re-evaluation, are, and must be, anticipated as far as possible in the system of meanings within which we, as consumers, must engage.

There are a number of further points to be made here. The first is made by Miller (1988, 175; see Carrier, 1990) himself when he draws attention to the constraints differentially operating on an individual's or a household's capacity to effect a transformative appropriation. For many, neither material nor symbolic resources are sufficient for them to do anything other than accept passively the embodied claims for meaning in technologies or mediated texts. And even for those who appear to have significant scope for resistance or transformation, except in the limiting case of complete rejection, it is unlikely that some aspects of public or systemically embodied meanings will not filter through.

This is true both for the appropriation of television as object, and for the appropriation of its transmitted meanings (see Morley (1980) for a discussion of television viewers' relationship to the texts of *Nationwide*, and compare this to Miller (1988) as well as Parkin (1972)).

OBJECTIFICATION

If appropriation reveals itself in possession and ownership, objectification reveals itself in display and in turn reveals the classificatory principles that inform a household's sense of itself and its place in the world (see Czikszentmihalyi and Rochberg-Halton, 1981). These classificatory principles will draw on perceptions of, and claims for status (see conversion, below) and will in turn define differences of gender and age as these categories are constructed within each household culture.

Objectification is expressed in usage (see incorporation, below) but also in the physical dispositions of objects in the spatial environment of the home.[10] It is also expressed in the construction of that environment as such. Clearly it is possible to see how physical artifacts of all kinds, in their arrangement and display, as well as in their construction and in the creation of the environment for their display, provide an objectification of the values, the aesthetic and the cognitive universe of those who feel comfortable, or identify, with them. An understanding of the dynamics of objectification of the household will also throw into strong relief the pattern of spatial differentiation (private, shared, contested; adult, child, male, female etc.) that provides the basis for domestic geography.

Once again television is no exception, as Ondina Faschel Leal suggests in her study of television in Brazilian homes:

> The TV is the most important element among the set of objects in a home of the working-class group. The TV set sits on its own small table, with the importance of a monument, and it is typically decorated with a crocheted doily. The TV, on or off, represents the owner's search for the social recognition of TV ownership which is why it has to be visible from the street. The old radio, next to the television, has already lost its charisma but is still there, documenting the earlier form of this status attribute. The television as an object is a vehicle of a knowledgeable and modern speech, it is rationality in the domestic universe where the rational order is, paradoxically, sacralized.
>
> (Leal, 1990, 24)

Television is one among many objects that can be displayed in this way, and not just by working-class households (though see the observations made by Baudrillard, cited above). And, as Charlotte Brunsdon (1991) points out in her discussion of the enforced display of the satellite dish, the messages communicated are not without their ambiguities nor are they always displayed with pride. It should also be pointed out that the appropriation and display of artifacts, in this case television, does not take place, nor can it be understood, in isolation. In the Brazilian example, the television, a vase, a painting, a plastic rose are all pointed out (by Leal) as significant, but significant as a collective expression of the systematic quality of a domestic aesthetic which in turn reveals, with varying degrees of coherence, particular dimensions of the moral economy of the household.

Objectification is not, of course, confined to material objects. Television programmes (and other mediated texts) are equally involved in the mechanics of display – in a number of ways. The first is through television programmes having (like material artifacts) the status of commodities. They can be, and are, appropriated in the same way that material objects are, their meanings not unequivocally fixed in production. And they can be objectified in the moral economy of the household through their physical display in photographs of soap-opera or rock-music stars. Finally one can see how the content of the media, and especially the content of television programmes, is objectified in the talk of the household, for example in the ways in which accounts of television programmes, the characters in soap operas, or events in the news, provide a basis for identification and self-representation (Hobson, 1982, 1989; Radway, 1984; Ang, 1986).

INCORPORATION

Through the idea of incorporation I want to focus attention on the ways in which television, like other technologies and objects, is used. Technologies are functional. They may be bought with other features in mind and they do indeed serve other cultural purposes. They may become functional in ways somewhat removed from the intentions of designers or marketers. Functions may change or disappear (for example in the case of those home computers originally bought for educational purposes which have become games machines or relegated to tops of cupboards or backs of wardrobes) (see Kopytoff (1986) on the biography of the object, and Chapter 2 above). To become functional a technology has to find a place within the moral economy of the household specifically in terms of its incorporation into the routines of everyday life. That incorporation may release time for other things (see Gershuny, 1982); it may facilitate 'control' of time, for example in the time-shift capabilities of the video or the microwave; it may simply enable some times to be better spent, for example in the use of the radio as a companion for the tea-break, or as part of the routine of getting up in the morning.

Whereas a concern with objectification principally identifies the spatial aspects of the moral economy, incorporation focuses, among other things, on its temporalities. Once again it is in research on television that this is most clear, and I have discussed this already in some detail in the last chapter in relation to the various ways in which broadcast television provides a framework both for the household's involvement in the sequencing of public time, and for the sustaining of domestic routines through the broadcast schedules. I argued there that these dimensions of television's temporality were subject to their incorporation into a household's temporality by virtue of that household's own clocking and temporal orientation (Silverstone, 1993).

Incorporation into the moral economy of the household also brings to the fore questions of age and gender, as well as questions of the visibility and invisibility of technologies. Technologies are incorporated into the household as expressions of gender (see Gray, 1987 and 1992 on the VCR) and age differentiation, as well as reinforcements or assertions of status. Teenagers will create a wall of sound in their bedrooms with their stereos. Battles will be fought and won over control of the remote switch for the television (Morley, 1986) or of the source of power for a whole room full of information and communication technologies (Silverstone and Morley, 1991). Ownership and use of the computer will follow and reinforce a family's gendered culture of technology (see Livingstone, 1992).

CONVERSION

Whereas objectification and incorporation are, principally, aspects of the internal structure of the household, conversion, like appropriation, defines the relationship between the household and the outside world – the boundary across which artifacts and meanings, texts and technologies pass as the household defines and claims for itself and its members a status in neighbourhood, work and peer groups in the 'wider society'.

The metaphor is a monetary one. Meanings are like currencies. Some are convertible; others – private, personal meanings – are not. A household's moral economy provides the basis for the negotiation and transformation of the meaning of potentially alienating commodities, but without the display and without the acceptance of those meanings outside the home, that work of mediation remains private: inaccessible and irrelevant in the public realm. The work of appropriation must be matched by this equivalent work of conversion if the first is to have any significance outside the home (see Douglas and Isherwood, 1980; Bourdieu, 1984).

Television provides an excellent example of this. I have already suggested that television is the source of much of the talk and gossip of everyday life (Hobson, 1982). The content of its programmes, the twists of narrative, the morality of characters, the stories behind the actors who play the soap-opera characters, anxieties about the news, provide in many places and for many of us, with greater or lesser degrees of intensity, much of the currency of everyday discourse (Fiske, 1989a). Computer software has much the same status for certain groups (from teleworkers to adolescents) (Haddon, 1992). Telephone conversations are as important as face-to-face conversation as a means of transmission (Moyal, 1992). Discussions about a recent or future purchase, a purchase prompted by television advertising perhaps, or by the particular culture of neighbourhood or class, are similarly ubiquitous. Once again one can point to the ways in which an integrated culture of communication and information technologies, with television plausibly at its centre, works within households and expresses the double articulation to which I have already referred: facilitating conversion (and conversation) as well as being the objects of conversion (and conversation).

Some individuals or households, of course, will resist (or not acknowledge) this aspect of the transactional system, and sometimes, as in the case of the satellite dish (Brunsdon, 1991; Moores, 1993), enforced display might prove to be a mixed blessing. But equally, the conversion of the experience of the appropriation of meanings derived from television, for example, is an indication of membership and competence in a public culture, to whose construction it actively contributes.

This final point brings us back full circle. For the cycle of consumption requires that the commodifying process, embodied in the activities of technologists, designers, market researchers and advertisers, as well as through the industrial structures themselves, take cognisance of the work done in objectification, incorporation and conversion. Market research is of course precisely an attempt to tap into this moment in the consumption cycle. There is no necessity to exaggerate the significance of consumption on the dynamics of commodification, but there is no need to underestimate it either. Increasingly technologists, increasingly the industries as a whole, are responding to the declared variations of taste culture as well as the particular responses to new technologies.

My discussion of consumption has been designed to do a number of related things. The first is to place it as a central motivating and mobilising dynamic at the heart of contemporary culture and society: to see it as both the oil and glue of structure and agency within everyday life. The individual, the domestic, the suburban and the techno-industrial are interrelated through consumption, where commodification and appropriation meet and are negotiated. Through consumption we articulate not just something of significance about our identity, but we draw, however vulnerably, the boundaries between public and private spaces and times. In this sense consumption is the operating principle, too, of the construction of an individual household's moral economy, and it provides the linking mechanism for a household's integration into, and separation from, the values and ideas of the public sphere. Television is both object and facilitator of this dynamic and transcending process: a technology in every sense of the word operating its insidious magic – its own poesis – through the endless normality of its daily communications.

Consumption is then at the heart of mobile privatisation: its content as well as its form: interweaving illusion and reality, commodification and possession, passivity and activity, in a web of social, cultural and economic relations which remain in essential tension. That tension – the tension of dependence and freedom, integration and isolation, which is so powerfully revealed within consumption practices – is one which now needs to be pursued further, only this time in relation to the television audience.

Chapter 6

On the audience

The history of television studies has been one of constant agitation, quite properly, around the question of the medium's influence. There have been arguments aplenty. The pendulum has swung between competing positions. The unfathomable complexities of the audience's significance (and how to understand it) have been raised by those defeated by what, on the face of it, seem to be both the most obvious and the most important questions of all: does television have any influence; does it matter what people watch?

Recent reviews (Curran, 1990; Morley, 1989; Fejes, 1984; Moores, 1990) have documented the pattern and the disputes very well, though these discussions sometimes seem to lose sight of the audience itself, perversely preferring methodology to substance. We have been offered accounts of the conflicts between behavioural and critical approaches, and pluralist and radical approaches. We have had illustrations of the usefulness of different methodologies and discussions of arguments about convergence and revisionism. As Ien Ang points out (1991), the audience has become increasingly problematic, not just for academic researchers, for whom it has tended to become de-reified to the point of invisibility, but also for commercial concerns, for whom it must be re-reified for them to maximise their share of it.

My argument in this chapter is based on a perception of audiences as individual, social and cultural entities, and as, in Janice Radway's terms, 'nomadic'. Even as television audiences move in and out of televisual space they are, literally, always present and in the present. Television audiences indeed live in different overlapping but not always overdetermining spaces and times: domestic spaces; national spaces; broadcasting and narrowcasting spaces; biographical times; daily times; scheduled, spontaneous but also socio-geological times: the times of the *longue durée* (see Scannell, 1988).

Television's influence is displaced and diffused by its position within these multiple times and spaces. Indeed the position of the audience in these multiple temporalities and spatialities is crucial. The failure to recognise this multiplicity or to measure the extent of its contradictions lies at the heart of the relative failures to understand television's role in everyday life. In this chapter, in which I take a more critical position in relation to existing research than I have hitherto, I want to illustrate and account for these failures, but also to identify the successes. In the final chapter I will offer a more synthetic account which involves placing the audience within the containing structures and practices of everyday life.

The power of television, or its lack of power, is constituted in its difference and its unevenness, dynamically. Audiences too have varying degrees of freedom to construct a relationship to the individual texts of the medium or to the medium as whole. Individuals can be deeply moved (for better and worse) by what they see and hear on the screen. Others can, and do, ignore those images and sounds, or let them slip away like water in the sand. For yet others, as I have argued, the continuities of soap operas or of television itself offer a kind of security otherwise unavailable through other media. And even more, there is the drip feed of the *longue durée*, the more or less consistent, more or less resistant, diet of ideology and entrenched values, invisibly informing and constraining all kinds of social action and belief.

The field of audience studies has been in tension, I suggest, because it has not really recognised these differences in audiences' positions in space and time, nor has it been able to incorporate the differences it has recognised into its methodologies. Our research has been undermined, ultimately, not just by the complexities of the place of television in everyday life, real as these obviously are, but by our relative failures, even in the new wave of audience research, to recognise both the limits of our claims and the incommensurabilities between them.

In this chapter I will try and disentangle the assumptions and implications of various influential approaches to the television audience. In doing so I will be suggesting that audience researchers also need to be 'nomadic'. They have to recognise, of course, that the problem of television's power does not admit an easy solution, but they also have to admit that no solution is even conceivable without an acknowledgement of the complexity of the social and cultural relations in and through which audiences are embedded. In this sense an enquiry into the audience should be an enquiry, not into a set of pre-constituted individuals or rigidly defined social groups, but into a set of daily practices and discourses within which the complex act of watching television is placed alongside others, and through which that complex act is itself constituted.

Emerging from the pages that follow, both in this chapter and the concluding one, will be, I hope, the basis both for a mediating theory of the television audience and a theory of, in the broadest sense of the term, mediation. I make no great claims for originality. Recent research has provided much in the way both of clues and demonstrations relevant to my argument.

Very broadly one can distinguish two distinct approaches to the study of the audience: that which focuses on the dynamics of mediation and derives some sense of the audience through an analysis of effects, influences or pleasures, depending on where it locates the key moments in the process of mediation; and one which focuses on reception and derives some sense of the audience through an analysis of their activity and passivity, their individual or social status, again depending on how the key moments of reception are located and understood. Running through both approaches are sets of assumptions which have significant implications for their commensurability and incommensurability – especially about space and time – about the locus and the temporality of audiences and audiencing.

MEDIATION

Mediation theories are those that privilege the medium itself as the critical site for the construction of the audience. In this sense the audience becomes a dependent variable, a consequence: it is the product, the creation of the media. Such theories and perspectives focus on the dynamics of mediation and extend along a continuum which begins with the audience as well nigh invisible and ends with the audience as effectively the only thing that can be seen, but still in a sense a product. Mediation-based theories can, as we will see, construct the audience as both passive and active, and of course as they move towards seeing the audience as active they cross the border between mediation and reception theories. Where they differ, and crucially differ, is where, once again, they locate their emphasis.

In discussing them I want to distinguish four non-discrete levels of mediation, each of which provides the starting point of a different conception of the audience, by privileging one of its dimensions. The first three, based on a technological, an ideological, and a cultural conception of mediation, tend towards analyses of television's influence on the audience as long-term and fundamental. The fourth, which sees the decisive moment of mediation in the text, offers a different temporality and therefore a more complex relation between the medium and its audience.

Technology

Technology-based theories of mediation offer the most fundamental socio-geology of television. The work of McLuhan, and following him Walter Ong, finds television's power in the particularities of its technological characteristics, generating a powerfully intrusive environment – an electronic space – which is universal and irreversible in its consequences:

> Most technology produces an amplification that is quite explicit in its separation of the senses. Radio is an extension of the aural, high-fidelity photography of the visual. But TV is above all an extension of the sense of touch, which involves maximal interplay of all the senses ... The TV

image reverses this literate process of analytic fragmentation of sensory life . . . The tactile mode of perceiving is sudden but not specialist. It is total, synaesthetic, involving all the senses. Pervaded by the mosaic TV image, the TV child encounters the world in a spirit antithetic to literacy.

(McLuhan, 1964, 332–4)

McLuhan's now-familiar rhetoric constructed the audience, implicitly, as merely an effect of the mediation of television. With television came a whole new kind of sensory experience, omnipotent and unconstrained by society or culture. Viewers of television were the slaves of the message of television, at the mercy of a transformative medium of communication, which above all shifted the ground from a literate to an oral culture. A linear culture of the fragmentary became an inclusive mosaic culture of integration – the global village – at every level of social life.

It is an argument picked up, though with some modifications, by Walter Ong (1977, and above). Ong offers a parallel but more subtle account which sees television as being responsible for the breaking up of the closed systems associated with writing and print, a breaking up which has major consequences for our perceptions of the world:

Television blurs the fictional with the real on a scale previously inconceivable. It does so not through deliberate choices made by executives, directors, writers, technicians, performers or viewers, but rather of its very nature. The 'tube of plenty' has generated an other-than-real world which is not quite life but more than fiction.

(Ong, 1977, 315)

Ong is saying that it is television's peculiar capacity to present presence and to blur the live and the staged, the real and the imagined, the spontaneous and the rehearsed, that marks it as an open system (as compared to the relatively closed system of writing and print). Television is narcissistic, but also participatory. While its audience is displaced and in a real sense a fiction, the identity of experience that a single shared viewing creates is a powerful force for community. The key to Ong's position is his view of television as a phenomenon *sui generis*, irreducible to society or culture. Television has a nature.

There are two slightly different ways of reading this. The first is to see in it a technological determinism in which the viewers are at best epiphenomenal. The other, slightly weaker version, is to recognise, as I think Ong himself does (see Silverstone, 1991b), that the issue is not a simple matter of determination, but of a new set of demands that accompany new technologies, demands of both sender and receiver, new (or fewer) skills, as well as a different relationship between message and referent.

The issue however in relation to the audience is easy to put. There are no audiences. Transformations occur simultaneously with the emergence of new technology both supra-consciously and unconsciously – a kind of Jungian coincidence of technology, myth and psyche, though without any, save the most mechanical, attention to the processes, particularly the psychodynamic processes, that link them. It is a view that appears, as I have already noted, in many of the critiques of the influence of television, critiques that do not involve detailed consideration of content, or if they do involve it, do so once again in terms of its dependence on the prior significance of the medium (e.g. Mander, Meyrowitz, Postman). This view does, however, involve, and this I think is important, a fix on the relationship between the medium and its viewers which is geological in its time-scale. Imperceptible but cumulative and fundamental changes take place in the audience's relations to the media, and in relation to each other, through their reception and reading, but not directly as a result of these activities. They take place as a result of a more or less total immersion in a technologically shifted and shifting culture. When we talk about the influence of television and other media on our everyday lives, this is an important dimension, one often overlooked by empirical investigation (for obvious reasons) or misunderstood.

Ideology

Theories of the television audience which originate from, and are located within, a Marxian or post- or sub-Marxian theory of ideology also tend to cast it as an epiphenomenon of forces active elsewhere. Theories of ideology – however else they differ – must accept as basic the capacity of a society to create and sustain a dominating and self-interested form of culture, generating representations and images, ideas and values, that disguise the realities of social existence (Hall, 1977). They must also accept, though with qualification, that the disguise is effective, in terms of both the support of the dominating groups of society and its acceptance, equally unchallenged, by those who receive it. Within such theories audiences are – *a priori* – dependent. Through ideology's capacity for legitimation, dissimulation, unification, fragmentation and reification (Thompson, 1990, 60), audiences are incorporated, and must be so incorporated, into an essentially 'false' culture.

The mass media, John Thompson argues, have not really satisfactorily been incorporated into these theories, though one might argue with his emphasis, since from the work of the Frankfurt School onwards, and including that of Gramsci, Barthes, Althusser and Habermas – let alone the theorists of the Birmingham School, the media have explicitly been seen as a central plank of what Althusser called 'the ideological state apparatuses' and what the Frankfurt School calls 'the cultural industries'.

Thompson's critique is based however on this acknowledgement of absence: that the media have never been seen as central to the workings of ideology. But it is also based on an acknowledgement that even those theories that do address the role of the media – he principally focuses on the early work of Jürgen Habermas – also fail to do justice to the complexity of mass communication in modern societies (Thompson, 1990, 121). This lack of justice relates both to the absence of any recognition of the mass media as formative of modern societies and, crucially for my own argument here, to the fact that that they also fail to recognise the limits of ideology's capacity to dominate and to incorporate individuals into the social order:

> It is all too easily assumed that, because individuals have been treated as passive consumers of images and ideas, they have *become* passive con-sumers ... This assumption ... commits the fallacy of internalism: it unjustifiably infers, on the basis of the production and characteristics of a particular cultural product, that this product will have a given effect when it is received by individuals in the course of their everyday lives.
>
> (Thompson, 1990, 116)

Thompson's own reformulation of ideology as a critical tool for the analysis of the role of the mass media integrates the audience, the viewer, the citizen, as actively engaged both in reproducing and producing (and, in pro-duction, to some degree challenging or transforming) mass-mediated culture.

It is a reformulation which both reproduces, and reflects on, the con-troversies around the very issue of determination which emerged in the pages of *Screen* and the arguments of the Birmingham School in the 1970s. These have been well discussed elsewhere (Morley, 1980; Moores, 1990) in the context of audience studies. *Screen* too offered an account of the audience as an epiphenomenon of the ideologies embodied in film and television texts, and despite the introduction of a more psychoanalytically informed account of that supposed relationship, it nevertheless denied the empirical audience any status or consequence. The audience was seen entirely as a shadow of the dominating forms, discriminations and power relations that were being defined and articulated elsewhere.[1]

But even *Screen* theory had already begun a move which was paralleled and sustained within an emerging but more widely based semiotics to recognise that the reader-subject-viewer-audience had to be struggled for and constructed within the text. This opened up, especially in the work of Hall and Morley (see below), a way of rethinking the relationship between text and viewer. But it also established a new reification – this time of the text itself – relatively disembodied from the political and economic structures and the institutional dynamics that created and sustained it. From the point of view of understanding the media audience, this was no great improvement, yet it provided an important intermediate step between ideological and institutional analysis on the one hand, and the audience on the other.

More recent attempts to sustain ideology as a plank of the critique of media in modern society (including Thompson's own, and see White, 1992) do so by offering a more fragmented version of it. They focus less on ideology's integrity and more on its contradictions; less on its uniformity and more on its variations; and they necessarily insist that despite a palpable breaking up of ideological formations in a post-modern society (a view which may have more to do with the theory than any reality) some forms of cultural domination are sustained. In these arguments the television audience, despite emerging from the shadows, remains vulnerable, for the workings of ideology demand invisibility. As Stuart Hall, in his discussion of common sense, paradoxically that most ideological of contemporary discourses, once noted: 'You cannot learn, through common sense, *how things are*: you can only discover *where they fit* into the existing order of things', (Hall, 1977, 325).

No analysis of the audience, its position in the social formation, its relationship to the texts and technologies of the media, can ignore the ways in which ideologies are formed and in turn claim subject positions for those who receive a constant diet of public communications. Television's unity in diversity, its naturalised and naturalising strangeness, its powers of legitimation and exclusion, its familiarity and taken-for-grantedness, are all easily recognisable as elements in an over-arching culture which contains and constrains alternatives, differences and oppositions. This work is done on another time-scale, this time historical, and social rather than technological; but it is still not easily amenable to empirical analysis based, as empirical analysis must be, on the details of cognitive or affectual response to specific items or threads of communication. The work of ideology is not measurable. And once again audiences, as such, disappear. They remain, even in their activity, shadows.

This is not to suggest, however, that attempts have not been made to measure its effects.

Culture

The work of George Gerbner and his team over twenty years has provided media research with a powerful, if controversial, analysis of the relationship between television and its audience that firmly grasps the nettle of television's empirical intransigence. Their work is based on a conceptualisation of culture that involves a concern with long-term changes in values and beliefs, and television's role in those changes. They call it cultivation analysis:

> Designed primarily for television and focusing on its pervasive and recurrent patterns of representation and viewing, cultivation analysis concentrates on the enduring and common consequences of growing up with and living with television: the cultivation of stable, resistant, and widely shared assumptions, images and conceptions reflecting the institutional characteristics and interests of the medium itself and the larger society. Television has become the common symbolic environment that interacts with most of the things we think and do.
>
> (Morgan and Signorielli, 1990, 23)

They too, take a long time-frame for their approach, claiming that it is television's ubiquity, its persistence, its redundancy and its pervasiveness at the heart of contemporary culture which secures its unique, and plausibly uniquely powerful, position as a definer of cultural reality, particularly for those who watch it intensely. Their definition of what they call 'mainstreaming' is an attempt to chart (indeed to measure) the consequences of heavy, long-term television viewing on the formation of beliefs and attitudes. Their particular concern, of course, is with the dominant sets of values embodied in the more or less consistent narratives and representations of television. Mainstreaming is a way of identifying the consequences of different intensities of viewing within social groups whose demographics and life-situations can be held broadly constant. Mainstreaming viewers articulate, they suggest, views of the world closer to those provided by television (in its presumed consistency) than would be expected given their social, cultural, or economic circumstances. Distinctions are made substantively and methodologically in the research between first-order effects (high viewers who describe the world through the distorting vision of television) and second-order effects (the more intangible effects in which the consequences of high television viewing are found in specific attitudes, for example, to law and order or personal safety rather than in a general belief that television offers an accurate reflection of the amount of violence in the world).[2]

In a recent review of their own output, Morgan and Signiorelli (1990) argue that cultivation analysis provides a way of examining and measuring the influence of television within the socio-geological time framework that I have so far indicated to be absent in the technological and ideological approaches to the audience. The ubiquity of television makes it very difficult to separate its influence from other equally plausible sources of influence such as personal experience or information, representations and images from other media but, they argue, given this ubiquity and the fact that everyone watches some television, then small but consistent variations in attitudes and their correlation with intensity and density of viewing must be significant.

Correlation is not causation, as Sonia Livingstone (1990) points out. The research has not proved to be easily replicable elsewhere (though this may be the result of a more diverse media culture in, for example, the United Kingdom) (Wober and Gunter, 1987). Indeed there are many methodological difficulties, including that of specifying what psychological processes are involved at the level of effects (that is the long-term, small-scale but significant effects seen as the nub by cultivation analysis). Equally problematic is the relative lack of attention to the social dynamics of television processing, within the family or household, as well as to the presumed unproblematic status of the activity of 'watching' television. Finally, for many researchers, their lack of attention to the specificities of genre and programme, to the indeterminacy of media content, as well as to the implications of technological change, seriously reduce the extent of the claims for what is after all (and despite all its own qualifications) a general theory of television and everyday life.

Despite these difficulties, there is a kind of prima facie plausibility in the arguments of the cultivation analysis research. Even those who in the past have been relatively hostile (and are still critical) point out that with the increasing homogenisation of television output (Wober, 1990) as well as the specificity of television's textuality (for example the redundancy in its various and only superficially distinctive narratives), which require a different kind of social psychology than that based on interpersonal communication (Hawkins and Pingree, 1990), cultivation analysis provides a powerful and relevant framework from within which to approach television's place in contemporary society.[3]

However the television audience still seems to emerge in this research rather like plankton floating on the surface of the Gulf Stream and the North Atlantic Drift – alive but entirely impotent to affect the dominant direction of the current.[4] It is part of a food (only in this case a cultural) chain. On the face of it, and without specifying the dynamics of the processes which are deemed to be so significant or the routes by which they can be deflected, this may seem like just another version of a mass society thesis: a kind of hybrid theory drawing on technological and ideological frames of reference but merely reformulated into a more sociologically sensitive account. What makes it plausible, nevertheless, are both its commitment to mediation as a constitutive process, and its identification of television as a symbolic force at those very levels at which individual television programmes and genres, individual acts of viewing, as well as the individual personalities who view, are situated. It acknowledges the continuities and ubiquities of television, and grounds its analysis of the medium's power precisely at this structural level of determination. In doing so, and in offering some, albeit flawed, justification in empirical observation and measurement, it provides an opening into a vision of the audience as properly situated in cultural, social and psychological space.

Text

The focus on the text as the site of television's mediatory power is perhaps the oldest of all. 'The message is the medium' is, after all, what McLuhan was explicitly denying in his own formulation. Effects research and its model of the audience as the patient receiving the influential syringe was devoted to understanding, mostly through laboratory experiments, what kinds of textual stimuli would generate the greatest effects. The Lasswellian encouragement to ask 'Who says what to whom in what channel and with what effect' depended for its answer, principally, on the relationship between text and viewer.

Within this empirical research tradition the text, though central, was seen as relatively unproblematic. Subjects would be shown snippets of violent or pornographic material and their responses measured. Research attention was focused on the differences between subjects, or viewing situations, but the text itself remained given and unchallenged. The text was content, not structure (see Burgelin, 1972). The text was also decontextualised, not only from its position alongside other texts within the flow of media content, but also, and crucially, from the contexts of reception in which the dynamics of viewing, the commitments to genre, as well as variations in social and demographic characteristics were taken for granted, and generally ignored as independent variables. In other words, neither empirically nor, even more significantly, theoretically, did these studies provide an adequate basis for an understanding of text–audience relationships and determinations.

This focus on the text as the site of influence and effects also brought with it, above all in the laboratory experiment, a different temporality and a presumption, too, that text–viewer relations were not dependent on location. Time was short-term; effects were measured as simultaneous with, or immediately sequential to the viewing. Few methodologies were developed to try and assess long-term effects. Equally the transposition of the viewing situation from the laboratory (where so much could be controlled) to the field (where very little could be controlled) did not necessarily involve a rethinking of the nature of the relationship between viewer and text. The flow was still in the same direction. The effects of text on audience were both measurable and measured: viewers were shown, within the limits of the various methodologies, to be vulnerable to influence (but for how long and in what ways?) in a number of different ways and as a result of a number of different stimuli (for a review see Comstock *et al.*, 1978).

With the application of structuralist, post-structuralist and psychoanalytic theories of language and discourse to the study of the televisual (and filmic) text, a more sensitive approach to the television and film text emerged. Nevertheless, these approaches, with their rejection of empirical enquiry, still framed the audience as an epiphenomenon. This was certainly the case, as I have just observed, with *Screen* theory. Analyses of that complexity, analyses of biases in content (in the nature of representations of, for example, minorities; in the frequency of appearances of, for example, women, the elderly or blacks; in the distortions of the 'truth' in news, current affairs, soap opera or situation comedy), as well as more intensive analyses of the structures – linguistic, narrative and more broadly discursive – which define the conditions under which a text can be read, also 'read' the audience into the text. 'Effect' was replaced by 'interpellation': the audience was not 'influenced' but 'hailed'. The text was seen as the site on which, with varying degrees of 'struggle' (Hall, 1977; Voloshinov, 1973), ideological power was exercised. The text was conceived as itself a technology working its ideological magic through the mechanics and machinations of its discourse.

These latter analyses of television's texts as multiply determining took a number of forms. They were seen, often within a structuralist framework, as offering together, or separately, an ideological, a mythic or a folkloric set of meanings. From analysis of the multiple levels of the classic realist text and the interpellations of viewers into an ideological and highly gender-specific textual frame to a view of the text as offering narratives of mythic resolution or domination, these text-based theories also left the audience nowhere at all. Both text and audience were inscribed in, and described by, the texts of the analysts themselves who offered accounts of preferred readings, of mythic narratives, or of 'the positioning of the viewer as subject' (Heath and Skirrow, 1977, 9) which brooked little, or no, qualification.

What these analyses did provide, of course, was an account of the television text as something much more complex (and as we will see, increasingly *in*-determinate and polysemic) than the early effects researchers had presumed. They also offered text-based accounts of the power of the medium which had recourse to ideological levels of analysis, and which consequently involved a much longer time-span of influence. While avoiding the insubstantial immediacy of behavioural explanations of text–viewer relations, they nevertheless replaced them with a different kind of insubstantiality: the result of projection from the analysts' own readings to the presumed vulnerability of an innocent viewer. Yet they also involved an evaluation, and to some extent also a validation, of television as a powerful cultural force in more than one dimension, offering individual pleasures as well as cultural pain, and seeing its texts as providing cultural resources as well as ideological domination.[5]

The shift away from this tyrannical textual preoccupation was marked by semiotic theory (Eco, 1972) and within an emerging cultural studies, particularly in the work at the Birmingham School of Contemporary Cultural Studies under Stuart Hall. The key lay in the identification of the text as a processual phenomenon. Not structure but structuration; and not text but textuality, in which texts were to be seen not as complete or static but as incomplete and dynamic – requiring the activity of reading for their completion (or in some more radical formulations, for their construction). These novel perceptions of the text, then, involved the recognition both of the polysemic and contested, or contestable, nature of the sign (which may or may not be the 'arena of the class struggle') and the recognition that 'every encoding requires a decoding' (Hall, 1981). Texts could no longer be seen as autonomous or determinant. Nor was their continued reification a possibility. Imminent analysis was a thing of the past. Texts could be variously open and closed, and could be seen to offer different (but still intensely problematic) degrees of determination and indetermination.[6]

What this opened up, of course, and this is reflected dramatically in the two halves of David Morley and Charlotte Brunsden's *Nationwide* study, is a refocus on the audience, and on reception rather than on mediation, as the site for the investigation of the power of television. As some recent commentators (esp. Curran, 1990) have noted, this seemed to involve a reinvention of the wheel, for audiences as active consumers or constructors of media messages had been part of the literature certainly since the pioneering work of Katz and Lazarsfeld (1955), as well as, in relation to the child audience, the early work of Schramm, Lyle and Parker (1961).

The 'discovery' of the audience as reader and the correlative (and tautological) 'discovery' of the text as polysemic has had, and continues to have, significant implications for our understanding of the power of television. But it has also enhanced (or done very little to resolve) the considerable indeterminacy at the heart of our understanding of the audience, of audience–text relations, and of the multiple but structured determinations of meaning and influence that need to be better resolved if we are in turn to understand the place of television in everyday life.

RECEPTION

The predominant route along which this diversity of meaning and interpretation has been explored has been that defined by the various examples of audience research based on the moment of reception. It is at this point, of course, that the otherwise presumed and unchallengeable authority and integrity of media messages is seen to begin to break down. The ensuing fragmentation creates a huge research problem for media analysts. As Denis McQuail observes:

> Media use can . . . be seen to be both limited and motivated by complex and interacting forces in society and in the personal biography of the individual. This is a sobering thought for those who hope to explain as well as describe patterns of audience behaviour.
>
> (McQuail, 1987, 236)

Denis McQuail's summary judgement on the challenges faced by audience researchers comes at the conclusion of a discussion of the research on audience activity, satisfactions and uses. The research with which he is concerned, often labelled 'uses and gratifications', has its origins in the post-war work of Katz and Lazarsfeld (1955). It focussed on the role of the individual in the mediation of information within society – information of all kinds, not just that provided by the media. This was an attempt to understand the individual, albeit the individual within the 'group', as a key element in the transmission and incorporation of publicly generated information into the patterns of action and belief in everyday life. From it stemmed a view of media-use based in turn on a view of the audience as active – active in an individual way, and choosing types of content according to both rational and emotional needs. It was this individualising of media use – a social psychology of the audience as decontextualised, if not from the interactions that make up the patterns of everyday life, at least from the more determining structures of social life, such as class, gender or ethnicity – to which David Morley (1980) took exception in his work on the television audience.

If uses and gratifications research posited, as it did, a contextualised individual, it was the individual as a member, or not, of a social network that counted. The defining context was that of interpersonal relations.[7] Katz and Lazarsfeld's argument was based on an idea of sociability: that the individual was embedded in a network of neighbourhood, community and group relations, and that media information passed through this, usually in a two-step flow via opinion leaders. Morley misread this, seeing Katz's problematic as essentially based in the decontextualised individual. The argument is more accurately put as being between the need to recognise other levels of sociality (rather than merely sociability) which Morley saw at the time as taking precedence over the empirically observable activities of everyday life.

McQuail's 'sobering thought' actually marks one of the essential tensions within the study of the audience, even once one grants that audience a dynamic role in the mediation process: it is the tension between the individual and the social. The other essential tension, of course, lies in the notion of the audience as either active or passive, though here, as I will argue, the tension is as much a product of the failure of media researchers to think through the specific ways in which both activity and passivity can be defined and used, as any ontological difference between activity and passivity.

THE INDIVIDUAL AND THE SOCIAL

Early – and all – research on media effects conducted in the laboratories of behaviourists and others, as I have already observed, inevitably both decontextualised the individual from his or her social location, and also, of necessity, constructed the relations between media and response as one to be explained in psychological terms. The power of the media was to be understood in the ways in which it was presumed to affect the isolated individual. Subjects could be classified according to sex or age, but classification was no substitute for social location, just as measurement was no substitute for understanding.

Katz and Lazarsfeld's move into an idea of sociability involved both empirical research outside the laboratory and a wider recognition of the determinations and mediations relevant to the study of the audience. Audiences were now seen as members of groups, as I have said, and their active engagement with the media continued, selected, transformed or rejected the information and ideas that the media provided. Here the model was still predominantly a cognitive one. Members of communities behaved rationally and their relation to the media was based on some (more or less articulable) idea of need as well as a sense of function.

There were a number of things missing from the framing of this research. The first was the absence of what James Carey (1975) called the 'consummatory' view of communication: a view of communication, still plausibly based on the individual, which recognised non-rationality, self-referentiality, and unpredictability as part of the viewing experience. The second was an absence of a sense of the individual as located within a political, economic and ideological world which was neither necessarily visible, nor expressed in daily patterns of interaction. And third, there was the absence of a reflection on different orders of temporality in the relation between the medium and its audience: the importance of the media was to be defined through the viewing experience, even if that viewing experience was conceived rather more broadly than simply watching. Media effects were, in this research, short run.

Nevertheless what Katz and Lazarsfeld can be seen to have done was to define a space for critical attention, and raise the question of the nature of the relationship between the social and the individual as elements in the dynamics of the audience's relationship to media output. That space has been crossed (and will continue to be crossed) in many different ways. Four of the more interesting – interesting because they take up different positions, but also because they come at the problem from different starting points – are the relatively recent works of Janice Radway, Sonia Livingstone, Elihu Katz and Tamar Liebes, and David Morley. These are interesting for what they achieve and also for what they fail to achieve.

Janice Radway, in *Reading the Romance*, offers an account of this relationship (only in this case the literary one of romantic fiction and its women readers) in terms of a model of the reading process grounded in what might be called a contextual constructivism. Readers construct the texts they read as members of 'interpretive communities'. The act of reading is, tautologically, governed by 'reading strategies and interpretive conventions that the reader has learnt to apply as a member of a particular interpretive community' (Radway, 1984, 11). Although not grounded, self-consciously, in a social psychology of mediation, Radway nevertheless finds in Dot (an employee in a local bookstore) the opinion-leader and the key figure in the two-step flow of information first identified by Katz and Lazarsfield. Her aim is to understand the relationship between text and reader through the readers' own work of reading; in this case the women of Smithton for whom romantic fiction looms enormously large. As she writes in her introduction:

> the following study is founded on the basic assumption that if we wish to explain why romances are selling so well, we must first know what a romance *is* for the woman who buys and reads it. To know that, we must know what romance readers make of the words they find on the page; we must know, in short, how they construct the plot and interpret the characters' intentions.
>
> (Radway, 1984, 11)

This involves Radway in an investigation of the institutional matrix of romance reading and above all in an 'ethnography' of the reading practices of a 'community' of women, all of whom buy their romance fiction from Dot. Radway has produced a fine-grained and extremely influential analysis of text–reader relations (see Moores, 1990; Thompson, 1990 etc.) and offers a model of that relationship to which I shall return on a number of further occasions during this chapter. My point in raising it here, however, is to focus on the relevance of this analysis for an understanding of the audience both as social and as individual.

Radway, perhaps not surprisingly, shows how individuals construct the meanings of the texts, and the interpretations of characters, actions, motivations and the narrative as a whole in their own terms – that is in accordance with their own belief systems. However her argument is that those belief systems are not idiosyncratic, but constructed within an interpretive community, which has an, albeit superficial, empirical reality in the network established around Dot as well as a phenomenological reality in the similarity of the readings and pleasures that they individually generate. The work is social, perhaps, only in this sense. The women in her study do not share their enthusiasms with each other; reading remains solitary and the interpretive community is an analytic construct. Nevertheless each reader is, individually, engaged in a shared task, and a task which is also defined by a shared position: as women in a patriarchal society for whom the romance offers a particular set of plausibly (but relatively impotent) transcendent pleasures.

Radway's work is important for its understanding of the dynamics of the relationship between public forms and private pleasures. It is an advance on the work of 'uses and gratifications' in its analysis of the multiple complexities of text–reader relationships which focuses on the texts as well as the readings in their mutual determinations. But the women in Radway's study are decontextualised from everything other than their status as women (though in her account, that is sufficient) and as readers of romance fiction. How they are to be understood as social beings in any other sense remains a mystery, and the dynamics of the integration, or non-integration, of their reading with the wider world of work, domestic duties or leisure is understood only in terms of a set of general presuppositions read from their status as women, but not investigated ethnographically nor theoretically in any other mode.

This observation has, I think, a number of implications for our understanding of the relationship between the individual and the social. Radway's subjects speak of their enthusiasms and display their active competence as readers of their preferred texts. Yet as I have just pointed out there is no evidence of how that activity feeds (if it does) into other parts of their lives, or indeed of how other parts of their lives (and their overall position in relation to the dominant structures of everyday life apart, that is, from those of gender and patriarchy) feed into that activity. Her readers are individuals only in their relationship to their texts and they are social only in one dimension – that of gender. For these reasons, as she herself acknowledges, her study is incomplete.

Gender, in Radway's study, is assumed, in all its subtlety, as a key sociological frame within which to understand text–reader relations and the key, even more problematically, to understanding the links between individual responses and social determinations. As Sonia Livingstone has suggested (1990, 108), such methodological and theoretical presuppositions may be distorting. Livingstone's own work examines and attempts to measure the nature of the relationships, the 'para-social' interactions (Horton and Wohl, 1956), between viewers of soap operas and the soap operas themselves. And it does so without any presuppositions about the likely sociological determinants which may affect the ways in which audience interpretations of media texts are generated.

Livingstone's studies (1990) are also oriented to the problem of understanding text–reader relations, and they do so also from within a social-psychological perspective, much influenced by uses and gratifications research, which seeks to understand the nature of the relevant processes. Both textual and social representations are seen to be relevant in providing the basis for the audience's work in constructing their relationship to soap operas. Multi-dimensional scaling and other methodologies are applied to small groups of respondents (both male and female, though predominantly the latter) in an attempt to extract 'naturally' a sense of the coherences and divergences across groups in their ability to read, and to read meaningfully, the television texts of which they are already significant consumers. Livingstone's research does however reveal a number of unexamined assumptions. The first is the presumed coherence of the soap-opera world and the assumption that this is, indeed, the basis for viewers' involvement. The second is a set of assumptions about how viewers watch. Subjects are invited to classify characters as keys to the structure and meaning of soaps according to a set of domains that they themselves define, and as a result of that classification Livingstone is able to 'map' the ensuing coincidences and consistencies of interpretation. The capacity to do this meaningfully presupposes a degree of engagement with the given soap opera that might be relevant to committed viewers but which is unlikely to extend beyond them.

Viewers were shown to be able to construct 'a coherent representation of the characters in television programmes' (though since that is what they were asked to do, it comes as no great surprise). But it is the divergences which she finds important, for they enable her to challenge those 'top-down' theories which suggest an homogeneous response to television. When Livingstone comes to assess the basis for divergence among viewers (though with a different sample, in a separate exercise), she finds herself able to classify them according to the consistencies with which they approach the various characters, the result being groupings which she labels as: the cynics, the romantics, the negotiated (or modified RS) romantics and the negotiated (or modified) cynics. This results in the following conclusion:

The results support Newcomb and Hirsch's (1984) argument that television provides a 'cultural forum', showing the '*range* of response, the directly contradictory readings of the medium, that cue us to its multiple meanings' (68). The determinants of this range were found to be not simply socio-logical (age and gender) but also psychological (identification, evaluation, recognition). Thus one cannot make straightforward assumptions about interpretations from a knowledge of the viewers' socio-structural position but one must also know how viewers relate to the characters. This is especially true of soap opera, where regular viewers build up substantial relationships with the characters over years.

(Livingstone, 1990, 183)

Livingstone's innovative and inventive research does suggest the ways in which individuals who are both socially competent and media-literate can and do construct a set of interpretive representations which are the product of both that competence and literacy. As such she has identified some of the psychological mechanisms by which viewers and audiences work with the texts that they see regularly, and has offered an analysis of what might provide a link between social- and text-centred explanations of audience activity.

But it remains open whether these kinds of processes, or the particular application of them, are equally relevant both to other genres of television programming (though of course they must be to some extent, for they are expressions of the baseline social psychology of everyday life), or to less committed viewing, even of soap operas. It also remains an open question whether the elementary psychological processes of identification, evaluation and recognition provide an adequate definition of the pyschodynamic relations between viewer, text and medium. Cynics and romantics clearly occupy different positions in relation to the texts, but none appear to subvert it, and all work within a framework which the texts themselves define. The idea of a cultural forum to which this research contributes is one which acknowledges a certain determinacy in the text (that is a forum has bounds) but it ignores almost completely the wider issues of power that must inform any under-standing of the relations between viewers and texts, as well as any under-standing of the relationship between the individual and the social.

So to what extent does this research open up any counterintuitive sense of the nature of the relationship between the individual and the social dimensions of audience activity as well as that between the individual and the text? Only, I think, in a limited way. Both subjects and programmes are de-contextualised from viewing situations and the uncertainties of everyday life. While homogeneously gendered, or class-based, interview groups may (as Livingstone herself argues) overdetermine results, the uneven and under-analysed class- and gender-base of her own subjects (despite the fact that on the face of it they do not offer significantly different interpretations) begs the questions of those differences and their significance. Are soap-opera viewers indistinguishable according to age, class or culture? Surely we can say more about the reading of soap operas than that it is, in the last instance, a matter of individual difference? While Livingstone has opened up the space between the individual and the social (as well as the reader and the text) in an interesting and provocative way, much remains to be done both theoretically and empirically before it is filled.

Elihu Katz and Tamar Liebes, and David Morley all offer a more socio-logically inflected account of the nature of the relationship between viewers and television programmes. Katz and Liebes' (Katz and Liebes, 1986; Liebes and Katz, 1988; Liebes and Katz, 1991) studies of audiences of *Dallas* focus on cultural differences and differential positioning in relation to the text. Relatively homogeneous groups of three (married) couples who were also friends and distinguished according to cultural, ethnic, background were invited to watch and discuss episodes of the programme principally in Israel (but also in the United States and Japan). Katz and Liebes are at pains to understand the dynamics by which viewers from different cultural back-grounds situate themselves in relation to the narratives of the programme, but also to understand how those differences could be identified in terms of discrete sets of social-psychological relationships. Results suggested that cultural and ethnic identity do provide a significant determinant of differ-ential relationships to the texts, differences which are an expression of the position of those groups culturally and politically in the wider society and their familiarity with the society represented in the programme, and which are in turn expressed through different kinds and degrees of critical distance from the texts.

Katz and Liebes distinguish between the referential (a critique which involves referring their reading of the texts to their own lives) and the critical (in earlier papers this was the poetic), a critique which involves either a semantic or syntactic engagement with the text itself. They also distinguish different degrees of intensity of distance, through the terms 'hot' and 'cool'. This results in another four-term matrix in which they distinguish four kinds of 'opposition' or critical distance: moral, in which the content of the programme is in some way strongly objected to; ideological, in which the framing of the text is identified and strongly objected to; ludic, in which the referential identifications are treated more playfully; and aesthetic, in which critical distance is expressed through references to the narrative and other dimensions of the text. They point out that most of the discussion in most of the groups was referential. And in a cross-reference to the findings of David Morley, they point out that both studies acknowledge that critical distance (of an aesthetic, a ludic or even a moral kind) does not necessarily involve challenging the basic referentiality of the text or its ideological force. Viewers can be critical but still accept the basic, dominant or structural meanings offered by the text. This seems to me to be both extremely important – it acknowledges the limits of the power of audience 'critique' – and self-contradictory, for it undermines the whole notion of critique as in some sense liberatory.

The reference to the work of Morley suggests a consideration of the degrees of convergence between his sociological research (as I have already noted he has nothing to say about psychological processes and is keen to distance himself from the individualism of uses and gratifications research) and the social-psychological approach to the audience. Morley's research is, to some extent, a story of the disappearing text, though not as completely as recent critics (e.g. Seaman, 1992; Morley, 1992) have suggested. The early *Nationwide* project involved analysis both of the codes and the ideological qualities of the texts of the programmes followed by a study of audience response. His later work on television in the family restructured that relationship once again into a 'natural' setting in which a broader range of determinations (especially gender) and indeterminacies (the patterns of viewing within the family) could be identified. But each step, in one sense at least, marked a recognition of the increasing 'power' of the viewer to define a relationship to the programmes on the screen.

Drawing on the work of Frank Parkin, Morley, in the *Nationwide* study, found, apparently to his surprise, that class was no simple indicator of reading, nor of the ability to distance one's own readings from those that were supposedly preferred by the texts. In addition, even for those who might, and did, articulate an oppositional reading to the texts of *Nationwide*, there was no guarantee that that opposition would extend to the dominant ideological frames of the programme as a whole. What Morley comes to argue is that viewers must be understood as being situated at the site of a number of overlapping and plausibly contradictory discourses, some having their origin in the media, but all needing to be accounted for if the specific nature of the relationship between text and reader is to be understood:

> We need to construct a model in which the social subject is always seen as interpellated by a number of discourses, some of which are in parallel or reinforce each other, some of which are contradictory and block or inflect the successful interpellation of the subject by other discourses. Positively or negatively, other discourses are always involved in the relation of text and subject, although their action is simply more visible when it is a negative and contradictory rather than a positive and reinforcing effect.
>
> (Morley, 1980, 162)

This is (or was) all very well. But the model did not emerge, nor indeed perhaps could it, since what Morley was saying, plausibly, but not terribly surprisingly, was that television viewing (and the relationship between text and viewer) was a complicated activity, and could not be examined simply either by the analysis of the text's supposed interpellations or by an over-simple account of class position.

Class, in any event, was to a significant extent replaced by gender in Morley's later work. Couples of a more or less homogeneous class position were interviewed about their television viewing. This work was informed by other research, particularly from within feminist cultural studies which sought to distinguish male and female relationships to the medium and to place those differences within the context of differential power relations both within and outside the family. Watching television was seen then to be a highly gendered activity, gendered in relation to the hierarchies of domestic politics, and in the consequent different qualities of time-use and control over space (see Seiter *et al.*, 1989, 230). Choices of programme, freedoms to watch favourite programmes, the interruptability or non-inter-ruptability of viewing, all were seen both as gendered and as subject to the dynamics of the culture of the family. Morley's later work with myself took some of these ideas further, both methodologically and theoretically, by attempting a more intensive ethnographic approach to the study of family life and media use (Morley and Silverstone, 1990), and I will have something to say about this shortly.

So Morley's research was, as I have suggested, resolutely sociological. The pleasures described by individuals in relation to particular programmes or genres were pleasures ultimately to be explained, with no intervening variables, by class or gender position. The dynamics of the relationship, the mechanisms of engagement or disengagement, were left open, an empty space. But despite this, what links his project with others I have so far discussed within this broad grouping of reception studies, is the view of the relationship between viewer and text as dialectical. Texts confine but do not confirm readings and viewings. Audiences create but, like Marx nearly said of history, not on the basis of texts of their own making.

Each of the analysts I have just considered finds a focus on a different component of that dialectic, constructing within his or her own theory both specificities of text: genre in the case of Radway and Livingstone, individual programmes in the case of Katz and Liebes, individual programmes and then 'television' in the case of Morley; and specificities of audience: individual 'fans' in Radway; focused groups in Katz and Liebes and Morley; individual interviewees in the case of Livingstone; and marital couples in the case of Morley. I have identified some of the methodological components of these studies precisely because they are material in defining both the way in which each researcher constructs the problem and of course the way in which the problem is perceived to have been solved.

All of this work advances our understanding of the crucial elements of audiences' activity (though what is meant by activity is still not yet clear) in relation to television's fragmented and continuous texts. Audiences them-selves have emerged as plural, and significantly so, particularly in the more sociological accounts. Yet none of these reception theorists and researchers has provided entirely satisfactory explanations of the relationship between sociological and psychological variables in the audience's relationship to television. The elements of the dialectic of the socially situated yet individual reader and his or her relationship to texts and social structures remains problematic. Social psychology has been unable to break through to the analysis of the structures within which the observable and discursible interactions of everyday life take place. Sociology, despite its claims, has yet to specify the ways in which individuals whose relationship to the medium, to its programmes and its genres, who may well be constrained by the material realities of social life, are nevertheless involved in complex processes of engagement with television *as* individuals. Without understanding the former we will have no sense of the kind, quality and power of the constraints affecting the viewer from political, economic and more broadly social structures, which are both extra-textual and embodied in the various forms of television's textuality. Without understanding the latter we will have no explanation of the bases for defining the differences and the dynamics of audiences' relations to the medium.

However for all its significance, the problem of the individual and the social as a basis for analysing audiences is only part of the story. The preceding discussion has certainly identified other areas which remain problematic, which overlap, but which can and should be addressed head on. The first is the identification by reception theorists of the audience as active. And the second, which I have already briefly addressed, is the problem of the relationship between audience and text. I shall now, albeit somewhat schematically, try to summarise what the issues are and how far we have come in resolving them.

VERSIONS OF ACTIVITY

What does it mean when we say, as we do, that television viewers are active? As Sonia Livingstone observes:

> The term 'activity' is the source of many confusions, for an active viewer need not be alert, attentive and original. Activity may refer to creative reading . . . but it may also refer to the more mindless process of fitting the text into familiar frameworks or habits.
>
> (Livingstone, 1990, 193)

Is activity the same as action or the same as agency? Max Weber has distinguished between different forms of action depending on their commitment to rationality, and extending from traditional action (behaviour by any other name) which is the result of a more or less mechanical engagement with the social world, to action guided by a rationality of both means and ends. Somewhere in the middle, as it might be, is emotional action and rational action oriented to a non-rational end. What kind of action is television watching?

James Curran (1990) is right to point out that the early research on media audiences, both for radio and television, acknowledged that they were both active and, in their activity, discriminating. Different audiences, even children, approached the media with different socially or individually defined characteristics, and came away with different meanings: 'different types of children, bringing different beliefs, attitudes, and values to the viewing of the show as a result of different socialization processes, are affected in distinctly different ways' (Meyer, 1976, cited in Curran, 1990, 149). The equation of social or individual difference and activity has been a constant theme in television research. It has been repeated to the point of banality (see Morris, 1990). It implies that viewers (all viewers? all viewers by definition?) construct their own meanings from their individual experiences of common texts. This notion of activity is associated with a notion of difference: different viewers create different meanings. Correlatively the idea that we may share meanings, or that the meanings that we do derive from our engagement with television are necessarily common (and in some sense determined), implies a kind of passivity.

So if I arrive home tired from the office, kick off my shoes, grab a can of Fosters and settle down for the evening in front of the 'tele' am I passively engaging with the medium? And if I account for my relative inactivity (I could be playing soccer with the boys) by saying that I really only watch television to relax, am I reaffirming that passivity? And is watching television more or less active than reading a book?

One can enquire into the ideological force behind the insistence that the audience is active: that it offers a defence against both the right and left who find in the media unacceptably untrammelled influence. But one can also recognise that the active audience is, minimally, a tautology. All audiences are by definition active in one way or another, and one of the crucial problems in these discussions is to specify precisely what kind of activity is being referred to.

Different audiences have different needs and different competences. Their capacity to discriminate and to draw from their consumption of television, meanings that are transformed or negotiated in accordance with psychologically or sociologically defined differences has now been well documented. This is obviously most dramatically but still problematically illustrated in studies of the child audience (Hodge and Tripp, 1986; Palmer, 1986). I have already referred to some of the more recent and parallel research on adults (Livingstone, Katz and Liebes and Morley etc.).

The key issue is not so much whether an audience is active but whether that activity is significant. We can grant that television viewing is active in the sense that it involves some form of more or less meaningful action (even in its most habitual or ritual mode). In this sense there is no such thing as passive viewing (an observation which simultaneously makes the simple descriptor 'active' redundant too). We can grant that television viewing offers different things, different experiences, to different viewers. But the recognition of difference is itself of precious little use without our being able to specify the bases for those differences. So we can ask: does that activity make a difference? Does it offer the viewer an opportunity for creative or critical engagement with the messages on the screen? And if we ask this we must also ask how that activity is constrained; how it is constrained by the social environment in which it takes place as well as by the potential or lack of potential available in the text.

Activity then becomes an analogical term, not a binary one. To understand its relevance in relation to television we have to see it in its mutual independence and dependence and be able to recognise the contradictions and potential indeterminacies that arise. Many have suggested that television (and other forms of popular culture) offer the possibility for 'truly' active enagagement of the kind that involves great pleasure and even transcendence. Theories of pleasure, or of fantasy (Burgin *et al.*, 1986) are one route to an exploration of that potential. But many of those who have worked in this field, particularly in relation to women's involvement as active television-viewers, have concluded rather more ambiguously (and even pessimistically) that all the television-related activity in the world does not necessarily lead to greater liberation, and may indeed (as it could be argued in relation to Radway's romance readers) only serve to provide private compensations for public hurt (see Ang, 1986; Geraghty, 1990).

These arguments tend to put into perspective the claims made, for example, by Hodge and Tripp (1986) or Palmer (1986) or Livingstone (1990) that their subjects were active. Of course they were.

Hodge and Tripp offer a sophisticated Piagetian account of child development in front of the small screen. Differentiating between children's competence at different ages in working with, or transforming, the meanings of the television text (their argument is largely dependent on empirical work with a five-minute extract from a TV cartoon), they acknowledge the increasing pressure of ideology to inform those readings as children are able to work with the text as a whole. As Rudd (1992) has pointed out, their argument is flawed on a number of counts, not least for their adoption of an overly cognitive version of child development and of the child's relationship to television. This view, he correctly suggests, limits the model of the individual to a single psychological strand and at the same time fails to integrate the social into the dynamics of development – seeing it as context rather than as an integral part of that development. Actually Hodge and Tripp are more catholic in their overall perception of the relationship between the child and television than Rudd grants. They acknowledge, though without any sense of a contradiction having to be resolved, both that the meanings gained from television 'have social status and effect' and that 'general ideological forms have an overall determining effect on interpretations of television' (Hodge and Tripp, 1986, 217).

Patricia Palmer's argument is very similar. She, too, sees in the potential within the relative openness of television's texts, in the variations of viewing and discursive contexts, as well as in the psychology of the child, the possibility for television to be a source of stimulation and a resource for creativity. She prefers, however, the term 'lively' to that of active, so as to distinguish a symbolic interactionist approach from a social-psychological one. 'Lively' implies activity of a social and symbolic kind rather than a cognitive or psychologically functional kind:

> The word 'lively' has been chosen to describe children as an audience because it was found that in their own talking and playing about the set, and in their viewing behaviour, children were not passive respondents. Rather, they were engaged in the human task of giving their own lives structure and meaning, using whatever was at hand to do so, within the bounds of their physical and social development. 'Lively' refers to children's conscious choice of favourite programs and to their activities in front of the TV set. Both of these demonstrate a relationship with television based on the ability to make decisions about salience of programs and the competing appeal of other activities.
>
> (Palmer, 1986, 139)

Methinks she doth protest too much. Can children ever be wrong about their choices? Does it matter what they are offered to watch? Is it only a matter of conscious choice and deliberation? Are children always in control? It would be wrong to suggest that Palmer does not consider some of these questions, but they are still raised nevertheless. A child's view of the medium, and a view of the relationship between the child and the medium as an active, or a lively one, still seems to me to beg too many questions for conviction. It also, and this a well-recognised feature of many of the 'active' theories, significantly romanticises the nature of that relationship. As such it disguises the very real determinations, cultural but also political, which the text and, through the text but also in other ways, other institutional realities impose.

If these discussions of the active child audience fail thoroughly to engage with the social as constitutive rather than as contextual then what of those theories of adult viewing that are resolutely social? Here too one can see the tendency towards a romanticisation of the free and unfettered audience.

John Fiske's analysis of the relationship between television and viewer is increasingly that of one between television's texts and the pleasures that audiences gain from them. Neither the audiences nor the texts are entirely disembodied from the world of hierarchical relations and political and economic interests, but neither are those relations or interests significantly material in affecting what he argues is the relative (but how relative?) freedom of meanings to circulate in semiotic space. A pretty polysemiosis, indeed.[8] Television delivers semiotic experiences, not programmes, and does so heteroglossically (by which I assume he means by offering multiple texts in multiple voices to multiple people):

> Television's segmentation and its democratic delegation of semiosis make it necessarily heteroglossic, and its heteroglossia is a precondition for its semiotic democracy and its segmentation.
>
> (Fiske, 1989a, 69)

And again:

> Social differences are produced by the social system but the meanings of these differences are produced by culture: the sense of them has to be constantly produced and reproduced as part of the subject's experience of these differences. Viewer-driven meanings made from texts and sub-culturally driven meanings made from social experience involve the pleasures of producing meanings rather than the subjection of those produced by them, and make it possible to maintain a consciousness of those abrasive, uncomfortable social differences that hegemonic common sense works so hard to smooth over. And television plays a crucial role in this.
>
> (Fiske, 1989a, 75)

Here is an argument that sees in television an institution of cultural democracy. But also more than that, television becomes a kind of fifth column, generating public meanings that provide discrete elements in the social formation with the opportunity to construct oppositional and, in the broad sense, private meanings at odds with the dominant tyrannies embodied and disguised in common sense.[9] Herein lies television's essential ambiguity – but it is an ambiguity without tension. Television can be, it appears, all things to all persons, or nearly so. Fiske seems to mistake ambiguity for polysemy, textual openness for lack of determination, and unfettered or challenging freedom for the kind of activities normally found in playpens.

There is no doubt, and I have been arguing it constantly throughout the pages of this book, that there are cultural spaces, and television both occupies and creates them, for individuals and groups, genders and classes, to be active, that is creative, in relation to what is seen and heard on the screen. That is no longer the issue. The issue is to specify under what circumstances and how, and as a result of what kinds of mechanisms and through what kinds of processes. Fiske, at the end of the paper already cited, calls for a 'tracing of actual instances of these links being made', but in his choice of the term 'links' he reveals his failure to recognise the need for an explanatory theory; and his implied appeal for some kind of extension of ethnography to the study of the television audience is likely to fall far short of the demands of that explanatory task.

David Morley offers a more circumspect, more reflexive but still limited account of the active viewer. It is, certainly, an active viewer released from the cold hand of class determination (1980) and inserted into the domestic

(1986) where, as he later (1989) argued, we need to identify the variety of subject positions that could be taken and negotiated in relation to television within the politics of the family. But not just the family; Morley recognises (as does Larry Grossberg, 1987) that television changes its meaning from context to context. Following Herman Bausinger, and drawing on work in family studies as well as James Lull's pioneering domestic ethnographies, he sees the problem of the audience as being one not so much of polysemy, but of poly-structure and poly-subjectivity:

> we should then be precisely concerned to examine the modes and varieties of attention which are paid to different types of programs, at different times of day by different types of viewers. It is precisely in the context of all these domestic complications that the activity of television viewing must be seriously examined.

(Morley 1989, 38)

At this point Morley and my positions coincided, and we did indeed write a number of papers together exploring television's domesticity and some of the methodological issues associated with its study.[10] We argued that it was essential to take into account the context of viewing in offering any meaningful account of the relationship between audiences and their screens. That context would have to be seen both in terms of its social dimension (principally the domestic setting) and its technological dimension (the fact that increasingly television is only one communication and information technology among many in the household).

However, on reflection, it seems necessary to make a number of points. The first is that there is a strong and almost irresistible pressure when considering both Morley's and my (1990) arguments and the empirical work designed to illuminate them, to overlook or underestimate the political and economic conditions within which contemporary domesticity and television's constructions within that domesticity are both historically and currently forged. There is a need not just to describe differences, but to explain significant differences. The spectre of 'difference', I have already noted, is a haunting one. It is, in itself, empirically compelling, but theoretically distracting. Second, there is the continuing problem in our work not so much of the subject (for the subject is after all a theoretical construct) but of the individual, and of the relationship between the social and psychological dimensions of viewing. And finally there is the problem of the explanatory theory. The relationship between television viewing and social structure is not explained but only mediated by a consideration of domesticity. Domesticity too, which is not in any sense simply coincident with home or hearth, has to be understood in its relationship to the changing balance of public and private spheres (but see my discussion in Chapter 7).

Reflections on my own work as well as that of others leads me to an irresistible conclusion. It is that the notion of the active viewer can no longer be sustained because it no longer has (if it ever did) a clear enough reference. Activity can, and does, mean too many different things to too many people. Those differences are not only obvious, as I have illustrated, but also complex. For buried beneath the manifestations of audience activity – in reading, watching, listening, constructing, learning, and taking pleasure – are the conflicting and contradictory constraints of different forms of temporality and multiple social, economic and political determinations. Instead of a simple term we need a theoretically motivated account of the dynamics of the place of television in everyday life and it is to this task that I devote my final chapter.

Chapter 7

Television, technology and everyday life

there is a certain obscurity in the very concept of *everyday life*. Where is it to be found? In work or in leisure? In family life and in moments 'lived' outside of culture? Initially the answer seems obvious. Everyday life involves all three elements, all three aspects. It is their unity and their totality, and it determines the concrete individual. And yet this answer is not entirely satisfactory. Where does the living contact between the concrete individual man and other human beings operate? In fragmented labour? In family life? In leisure? Where is it acted out in the most concrete way? Are there several modes of contact? Can they be schematized as representational models? Or must they be reduced to fixed behaviour patterns? Are they contradictory or complementary? How do they relate? What is the decisive essential sector? Where are we to situate the poverty and wealth of this everyday life which we know to be both infinitely rich (potentially at least) and infinitely poor, bare, alienated; which we know we must reveal to itself and transform so that its richness can become actualized and developed in a renewed culture?

(Lefebvre, 1991 (1958), 31)

Henri Lefebvre, writing a foreword to his *Critique de la vie quotidienne* (1947) in 1958, reflected on the intensely complex but vital problem of everyday life: on its material invisibility; on its contradictions; on its vitality and its capacity for transcendence. He wrote as one of a number of voices within the Marxian tradition who had engaged with everyday life as the site for the exploration of alienation as a key dimension of life under capitalism, both within French philosophy, sociology and history and within German social critique. Their analyses still provide, despite and perhaps even more because of recent history, timely and chastening insights into the 'problematic' of everyday life; thorns in the flesh of the new romanticism; and a stimulus for the kind of investigation that I have thus far been undertaking into the relationship between television and everyday life.

This investigation has involved considerations of a number of dimensions of that relationship. But the discussion remains incomplete. The paradoxes –

the essential tensions – have been expressed in a number of different ways. They appear in the relationship between anxiety and security; in that between activity and passivity, creativity and addiction; in that between the public and the private; in that between dependence and independence; and in that between consumption and production. They appear in a number of different domains: in the domestic; in the suburban; in the management of time and space; and in the construction of technology. And although these various dimensions of analysis do indeed address the problematic of everyday life as it was conceived by Lefebvre they do not do so in a direct or coherent way. They do not confront everyday life as politics, as a political domain.

This is what I want to attempt in this last chapter. I do not expect to succeed, if by success is meant the production of a *theory* of everyday life. Post-modernism has taught us, if nothing else, that the time for such an undertaking is now past. But I do want to try and offer a route through some of the paradoxes. Stephen Heath, whom I cited in Chapter 1, referred to the seamless equivalence of television with everyday life. Television was more than the totality of its transmitted programmes: and television was coincident with everyday life in its extensiveness, expansiveness, instability, interminability, and ubiquity. This is fine, and it leads him, too, to consideration of television as essential to the politics of everyday life. He asks: 'can anyone in our societies be outside television, beyond its compulsions?' (1990, 283). Yet this seamlessness, these compulsions, this incorporation of television by and within everyday life, is still only restating the problem in another way, for it is only in our capacity to unpick the seams, and to understand the process of that incorporation – the interweaving of television and everyday life – that we can begin to think critically about it. It is all very well, too, to talk of the 'complexity' of those relationships. The complex, like the seamless, returns the problem to where it began: it consigns it, once again, to the invisible.

Michel de Certeau also reminds us of the politics of everyday life, and does so in a particularly distinct and important way, for he links everyday life with the sphere of the popular, and the popular he sees as a site of opposition. But his influential intervention has itself to be understood within a broader historical context, and one in which the terms of analysis are often transposed. On the one hand we are confronted by the approaches defined by the post-Lukacsian critiques of the Frankfurt School, by versions of French Marxism, such as those of Lefebvre, Bourdieu and also Foucault, as well as by the mass society critics of the 1950s, all of whom see in everyday life an expression of a defeated politics, politics mistaking play for power. On the other hand de Certeau and representatives of the new populism see in everyday life the possibilities for a transcending, if albeit limited politics, real in its consequences; a politics in which play is power. They represent and preserve a dichotomous approach to the study of everyday life which tends to preserve and reinforce the equivalent, dystopian and utopian, dichotomies of common sense. These dichotomies can no longer be sustained.

Against this I want to interpose a hopefully more measured approach, an approach based on an understanding of the dynamic and uneven politics of everyday life; and an approach based both in cultural critique and empirical research. That approach does seem to require a breaking down of the binary-ism of contemporary theories in favour of a more processual, perhaps a more provisional form of thinking. And it involves placing television and the television audience at its centre in such a way as to identify each as multiply structured and structuring, making, remaking and unmaking meaning as they both respond and contribute to the twists and turns of social and technological change. Let me begin, then, with a brief account of the questions that have been, or can be, asked about everyday life.

There are, it seems to me, three ways in which the problem of everyday life can be framed. The first takes as its starting point the early writings of Marx (in the Philosophical Manuscripts of 1844) in which he offers an account of life under capitalism in terms of alienation and reification (Meszaros, 1970). The second involves theorising the popular and issues of pleasure and resistance. And the third involves a much more hesitant approach released by object relations theory, which identifies the fundamental paradoxes at the heart of creativity.

In fact of course the first two theories of everyday life are not simply dichotomous, since from Marx's early formulations onwards (e.g. *Capital*, I, 487–8, cited in Swingewood, 1975) there has been a recognition, albeit differently inflected, that everyday life is constructed within capitalism at once in both its negative and positive aspects. Capitalism's efforts are directed at creating a pliant and productive workforce, but one in which the worker is encouraged, for the sake of 'modern industry', to develop his own 'natural and acquired powers'(Marx, ibid.). The worker is seduced by, and into, the false realities (or real falsehoods) of the culture of everyday life and into believing in his or her own freedoms and authenticities. Fulfilment is a motivated and contained fulfilment, for under capitalism there is no escape from the alienation that lies at its core and which is embodied in all acts of exchange and communication.

Informing this critique, which in varying degrees is an essential dimension of any radical approach to everyday life, is a sense of another form of life, perhaps once lived, but in any event not difficult to imagine, against which to judge the tragedies of the present. Lefebvre himself counterposes the 'everyday' – the vital and the authentic, the active and the original – with 'everyday life' – life under capitalism, life in 'the bureaucratic society of controlled consumption' (Lefebvre, 1984, 68ff.). The latter has replaced the former though not without the hope of its return. For in the critique of everyday life lies the hope of its transcendence in the everyday, and of the realisation of the otherwise denied potential of festival, carnival (see Bakhtin, 1984). Here are reverse images, still visible in the avant-garde, in the drama of Brecht and in the films of Chaplin (Lefebvre, 1991, 3–51).

It is not always easy to endorse even this limited optimism, though the space Lefebvre leaves for the 'reverse image', for the alternative and the resistant, is one which later theorists will be perversely keen to exploit (perversely because much of their analysis leaves the basic structures of society unexamined or unchallenged). Indeed Lefebvre leaves the contradictions of capitalism intact in his own theory, insofar as he appears to recognise that everyday life is both the site of a potential critique and the necessary object of critique; everyday life is both genuine and false at the same time. He argues that everyday life consists in a complex of activities and passivities, of forms of sociability and communication which

> contain within themselves their own spontaneous critique of the everyday. They *are* that critique insofar as they are *other* than everyday life, and yet they are *in everyday life*, they are *alienation*. They can thus hold a real content, correspond to a real need, yet still retain an illusory form and a deceptive appearance.
>
> (Lefebvre, 1991, 40, italics in original)

A real need falsely met. More pessimistic, perhaps, and less closely grounded in a theory of alienation, are the arguments of the Frankfurt School. They too recognise in the developing industrialism of capitalist society, and the extension of the forms of order and regiment that extend beyond the sphere of production and into the sphere of consumption, an increasing and increasingly irresistible reification of culture (see also Heller, 1984, 148ff.). In this reification, objects are humanised and humanity becomes objectified.[1] The iron cage of a false rationality leaches all originality from everyday life, leaving an empty husk of false gods, false goods and false desires. The theories of Adorno, Horkheimer and Marcuse are familiar and uncompromising. There is little hope of transcendence simply because the world of everyday life is so completely dominated by and through the combined pressures of bureaucratic and scientific reason, technology and mass culture. Central, of course to this domination is television (Lodziak, 1986) and other information and communication technologies (Robins and Webster, 1988).

Despite the fact that both Bourdieu (1984) and Foucault (1977; Gordon, 1980) provide accounts, both explicitly and implicitly, of everyday life as dynamic either in terms of taste or power, they both see it still, to a significant extent, as the result of social and political processes taking place elsewhere in the social structure. Michel de Certeau, as I have noted, objects to both kinds of totalising theory (1984, 45–60) and sees in even such a sensitive and suggestive concept of the habitus a form of closure against the everyday which denies its dynamics, its contradictions and its indeterminacies. And it is de Certeau's theories, and especially his consideration of the potential for resistance within the tactical times of everyday life, that have provided the intellectual space for a more strident populism, especially suggestive in the work of John Fiske (1989a).

However de Certeau's work is itself actually still quite ambiguous and contradictory and the metaphors he uses to encapsulate the dynamics of popular resistance are inconsistent. So within the seized times of everyday life we are told that we are engaged in a guerrilla warfare and a kind of terrorism (note that Lefebvre uses the term terrorism to describe the activities not of the subordinate but of the dominant), but we are also told that we are merely renting (de Certeau, 1984, xxi), and as renters we do not make property our own. We are condemned to the leasehold: temporary and provisional occupiers. And elsewhere de Certeau describes these activities as stealing and playing. Each of these metaphors for the dynamics of the quotidian, as ways of conceptualising the uses that we make in our daily lives of the objects and strategic spaces of social life, offer a different inflection, and a different politics, of that activity. Brilliant those activities may be (Miller, 1987) from time to time, but they will not always be so. And a mistake is often made when the everyday and the popular are treated as coterminous, as in John Fiske's summary:

> Everyday life is constituted by the practices of popular culture, and is characterized by the creativity of the weak in using the resources provided by a disempowering system while refusing to submit to that power. The culture of everyday life is best described through metaphors of struggle or antagonism . . . These antagonisms, these clashes of social interests . . . are motivated primarily by pleasure: the pleasure of producing one's own meanings of social experience and the pleasure of avoiding the social discipline of the power-bloc.
>
> (Fiske, 1989a, 47)

This is simultaneously an oversimplification of de Certeau's arguments and also a misreading of the politics of everyday life.[2] It is however, even in its own ambiguities and contradictions, an identification of that other space, that of the everyday, in which the popular is constructed, and one in which everyday life can be seen, through the products and commodities of mass culture, to have become aestheticised. This is an aestheticisation which another critic has also identified, though in this case in terms of more subtly controlled freedom (Featherstone, 1991, 27).[3]

The argument is not that we should replace one analysis by another. It is not that there is a choice to be made between utopianism and dystopianism, between control and freedom or between ideology and popular culture. Neither is it that we can adjudicate conclusively, as I have already suggested, between activity and passivity in the context of the audience's relations to the media. In a sense these questions are falsely posed, and these dichotomies are the wrong ones. Lefebvre is offering a critique of domination which sees in the 'everyday' the hope that capitalism has denied in its domination of 'everyday life'. Horkheimer and Adorno offer even less. Fiske provides an analysis of the popular which is only to be valued in its capacity for resistance and transcendence. De Certeau requires us to focus on the everyday as a site for significant action. It is significant because in the everyday our lives become meaningful, and without those meanings and without understanding those meanings and properly locating them within social space, we who participate (and also observe) will miss the dynamics of the social, and fail to comprehend its politics.

Yet none have satisfactorily posed the question. None have quite accepted the paradox of the everyday – a paradox that Winnicott elegantly identifies in the context of the symbolic significance of the transitional object:

> I should like to put in a reminder here that the essential feature in the concept of transitional objects and phenomena . . . is *the paradox, and the acceptance of the paradox*: the baby creates the object, but the object was there waiting to be created and to become a cathected object. I tried to draw attention to this aspect of transitional phenomena by claiming that in the rules of the game we all know that we will never challenge the baby to elicit an answer to the question: did you create that or did you find it?
>
> (Winnicott, 1974, 104, italics in original; and see Chapter 1 p. 14)

'Did you create that or did you find it?' This seems to me to be the key question at the centre of the problematic of everyday life, but it is the one question that Winnicott suggests that we cannot ask. If it were to be answered – and popular culture does answer it in its own way – then the reply would be both and neither. Everyday culture is in this sense, and within this paradox, transitional. Everyday life appears in use, in practice, as de Certeau is at pains to argue, but that use is itself preconditioned by a 'capacity' in Winnicott's (psychodynamic) terms, by symbolic capital in Bourdieu's (sociological) ones: a competence and a facility no less relevant, then, to the individual than to the group. And the terms of that paradox – the found object and the created object – the imposed meanings and the selected meanings – the controlled behaviour and the free – the meaningless and the meaningful – the passive and the active – are in constant tension. These tensions can be observed in everyday behaviour and traced through the study of the individual and the group. They can be deciphered through ethnographic or psychoanalytic case studies – studies which must be firmly grounded in the mutuality of empirical and theoretical understanding. For it is in the dynamics of the particular that we will be able to identify, if not fully comprehend, the forces of structure: the forces both of domination and resistance.

In this sense the problematic of everyday life is not one of strategies and tactics which are, albeit unequally, opposed. On the contrary it is the expressions of activity and creativity *within*, and constitutive of, the mobile forces of structure. If this is what Giddens means by structuration then my argument follows very closely the models that he has explored. Everyday life becomes then the site for, and the product of, the working out of significance. The meanings that we produce, the representations that we reject or appropriate, the identities we attempt to secure, the rituals which we accept, are all both found and created within a shared, often disputed and always highly differentiated social space. In the paradox of finding and creating – and in the constant tension that results – structures are simultaneously accepted, exploited and challenged. Herein lies the possibility, indeed the necessity and inevitability, of change. Herein too lie the ambiguities at the heart of the popular, and the source of the essential tensions that I have recognised in so many dimensions of my analysis of television's role in everyday life thus far.

One dichotomy is perhaps salvageable as long we recognise that it too is only meaningful in the same terms of the essential tension that I have insisted on in relation to the others. It is that between security and anxiety. Both psychoanalysis and sociology have indicated the fundamental significance of both. And I too have begun this argument with an attempt to locate the media's role in the articulation of the relationship between the two, both for the individual and the social. To talk of existential anxiety and ontological security, as I have done, is not to offer a reductive account of the social or the everyday, but to provide an account of the ground base, of the preconditions, of the possibility, of the social and, most importantly, of the increasing significance of the media in the dynamics of that possibility. Our everyday lives are the expression, in their taken-for-grantedness, as well as (in popular culture) their self-consciousness, of our capacity to hold a line against the generalised anxiety and the threat of chaos that is a *sine qua non* of social life. In this sense everyday life is a continuous achievement (Garfinkel, 1967; Goffman, 1969) more or less ritualised, more or less taken for granted, more or less fragile, in the face of the unknown, the unexpected or the catastrophic. Indeed the catastrophe is by definition that which breaks through the line that bounds anxiety and contains trust (Doane, 1990). And since trust is what emerges (or does not emerge) through the mediated experiences of social life, in the dynamics of child development and in the ongoing accomplishments of everyday interaction, a concern with its preconditions and possibilities must be a central component of any analysis of the role of the media in everyday life.

I want to pursue this argument now a little further, by integrating into it a more focused concern with television and other media. In so doing I will offer an account of the dynamics of the relationship between media and everyday life that hopefully avoids all but the most quintessential of the dichotomies and centres on three pivotal dimensions of that relationship, which I shall call agency (referring to process), modernity (referring to content) and domesticity (referring to context).

AGENCY

Anthony Giddens (1984) defines his sociology through, *inter alia*, the centrality of agency, by which he means the capacity for historically situated reflexive and purposive behaviour. It is a component of a sociology which is sustained and mobilised in a critique of the implications of ontological passivity in the pessimisms of Christopher Lasch (1977) and Richard Sennett (1977) (a pessimism that has its equivalence in the writings of some of those I have already considered in this chapter). Agency involves both individual and collective actions, whose consequences are not, he argues, limited only to micro-social settings:

> If we do not see that all human agents stand in a position of appropriation in relation to the social world, which they constitute and reconstitute in their actions, we fail on an empirical level to grasp the nature of human empowerment. Modern social life impoverishes individual action, yet furthers the appropriation of new possibilities; it is alienating, yet at the same time, characteristically, human beings react against social circumstances which they find oppressive.
>
> (Giddens, 1991, 175)

This characterisation raises of course more questions that it can hope to answer (in relation to the particular characteristics of modernity; in relation to the meaning and reach of empowerment) but nevertheless it is perhaps worth observing that if this reflexivity and 'empowerment' is a fundamental constitution of social life *sui generis*, then to suggest that it is a particular product of certain forms of mediation or popular culture makes no sense. And equally if social life is by definition the product of action, then to talk of passivity in relation to viewing behaviour, once again, begs the question.

But what is the question? It seems to me that the question is that of what an earlier generation of sociologists would have called 'the taken for granted' in social life, and I, for want of a better term, wish to call its ordinariness.[4] By that ordinariness I mean the more or less secure normality of everyday life, and our capacity to manage it on a daily basis. As Scannell and Cardiff have argued, this ordinariness (which is sociologically and culturally differentiated by region or nation) is something that had to be recognised, addressed and embodied in the increasingly democratised *forms* of talk progressively delivered by the BBC. They have argued that it was through an emerging but insistent communicative ethos that this normality was inscribed in broadcasting talk and through that talk reinscribed into the culture of the everyday (Scannell and Cardiff, 1991, 178). But the *forms* of talk are only one element in the mediation of the ordinary that broadcasting in particular has been so (but never entirely) successful in accomplishing. Behind the forms of talk are the forms of thought, order and expression that provide the content of the media and which provide the basis for agency, for our capacity to act in the ordinariness of everyday life.

I have argued on a number of occasions that the ordinariness of everyday life is sustained within our society, as within others, by forms of culture which it has been most easy (but still intensely problematical) to call myth (Silverstone, 1981; 1988). Mythic structures and functions within contemporary communications can be identified, and arguments about their significance sustained, as long as it is recognised that myths, like so much in culture, are Janus-headed. They provide in their narratives and in the formalities of their delivery within ritual or on neo-ritualised occasions, a framework for the creation and sustenance of ontological security. These narratives explore, through both form and content, the fundamental aspects of human existence: origins, mortality, the relations between culture and nature, the relations between the sexes. But recognising this also requires an equivalent recognition that the form and content of a mythology of a given society can only be sustained within an ideology, and through ideology the particular values of dominance – coded – encoded – disguised – will be represented (see Hall etc.).[5]

Mythic forms of communication, often recounted in highly charged ritual times and spaces, clearly demarcated the more or less sacred times from the secular ordinariness of everyday life. Yet they could be considered as always part of the everyday, by virtue of their capacity both to reflect and reflect upon the everyday. This is so despite, or even because of, their more or less intensely marked difference from everyday life (see Bakhtin on carnival for example). But they were also part of the everyday because they generated the forms of culture which could then be seen to be incorporated through more practical or mundane attitudes and behaviours into the daily round. The 'sacred' spaces occupied by the media have this quality, and our relationship to them reinforces it. The spoken and displayed narratives of television have their equivalent and their extension in the lived narratives of daily life, and of course both gain their meaning precisely through this constant juxtaposition (Ricoeur, 1984).

Once again de Certeau recognises the persistence of this and also the disjunction which it marks, for the myths of public texts and strategic culture are not simply reproduced in the storytelling of everyday life. The rhetorics of the dominant in strategic places are matched and both explored and exploited by the disjunctive tactical rhetorics of everyday life. In a passage in which he addresses the specific example of television de Certeau appears to recognise this tension, for television has the capacity, and at the moment of reception, it fulfils that capacity ('The television viewer cannot write anything on the screen of his set') of turning the viewer into a 'pure receiver' and television itself becomes a 'celibate machine'. But in reality the consumption of television is no different from other acts of consumption, revealing in *use* the contrary capacity to turn a trick or two with the objects and logics of a 'rationalized, expansionist, centralized, spectacular and clamorous pro-duction' (De Certeau, 1984, 31).

The tricks that are turned, in the gossip, the rhetoric and the rumours of everyday life, the metaphors and myths of the stuff of everyday experience and discourse, depend crucially on the raw material, albeit highly refined raw material, that the media, both in their primary and secondary textu-alities, produce. At the core of the experience of everyday life is a form of practical rationality that we recognise as common sense, and within which the forms and order of our capacity to manage the ordinariness of the everyday are embodied and expressed. Agnes Heller (1984; see Bourdieu, 1977) describes common sense as *doxa* and distinguishes it from scientific rationality (*epistémé*):

> Certain items in our everyday knowledge can be much firmer, less subject to change, more 'eternal' than our stock of scientific information . . . We have known that we can buy things for money for several hundred years; monetary theory has changed several times in the same period . . . *doxa* is inseparable from practical activity: it is in practical activity and nowhere else that *doxa* is verified . . . *Doxa* is the knowledge for which the information and values contained in the world of everyday knowledge and everyday norms are obvious or self-evident.
>
> (Heller, 1984, 203–4)

And *doxa* is the product not only of direct experience but of mediated experience, as our knowledge of the world, and especially our taken for granted knowledge of the world, is conditioned by our consumption of information, ideas and values that television and other media provide. There is no mystery in this, nor is it necessarily to be condemned, since that knowledge too has to be tested in practice in and through the forms of communication that in turn define our capacity to act – our status as agents in the management of our daily lives. Everyday life has the paradoxical character of being both creative and blind to its own creativity, even in most of the forms of popular culture (it is usually only analysis that makes popular culture 'see').

Yet the ordinariness of everyday life, its taken-for-grantedness, is not homogeneous. Not only is it profoundly differentiated by virtue of culture – ethnic, religious, class, national or gendered culture – but it is also uneven in its formal quality. Everyday life is marked by a continuous, predictable and unpredictable, series of shifts between the marked and the unmarked, the sacred and the profane. Daily life is studded with ritual times and spaces in and through which the insistence of the daily round is momentarily put to one side. Stolen moments in front of the television set. The scheduled rituals of the annual calendar, informed and prescribed now in broadcasting. In each of these events and in our participation in them (with or without the media) we move perceptibly from one domain of everyday life into another, crossing a boundary or a threshold into a clearly if often weakly marked ritual space: a space where the intense ordinariness of the everyday is replaced by a different kind of intensity – heightened and symbolically charged. In these ritual spaces the culture of everyday life is reinforced. In our participation in them, and especially in those ritualised activities that by virtue of mass production, most of us can share – for example reading the morning newspaper (Anderson, 1983; Bausinger, 1984), or watching a favourite soap opera – our place and position in the world is symbolically defined. And that definition is reinforced by our activities once we return to the mundane and the quotidian, in the talk and gossip, in the sharing of information: in our mutual construction of the news of the world.

Some have seen this shifting in and out of the mundane as a form and expression of play, and one at least (Stephenson, 1988) has gone so far as to construct a theory of mass communication as play on the strength of it. The theory itself is disappointing and inconclusive, but along the way it draws attention to the seminal work of a number of play theorists (Huizinga, 1959; Callois, 1961) each of whom, though in different ways, finds in play a (the) source of culture. Play is pursued within a distinct and distinguishable social and cultural space. It is rule-governed but protected and differentiated from the rule-governed normality of other (principally work-related) spaces of the rest of everyday life. There are difficulties with many of these theories, not least the elision of play and leisure, but what makes them collectively suggestive (and it should be remembered that Winnicott's own theories of child development also insist on play as a central component of cultural experience) is their stress on the privileged kinds of creativity that are possible in the more or less clearly differentiated times and spaces which in turn, make play possible. Within play 'realities' are suspended in favour of fantasies, since the rules of play are not those of ordinary everyday life. Indeed de Certeau also draws on game theory, only this time to make the case for the transcendence of playing the game (tactics) over the rules of the game, the game itself (strategy). While the game is defined by the governing rules which make it playable, it is in the play itself that the game comes alive and, in that vitality, gains its uniqueness and significance.

Implicit in these arguments, especially of the boundedness of play, and indeed in the identification through everyday life of the notion of agency, as well as of *doxa*, is a critique of those other arguments that imply that within everyday life, and particularly through the highly mass-mediated everyday life of contemporary societies, the boundaries between fantasy and reality are becoming less and less clear. One might be inclined to think that they are indeed no longer as clear as they once were, and that television's habit, both in its primary and secondary textuality, to elide the real and the imaginary, is telling. Yet empirical evidence, as well as the kind of theoretical arguments that I have been advancing, suggests that this boundary is still held by most of us, and the theory requires that it should be the case, since the practicalities of everyday life require and depend on it.

Agency then, our capacity to act within the ongoing normality of everyday life, is a precondition for our involvement with television and other media. And to present the argument in this way makes the idea of a passive viewer a nonsense, and the dichotomy of activity and passivity, as I have suggested, redundant. Instead we are confronted with a different kind of empirical problem, which is not to discover presence or absence, activity or passivity, but on the contrary to understand engagement. That engagement might be weak or strong, positive or negative in its implications. But it is, in the sense in which I have identified it, always dynamic, and dynamic in the specific sociological sense of agency. We engage with television through the same practices that define our involvement with the rest of everyday life, practices that are themselves contained by, but also constitutive of, the basic symbolic, material and political structures which make any and every social action possible.

MODERNITY ETC.

But the particular character and content of that agency remains to be addressed. The society in which we live is changing, some would say rapidly and fundamentally changing, and these changes are most significantly expressed in the practices of everyday life. Agency by itself is a conceptual abstraction, and we need to think what it might mean to be acting within the heavily mediated society of contemporary times. Does television make a difference; does it 'signify'?

I want to approach this question through some reflections on modernism and post-modernism as distinct aesthetics, and modernity and post-modernity as supposedly new forms of social and cultural organisation, and in particular to examine both modernism's and post-modernism's close identification with the urban experience, with the city. I do not intend to try and settle the matter of post-modernity's or post-modernism's distinctiveness with respect to modernity and modernism, though I take it as axiomatic in matters of social and cultural life that revolutions and epistemological and aesthetic breaks are likely to be found more often in theory than in experience. Indeed I can begin by pointing out that one of the classic examinations of the paradoxes of the experience of modernity (Berman, 1983) draws attention to the significance of the city for the definition and indeed the collapse of modernist culture. This preoccupation with the materiality and culture of *urban* space is continued within many discussions of post-modernism (Harvey, 1989; Lash, 1990; *Zone 1/2*), where the significance of the metropolitan urban experience, however differently conceived and imprinted by a supposedly newly emerging post-modern aesthetic, remains.

For both Harvey and Lash, though with different emphases, the city is where both modernism and post-modernism are forged and most dramatically find their clearest expression. Modernism, its order, its standardised functionality, is expressed in the urban fabric, an urban fabric which makes 'modernism happen' (Lash, 1990, 31), but which also expresses it. Modernism is embodied in the confidence of urban design, in the boulevards of Huyssmans, the urban freeways of Moses, in the grids of the city and the standardised units of office blocks and housing developments. But as Berman reminds us, there is also a modernism of underdevelopment (expressed in the building of, and living in, St Petersberg) and most crucially there is in modernism a self-destruction, a built in obsolescence of the city itself (Berman, 1983, esp. 307). At the root of modernism's elective affinity with the city are the changing relations to space and time which they both address and express.[6] And similarly post-modernism, in its address and expression has defined a more fragmented diverse, human and supposedly democratic aesthetic which is the product of – collectively – technological, industrial and cultural change. The cities, then and now, were the site too not just of architectural or spatial expression, but also of distinct forms of social life. They provided the infrastructure for the 'melting-pot', for the intermixing and movement of peoples and cultures forced, however temporarily, together, and thence to be moulded by the combined effects of ideology and urban design.

Against the authority of the modernist city, critics identify Los Angeles as the exemplary post-modern urban environment, one which breaks free of the grand narratives and superordinate ideologies of modernism, through its diverse and fragmentary, dispersed and displaced, mobile collage of malls, freeways and (sub)urban sprawl. Los Angeles is not so much a melting-pot as a pot that is melting, as recent events in Watts have once again reminded us:

> It is a city of pragmatic adaptation to the innumerable differentiated urban micro-orders which constitute it, and which collectively make up an unplanned mega-space . . . , which threatens the meta-narrativistic principles upon which the theory and practice of Western urban planning and design have been based for millennia. It is, finally, a city which cannot be reduced to a single principle: not the motor car, not the freeways nor the railway system that preceded them, not its lack of history . . . not Hollywood and the dream factory, not the giant corporation, not the high technology company, not the beach, not the smog, nor the sun.
>
> (Boyne and Rattansi, 1990, 20)

Los Angeles may have been seen as the embodiment of all that post-modernism represents for the city, yet it also expresses another history, a history which is both the reverse image of that of the city, and one to which the media, firstly radio and then television, have made indelible contributions. This is a history of the suburb and it is a history not just of a particular form of material and social space, but a history of an emerging cultural formation. The suburb represents the soft underbelly of modernity, a kind of Achilles' heel, for it is both persistent, and increasingly dominant as an environment in which we either live, or aspire to live. The suburb is that soft underbelly because it has emerged, both by accident and design, as a form of life that modernism has created almost to escape from itself. The writings of Ebenezer Howard and the subsequent Garden City movement, provided a catalyst for an alternative vision of modernity, one that would freeze the atavistic utopia of the rural idyll and transplant it into the body of the city. The suburbs came to represent that strange hybrid (arguably, but never entirely, sterile) which simultaneously denied its origins and its compromises, and trumpeted as the residents of Crestwood Heights trumpeted, that those who lived within them had got the best of both worlds. They had not got the best of both worlds of course, but neither had they got the worst. What they got was a form of life, remarkably persistent in its appeal and one which at the level of everyday life somehow seems to be making the transition from modernity to post-modernity, providing as it does precisely that mix of strategic mass production and tactical appropriation (see Miller, 1988) that the new forms of consumerism both stimulate and depend upon.[7]

The suburb, ubiquitous but invisible, desired but derided, domestic and defensive, embodies many of the contradictions of modernity – particularly those of inclusion and exclusion – but adds a few of its own. The functional order of a Levittown or a Milton Keynes created to erase the challenging complexity and confusion, as well as the grinding poverty and social grime, of city life; the standardised dwellings of inter-war ribbon development – home, hearth, ownership; the logics of new-found ersatz community life, distancing yet connecting through self-interest; all of these marked a new form of social order that contained and dominated, as well as liberated, its inhabitants. And this is not to mention its capacity to exclude those who did not fit into the tightening straight-jacket of the suburban ideal.

As I argued in Chapter 3 the contradictions at the heart of the suburb are those that focus on the relationship between public and private spaces and cultures. But the suburban ideal marks a much deeper cultural process – I described it, following Marilyn Strathern, as a process of hybridisation. As she suggests 'suburbia is neither urban nor rural' (1993, 191). And in the conflation of both it comes to represent a new kind of fused and fusing reality, in which boundaries: between nature and culture; the country and the city; and perhaps also between fantasy and reality, become indistinct and in-adequate. Indeed for Strathern the suburbs, precisely in this hybridisation, become the harbinger, symbol and crucible for the post-modern rather than the modern. The suburb, like all good myths, is multiply useful, and suburbia has become the articulating myth both for modernism and post-modernism, at least in many of their most significant respects.

The floodlit privacy of the suburb has been sustained and is suffused by television. The rapid development of the suburb in the United States after the Second World War was supported by television's insistence, through sit-com and soap opera, that the ideals of suburban life – ideals that were unlikely to have been met in reality as newcomers discovered rather less of a rural idyll and rather more of a standardised and claustrophobic reality – were actually sustainable. Lynn Spigel, while plausibly exaggerating the sense of horror that the suburbs engendered in their first inhabitants, nevertheless correctly recognised the ideology of television at the time: 'to provide an illusion of the ideal neighbourhood – the way it was supposed to be' (Spigel, 1992, 129).

The British experience of rapid suburbanisation was both earlier and different and, in significant respects, it was radio, both as domesticated technology (Forty, 1986) and medium (Lewis, 1942, cited in Frith, 1983) and not television that provided the support for its expansion during the 1930s. And here too the ideal was less a model of the privatised neighbourhood and, arguably, more an expansive ideal of national family (Scannell and Cardiff, 1991). Indeed as Oliver *et al.* (1981) note, the suburb itself was remarkable mainly for its material absence both from radio programming and from the cinema, at least until after the war.

Nevertheless, both in the 1930s in Britain and in the 1940s and 1950s in the United States (and of course elsewhere too), the broadcast media were central in articulating a culture of, and for, suburbia: principally for the white middle classes and for those who could aspire to that status. The suburban oxymoron captured so well by Williams' description of it as 'mobile privatisation' – despite the fact that this most accurately referred to the consequences of the motor car and public transport – had both a sociological and a cultural dimension. Populations were indeed simultaneously displaced and connected; and simultaneously sedentary and mobile. But they were also presented with, and increasingly incorporated into, a publicly produced culture which materialised in the scheduled but interruptable flow of the broadcast.

This culture was suburban in another, and most significant, respect. It produced a fundamentally hybridised culture: neither–norist as well as both–andist; a form of mediated experience which knew few bounds and had few boundaries; an encompassing and increasingly inclusive culture in which everything was within reach, everything possible, everything connected, everything explained, if only for a moment and if only for now. Lynn Spigel, once again, notes how one element of that hybridisation was expressed in an emerging form of television: in the merging of two traditions of American popular culture – the live and the narrated; the theatrical and the vaudeville, and in the production of what she identifies as a middle-ground aesthetic:

> Blending the wild spontaneity of vaudeville performance with the more genteel – and decidedly noncontroversial – aspects of theatrical realism, this genre [situation comedy] became the networks' preferred form for reaching a family audience.
>
> (Spigel, 1992, 144)

This middle-ground aesthetic arguably also drew on the power of the media, both in sound and then in image and sound, to merge reality and illusion, though as I have suggested, the novelty of this should not be exaggerated, even if its insistence can barely be denied. What it does, of course, is to leave everything in place. In such a hybrid, illusion cannot challenge reality nor reality puncture illusion. Suburban broadcast culture is, despite this radical hybridisation, fundamentally – and in every sense of the term – conservative. Perhaps one can also see it as being opposed to the urban cinema on the one hand, and as being increasingly vulnerable to the privatising impulse of narrowcasting on the other.

I have been trying to suggest that the emerging broadcast culture of radio and television was a key component of a new social, political and geographical reality embodied both materially and symbolically, physically and ideologically, in suburbia. In the suburban, correlatively, a new form of culture emerged, different from, and opposed to, the abrasive challenges and uncertainties of the city, and plausibly more significant even than the city in the formation of modern and post-modern culture. In this sense, the question I asked at the beginning of this section can be answered in the affirmative. Television does make a difference. It does signify, but it does so as part of a tele-technological system in which the crucial component is its broadcast form. Here modernity and post-modernity are expressed in the content of television and in its active hybridisation of public–private culture. How far this is or will be threatened by the privatising of the media, most powerfully expressed in the video, but also in the fragmenting of broadcasting through satellite and cable, is still unclear, though there is little doubt that the suburban hybridisation of broadcast culture is no longer quite as secure as it might once have been.

DOMESTICITY

Agency and modernity (and post-modernity) meet in the domestic and that meeting is expressed in the ideology and activity of consumption. The particular character of everyday life as it is lived under contemporary capitalism requires a consideration, finally, of this third term.

Domestication is a process both of taming the wild and cultivating the tame. It is where nature becomes culture. One can think of domestication too, as both a process by which we make things our own, subject to our control, imprinted by, and expressive of, our identities; and as a principle of mass consumption in which products are prepared in the public fora of the market. In a sense the commodity is already domesticated, and it is in this 'anticipation of domesticity' which the commodity embodies that we must understand the context of our own domesticity and of the role of television in creating and sustaining it. As Igor Kopytoff suggests:

> in any society, the individual is often caught between the cultural structure of commoditization and his own personal attempts to bring a value order to the universe of things.
>
> (Kopytoff, 1986, 76)

So the commodity, in a sense, is already pre-digested. Consumption presents us not with the alienated object (Miller, 1987) but with the already pasteurised object, pasteurised against the threat of indigestibility. Consumption is always a participative process and only sometimes a transcendent one, though that does not mean that we are not able to appropriate mass-produced objects into our own image and into our own particular expression of domesticity. What it does mean, however, is that domesticity, like so much of everyday life, is simultaneously both found and created, and that the identities constructed through our active engagement in consumption are already available, somewhere, even in their uniqueness. We talk, for example, of having just 'found a little shop', or 'discovering a restaurant' in an unfamiliar town. We take perverse and contradictory pleasure if we later discover that the shop or restaurant is already well known, as if that prior knowledge guarantees our good taste (though we may feel offended by the undermining of our private and individual competence and skill).

Television is both object and medium within this domesticity. Our choice of technology, our incorporation of it into the private spaces, times and practices of our homes is paralleled by the same kind of choices that we make with respect to programmes and the work we do on them both inside and outside our domestic space: to make them our own. But given this kind of prior domestication (they are 'user-friendly') which makes both objects and texts more or less easily appropriated, then it is clear that both the acts of appropriation and the domestic itself are exclusively neither part of the private nor the public spheres. Consumption too is never simply a private activity. It depends on a whole slew of public meanings, a public language, constantly changing but preserving, like written language, a much more resilient and material structure. Our individual acts of consumption therefore, private as we imagine them, are dramatic expressions, gaining their significance not just in private statements but through the attention of public audiences. The shopping mall takes that extension of domesticity a step further by providing protected spaces, simultaneously public and private, within which to demonstrate (to ourselves and others) the skills that mark full participation in the suburban world.[8]

So there is an added dimension to our domesticity. The pre-digested commodities of contemporary culture still have to be selected, bought and owned. They enter a social space, a moral economy, that will use them to help define its own identity and integrity. Clearly commodities are not the only things that fulfil this role, and families and households may not find in them anything much of symbolic value. However it is in this process of bringing things and meanings home that the empirical diversity of our own domesticity is produced and sustained. And it is in this struggle with or against the commodities – both objects and texts – of the mass market, that many of the structures of everyday life are revealed. It is in the everyday (which is not of course coterminous with the domestic any more than the popular is) that the functional and the cultural dimensions of media are worked through. New technologies, old social forms: both of course are changing, though at different speeds and unevenly. Everyday life in general and domesticity in particular can resist, but such resistance is, like so much in everyday life, paradoxical. Through it are expressed both the marks of difference and, in their significance, an acknowledgement that they are to be recognised and shared by others.

The television audience is at one in all of this. The audience is, and always was, a consumer. And the terms of trade – the material and symbolic terms of trade – are set but not determined by a political economy of the media which is becoming increasingly globalised, integrated and technologically diverse. The unchallenged age of broadcasting may be over. In which case audiences will increasingly become, more literally, consumers, buying and owning software and hardware, and paying for telecommunicated services. There is a politics here, of course: a politics of access and equity (Golding and Murdock, 1991), a politics that broadcasting perhaps took for granted. Yet the position of the audience, and our capacity to make sense of that position in a changing world, still depends on its location within the public and private structures of everyday life. And our understanding of those structures and the practices that both sustain and change them is still a precondition for understanding the process of mass media and mass communication.

The politics of everyday life, then, consists in the uneven relationship of public and private spheres: of agency, modernity and domesticity. It is a politics mediated and translated through consumption. Nicholas Garnham is in little doubt as to its quality:

> Political communication is forced to channel itself via commercial media . . . Public communication is transformed into the politics of consumerism. Politicians appeal to potential voters not as rational beings concerned for the public good, but in the mode of advertising, as creatures of passing and largely irrational appetite, whose self-interest they must purchase . . . the citizen is addressed as a private individual rather than as a member of a public, within a privatized domestic space rather than within public life.
>
> (Garnham, 1991, 111)

Stephen Heath similarly talks of the depoliticisation of political communication. In the commodification of the public sphere, it has been argued, citizens have been turned into consumers (see Elliott, 1982, 244). Conversely, others (Giddens, Scannell and Cardiff, Thompson) suggest that the contemporary politics of everyday life has been transformed by the media, and a new kind of public sphere has emerged (see esp. Thompson, 1990, 246 and my discussion Chapter 3). Have we come full circle? How do we resolve this final dichotomy?

Perhaps we cannot. There is a difference between a domesticated politics and a politics of the domestic. Garnham and others bewail the emergence of the first; Thompson celebrates the arrival of the second. Neither disagree that it is television's mediation of political life which is the significant factor in what is seen by both as more or less dramatic change. I have described this situation in terms of the suburbanisation of the public sphere, which among other things involves not only an extension through the media of the power of the centralised State but also in that extension, and as a result of the same mechanisms, possibly its intermittent weakening. Television extends rather than deepens, and its capacity to mediate politics involves a thinning of the fabric of control within the public sphere, such that holes can and may appear: challenges, mobilised through the same media that have previously and successfully been used to contain them, but which offer scope for both focused and unfocused, and occasionally successful, participation of private consumer-citizens in public affairs.

It is certainly the case that contemporary politics are being fought out in the media, on the screens of television sets and the pages of newspapers. It is also certainly the case that the political system remains for the most part protected, inviolate (though by no means everywhere). But it is equally certain that the politics of everyday life is not entirely contained by this media appropriation, that consumers are intermittently also citizens, and that it is in the deepening of our understanding of the essential tensions that mark the interrelationship of television, technology and everyday life that we will better be able to participate in them.

Notes

PREFACE

1 Strictly speaking it is the second: *Consuming Technologies: Media and Infor-mation in Domestic Spaces*, edited by Roger Silverstone and Eric Hirsch, was published by Routledge in 1992.

2 TELEVISION AND A PLACE CALLED HOME

1 'Home is no longer just one place. It is locations. Home is that place which enables and promotes varied and everchanging perspectives, a place where one discovers new ways of seeing reality, frontiers or difference. One confronts and accepts dispersal and fragmentation as part of the constructions of a new world order that reveals more fully where we are, who we can become' (bell hooks, 1991, 149, cited in Massey, 1992, 15).

2 Work in family therapy is vulnerable to significant critique of course, not least for its hypostatisation of the family as a norm. In following some of the arguments of this literature I do not intend to endorse the judgements of pathology or normality mostly associated with family therapy literature or to reify the family as a necessary or even desirable social unit.

3 Ure (1835) describes the newly emerging factory system as a moral economy. Apart from the discussions that follow in which the term and the idea of an alternative set of economic values, distinct from those embodied in public and market oriented economics, is variously discussed, one can also point to the emergence of institutional economics (Adams, 1980) in which economic theory is grounded in a perception of institutional specificity.

4 e.g. 'Time orientation may be particularly evident in the kind of economy constructed for the household; in situations where there is a choice, the balance among savings, income from investment, and credit may reflect a difference in orientation. A household economy based substantially on credit may be clearly present-oriented; savings may reflect a future orientation; income from invest-ments may reflect a family living on the accumulated wealth of several generations and hence constitute a strong root in the past' (Reiss, 1981, 233).

3 THE SUBURBANISATION OF THE PUBLIC SPHERE

1 George Cadbury, one of the early pioneers of suburban utopias and builder at the end of the last century of Bournville, an industrial village near Birmingham, wrote

in a familiar vein that 'the only way [to improve social conditions in the smoke and grime of crowded industrial areas] was to bring men out of the cities into the country and to give every man his garden where he can come into touch with nature and thus know Nature's God' (quoted in Gill, 1984, 111).

2 This is, of course, not particular to the newly mobilised middle classes of the American suburbs. It is equally true, among others, of the English working classes (see Roberts, 1973; Martin, 1981) and of the Brazilian (Leal, 1990).

3 See Tomlinson, 1990; and Willmott and Young, 1960, 27: 'The husbandman agriculturalist is back in a new form, as horticulturalist rather than agriculturalist, as builder rather than cattleman, as improver not of a strip of arable land but of the semi-detached family estate at 33, Ellesmere Road'.

4 I shall be discussing both these issues more fully in Chapter 6.

5 Lyn Richards (1990), in particular, in her detailed analysis of the social relations of a newly created Australian suburb, points to how the Residents' Association and the self-help groups which emerged in the community, and through which its own internal politics were conducted, were also the site for a politics of class and gender which reproduced the expected structures of division and control.

6 Lynn Spigel (1992) addresses the relationship between both soap operas and sit-coms and the merging culture of suburbia. For her the nuclear family and the suburb are increasingly synonymous, and the two genres functionally indistinguishable. Nevertheless I think it is important to separate them, for in doing so a range of issues that Spigel herself does not raise can be addressed. In the present context these include above all the systemic nature of television's suburbanness, and its particular embodiment in the contemporary soap opera.

7 'Well, it was about Meg Richardson, the widow who'd suddenly found herself in a big house which she couldn't afford to run, didn't want to leave it and they built a motorway through the land, and so she decided to capitalise on it, because at that time motels were very new in this country, and the producer, being an Australian, was very conscious of motels' (Margaret French, production manager of *Crossroads*, quoted in Hobson 1982, 41). On the motel as a 'transitional object', see Morris (1988).

8 Another problem with the Lévi-Straussian position is in the definition of the boundaries of the system. Soap opera is by no means a clearly bounded system. Its generic character is unstable and, at the margins, diffuse. It is constantly transforming itself (as Lévi-Strauss would acknowledge) but it also shades into other forms of television storytelling (on the limits of the notion of genre in television studies, see Feuer, 1992).

9 There is much more to be said about soap opera specifically and the television audience more generally in terms of gender. I will address these issues again in Chapter 6.

4 THE TELE-TECHNOLOGICAL SYSTEM

1 'The revealing that rules throughout modern technology has the character of a setting-upon, in the sense of a challenging-forth. That challenging happens in that the energy concealed in nature is unlocked, what is unlocked is transformed, what is transformed is stored up, what is stored up is, in turn, distributed, and what is distributed is switched about ever anew. Unlocking, transforming, storing, distributing, and switching about are ways of revealing. But the revealing never comes to an end' (Heideggar, 1977, 16).

2 This is evident even in Michel Callon's original formulation: 'The actor network can thus be distinguished from the traditional actors of sociology, a category

generally distinguished excluding any nonhuman component and whose internal structure is rarely assimilated to that of a network. An actor network is simultaneously an actor whose activity is networking heterogeneous elements and a network that is able to redefine and transform what it is made of' (Callon, 1987, 93; and see Callon, 1986, 20ff.).

3   Knut Sørenson (1990, 17–18), in his study of the motor car in Norway, makes two additional points in relation to actor-network theory in its strong form. The first is that it underestimates the significance of 'extra-scientific and techno-logical' institutions and the second is that it underestimates the resilience of the established network structures to subsequent actor initiated changes.

4   'Such an analysis – focused on the consumer, extending its causal reach into other socio-economic realms, open to various criteria for "betterness" – seems to me to be essential in making sense out of the history not only of stove technology, but of all technologies' (Cowan, 1987, 273).

5   'What is . . . significant is the place of the car in the only global system we have identified, the system of substitutes; as a substitute for eroticism, for adventure, for living conditions and for human contact in large towns the car is a pawn in the "system" that crumbles away as soon as it has been identified' (Lefebvre, 1984, 101).

6   On the motor car as a leading object, though not explicitly so, see for example: Barthes, 1972; Bayley, 1986; Flink, 1988; and for a national study of the emergence of the motor car as a socio-technical system, see Sorenson, 1990.

7   'Postmodernism is both a symptom and a powerful cultural image of the swing away from the conceptualization of global culture less in terms of alleged homogenizing processes (e.g. theories which present cultural imperialism, Ameri-canization and mass consumer culture as a proto-universal culture riding on the back of Western economic and political domination) and more in terms of the diversity, variety and richness of popular and local discourses, codes and practices which resist and play-back systemicity and order' (Featherstone, 1990, 2).

8   A number of recent publications have reviewed these various trends, both in relation to the specific circumstances of Europe (e.g. Siune and Truetzschler, 1992) and more widely, (e.g. Mattelart et al., 1984).

9   See Eisenstein (1979, 704) 'Since the advent of movable type, an enhanced capacity to store and retrieve, preserve and transmit has kept pace with an enhanced capacity to create and destroy, to innovate and outmode. The somewhat chaotic appearance of modern Western culture owes as much, if not more, to the duplicative powers of print as it does to the harnessing of new powers in the past century.'

10   It is equally dangerous, of course, to pursue the opposite line: that is to discount television (and other media) as immaterial to the kinds of social and cultural changes currently being considered. This is what Lodziak (1986, 190–1) appears to be arguing when he suggests that: 'television's "capturing of time-space" [is] something other than it . . . appears. Our time-space is already "captured" as a consequence of economic and state practices in a context which has been heavily shaped by those practices.'

11   Bastide (1978) on the religions of Brazil; Parry and Bloch (1989) on money; Ferguson (1990) on media technology; de Certeau (1984) on everyday life; Hebdige (1988) and Miller (1987) on contemporary culture, all address, from one point of view or another, this issue. In doing so they pick up a familiar theme in anthropology (e.g. Redfield, 1960) and history (e.g. Burke, 1978) which seeks to explore the relationship between the great and the little tradition.

12   Haralovich (1988, 39–40) offers an analysis of 'a historical conjuncture in which institutions important to social and economic policies defined women as home-makers: suburban housing, the consumer product industry and market

research. *Father Knows Best* and *Leave it to Beaver* [two US sit-coms of the period] mediated this address to the homemaker through their representation of middle class family life. They appropriated historically specific gender traits in a realist mise-en-scène of the home to create a comfortable, warm and stable family environment.'

5 TELEVISION AND CONSUMPTION

1 The French word 'consommer' preserves a double meaning, that of being fulfilled and annulled (see Baudrillard, 1988, 22), which can only be expressed in English through different words: 'consumption' (Lat. *consumere*) and 'consummation' (Lat. *consumare*). Of course it is precisely in the ambiguity of the French 'consommer' that much of the discussion of this chapter takes place.

2 This is what I have called elsewhere its double articulation (Silverstone *et al.*, 1992).

3 See note 1 of this chapter. Baudrillard is using the French term 'consommation' in its sense of consummation.

4 For a recent critique of Baudrillard, see Kellner, 1989; and for a defence, see Gane, 1991.

5 In *Symbolic Exchange and Death* (Baudrillard, 1988, 135ff.) Baudrillard distinguished between three orders of simulation: the counterfeit associated with classical culture from the Renaissance to the Industrial Revolution; production, (Walter Benjamin's 'reproduction') of the industrial period; and simulation proper: the eternal reproduction and self-referentiality of signs governed by a 'cybernetic' code.

6 'A class is defined as much by its being perceived as by its being, by its consumption – which need not be conspicuous in order to be symbolic – as much as by its position in the relations of production (even if it is true that the latter governs the former)' (Bourdieu, 1984, 483).

7 'The stream of consumable goods [into the home] leaves a sediment that builds up the structure of culture like coral islands. The sediment is the learned set of names of sets, operations to be performed upon names, a means of thinking' (Douglas and Isherwood, 1979, 75).

8 'This misunderstanding assumes that "assimilating" necessarily means "becoming similar to" what one absorbs, and not "making something similar" to what one is, making it one's own, appropriating or reappropriating it' (de Certeau, 1984, 166).

9 The arguments offered in this section are based on, and extend, material published in Silverstone *et al.*, 1992.

10 'What science has to establish is the objectivity of the object which is established in the relationship between an object defined by the possibilities and impossibilities it offers, which are only revealed in the world of social uses (including, in the case of a technical object, the use or function for which it was designed) and the dispositions of an agent or class of agents, that is, the schemes of perception, appreciation and action which constitute its objective utility in a practical usage' (Bourdieu, 1984, 100).

6 ON THE AUDIENCE

1 '"*Screen* theory" constantly elides the concrete individual, his/her constitution as a "subject-for-discourse", and the discursive subject positions constituted by discursive practices and operations' (Morley, 1980, 169).

2 Hawkins and Pingree (1983 and 1990) offer a critique of the cultivation analysis research on a number of grounds, not least the difficulty of providing psychological or social-psychological explanation for the revealed correlations (i.e. at an individual level). They also point out that they have no evidence that first- and second-order beliefs are correlated, so that it is by no means clear how, if at all, the two are related and how television viewing is to be understood in this relationship (or lack of it) (Hawkins and Pingree, 1990, esp. 43ff.).

3 Sonia Livingstone, in yet another recent review disagrees: 'its relative theoretical naivity in the conception of the effects process (an unspecified process of cultivation), its reliance on the much criticised method of content analysis to determine programme meaning . . . and its use of social statistics and opinion polls . . . make cultivation analysis one step in a long theoretical development' (Livingstone, 1990, 16). A long step in a misguided theoretical development, palpably. I discuss Livingstone's own approach below.

4 This process is not really undermined by Gerbner's insistence on the process of cultivation as a 'gravitational' one rather than a 'unidirectional' one, since in his own words: '[Different] groups of viewers] may strain in a different direction, but all groups are affected by the same central current. Cultivation is thus part of a continual, dynamic, on-going process of interaction among messages and contexts' (Gerbner et al., 1986, 24).

5 For a more recent, and significant, study of television's influence, particularly in relation to the audience's ability to learn and to reproduce what they see on television news, and thereby its functions as an agenda-setting medium, see Philo (1990, esp. his conclusion pp. 154–5). Philo also links his findings to, though claims greater precision than, the work of Gerbner et al.

6 Eco was at pains to distinguish openness and indeterminacy. As Sonia Livingstone points out, it is a distinction which many recent analysts have overlooked: 'As for aberrant presuppositions and deviating circumstances, they are not realizing any openness, but, instead, producing mere states of indeterminacy. What I call open texts are, rather, reducing such an indeterminacy, whereas closed texts, even though aiming at eliciting a sort of "obedient" co-operation are, in the last analysis, randomly open to every pragmatic accident' (Eco, 1979, 6–7, cited in Livingstone, 1990, 42).

7 'Communications research aiming at the study of short-run mass media effects must take systematically into account an individual's relatedness-to-others . . . No longer can mass media research be content with a random sample of disconnected individuals as respondents. Respondents must be studied within the context of the group or groups to which they belong or which they have "in mind" – thus, which may influence them – in their formulation of opinions, attitudes or decisions, and in their rejection or acceptance of mass-media influence-attempts' (Katz and Lazarsfeld, 1955, 131).

8 See Klaus Bruhn Jensen (1990, 74): 'The polysemy of media texts is only a political potential, and the oppositional decoding of media is not yet a manifestation of political power.'

9 It is easy to exaggerate and parody some of Fiske's writings. He is aware of those dangers, and also of the links between his version of culture and the accounts of the relationship between the popular and the elite, and the public and the private which have already established their symbiotic and dialectical relationship to each other. The key terms here are carnival and dialogia; and the key theorist Bakhtin – though see also Burke (1978).

10 David Morley, Eric Hirsch and I combined on an ESRC/PICT funded study on information and communication technologies in the home (see Silverstone, 1991a; and Silverstone et al., 1992). Many of the arguments offered within this book arose

as a result of that empirical work, and in discussion. I am enormously grateful for both my colleagues' involvement in the project.

7 TELEVISION, TECHNOLOGY AND EVERYDAY LIFE

1 One needs to be careful here, for the concept of 'objectification' actually is a more subtle and less evaluative one in Marxist theory, referring as it does to the basic processes by and through which the structures of (everyday) social life are defined and maintained. Agnes Heller's (1984) discussion of everyday life takes as its starting point this more basic sense of objectification and avoids the evaluative connotations implied by 'reification'.

2 As it happens Fiske also offers a misreading of Lefebvre in the same chapter, offering an edited quote from *Everyday Life in the Modern World* which excludes from a continuous paragraph, Lefebvre's reference to the work and power of ideology (Fiske, 1989a, 37; Lefebvre, 1984, 31–2).

3 'Today's consumer culture represents neither a lapse of control nor the institution of more rigid controls, but rather their underpinning by a flexible underlying generative structure which can both handle formal control and de-control and facilitate an easy change of gears between them' (Featherstone, 1991, 27).

4 Ordinariness might be opposed to the 'popular' (Fiske) and the 'mediocre' (Lefebvre) as a way of characterising everyday life. It appears to me to be both sociologically more accurate and evaluatively less extreme.

5 In my first excursion into these issues (Silverstone, 1981) I rather cavalierly and incorrectly opposed myth to ideology in an attempt to distance an anthropological and structuralist account of contemporary culture from a more politicised and, originally at least, a literary one. It was a mistake.

6 'Urban form is no longer designated by a line of demarcation between here and there, but has become synonymous with the programming of a "time-schedule" . . .
In this realm of deceptive appearances, where the populating of transportation and transmission time supplants the populating of space and habitation, inertia revives an old sedentariness (the persistence of urban sites). With the advent of instantaneous communications . . . arrival supplants departure: everything arrives without necessarily having to depart' (Virilio, n. d., 19).

7 Yet it is worth noting that the author of a recent history of the American suburb notes that the suburb is becoming increasingly city-like: more diverse socially, and more threatened by the cultural and environmental instabilities that have previously been confined to the city (Marsh, 1990, 187).

8 John Fiske (1989a) and others have suggested that shopping malls also provide spaces for their reappropriation through the tactics of the young or the disadvantaged. Such activities, while they might signify the expression of alternative and contrary freedoms, nevertheless do not alter the strategic significance of the mall as a domestic temple, as a shrine to consumption.

References

Adams, John (ed.) (1980) *Institutional Economics: Contributions to the Development of Holistic Economics*, Boston, Martinus Nijhoff.

Adorno, Theodor (1957) 'Television and the Patterns of Mass Culture', in Rosenberg, Bernard and White, David Manning (eds) *Mass Culture: The Popular Arts in America*, New York, Free Press, 474–88.

—— (1991) *The Culture Industry*, Bernstein, J.M. (ed.), London, Routledge.

Alexander, Jeffrey C. (1986) 'The 'Form' of Substance: The Senate Watergate Hearings as Ritual', in Ball-Rokeach, Sandra and Cantor, Muriel (eds) *Media Audiences and Social Structure*, Newbury Park, Sage, 243–51.

Anderson, Benedict (1983) *Imagined Communities: Reflections on the Origin and Spread of Nationalism*, London, Verso.

Ang, Ien (1986) *Watching Dallas: Soap Opera and the Melodramatic Imagination*, London, Methuen.

—— (1991) *Desperately Seeking the Audience*, London, Routledge.

Appadurai, Arjun (1986) *The Social Life of Things: Commodities in Cultural Perspective*, Cambridge, Cambridge University Press.

Appleby, Sam (1990) 'Crawley – a Space Mythology', *New Formations*, 11. 19–44.

Archer, Margaret S. (1988) *Culture and Agency: The Place of Culture in Social Theory*, Cambridge, Cambridge University Press.

Bakhtin, Mikhail (1984) *Rabelais and his World*, Bloomington, Indiana University Press.

Barnes, Gill Gorell (1985) 'Systems Theory and Family Therapy', in Rutter, M. and Herzov, L. (eds) *Child and Adolescent Psychiatry: Modern Approaches* (2nd edition), Oxford, Blackwell, 216–29.

Barrett, Michele (1980) *Women's Oppression Today: Problems in Marxist Feminist Analysis*, London, Verso.

Barthes, Roland (1972) *Mythologies*, London, Jonathan Cape.

Bastide, Roger (1978) *The African Religions of Brazil: Towards a Sociology of the Interpretation of Civilizations*, Baltimore, Johns Hopkins University Press.

Baudrillard, Jean (1981) *For a Critique of the Political Economy of the Sign*, St Louis, Telos Press.

—— (1983) *Simulations*, New York, Semiotext(e).

—— (1988) *Selected Writings*, Poster, Mark (ed.), Cambridge, Polity Press.

Baumgartner, M.P. (1988) *The Moral Order of a Suburb*, New York, Oxford University Press.

Bausinger, Hermann (1984) 'Media, Technology and Daily Life', *Media, Culture and Society*, 6 (4) 343–52.

Bayley, Stephen (1986) *Sex, Drink and Fast Cars*, London, Faber.

Benjamin, Walter (1970) *Illuminations*, London, Fontana.

—— (1976) *Charles Baudelaire: A Lyric Poet in the Era of High Capitalism*, London, Verso.

Berger, Peter, Berger, Brigitte, and Kellner, Hansfried (1974) *The Homeless Mind: Modernization and Consciousness*, Harmondsworth, Penguin.

Berger, Peter and Luckmann, Thomas (1967) *The Social Construction of Reality*, Harmondsworth, Penguin.

Berman, Marshall (1983) *All That is Solid Melts into Air: The European Experience of Modernity*, London, Verso.

Bernardes, Jon (1986) 'In Search of "The Family" – Analysis of the 1981 United Kingdom Census: A Research Note', *Sociological Review*, 34 (4) 828–36.

Bernstein, Basil (1971) *Class, Codes and Control Vol. 1.*, London, Routledge & Kegan Paul.

Betteridge, Jennifer (1992) 'The Settlement of Modernity', Ph.D. Thesis, Brunel University.

Boddy, William (1986) 'The Shining Centre of the Home', in Drummond, Phillip and Paterson, Richard (eds) *Television in Transition*, London, British Film Institute, 125–34.

Bott, Elizabeth (1971) *Family and Social Network*, (2nd edition), London, Tavistock.

Born, Georgina (1993) 'Against Negation: For a Politics of Cultural Production: Adorno, Aesthetics, the Social', *Screen*, 34 (4) 223–42.

Bourdieu, Pierre (1977) *Outline of a Theory of Practice*, Cambridge, Cambridge University Press.

—— (1984) *Distinction: A Social Critique of the Judgement of Taste*, London, Routledge & Kegan Paul.

Boyd-Barrett, Oliver (1977) 'Media Imperialism: Towards an International Framework for the Analysis of Media Systems', in Curran, James, Gurevitch, Michael and Woollacott, Janet (eds) *Mass Communication and Society*, London, Edward Arnold, 116–40.

Boyd-Barrett, Oliver and Thussu, D.K. (1992) *Contra-Flow in Global News: International and Regional News Exchange*, London, John Libbey.

Boyne, Roy and Rattansi, Ali (eds) (1990) *Postmodernism and Society*, London, Macmillan.

Brodsly, David (1981) *LA Freeway: An Appreciative Essay*, Berkeley, University of California Press.

Brody, Gene H. and Stoneman, Zolinda (1983) 'The Influence of Television Viewing on Family Interaction: A Contextualist Framework', *Journal of Family Issues*, 4 (2) 329–66.

Brunsdon, Charlotte (1991) 'Satellite Dishes and the Landscapes of Taste', *New Formations*, 15. 23–42.

Brunsdon, Charlotte and Morley, David (1978) *Everyday Television: "Nationwide"*, London, British Film Institute.

Bryce, Jennifer (1987) 'Family Time and Television Use', in Lindlof, Tom (ed.) *Natural Audiences*, New Jersey, Norwood Ablex, 121–38.

Burgelin, Olivier (1972) 'Structural Analysis and Mass Communication', in McQuail, Denis (ed.) *Sociology of Mass Communications*, Harmondsworth, Penguin, 313–28.

Burgin, Victor, Donald, James and Kaplan, Cora (eds) (1986) *Formations of Fantasy*, London, Methuen.

Burke, Peter (1978) *Popular Culture in Early Modern Europe*, London, Maurice Temple Smith.

Buttimer, Anne (1980) 'Home, Reach and the Sense of Place', in Buttimer, Anne and Seamon, David (eds) *The Human Experience of Space and Place*, London, Croom Helm, 166–87.

Byng-Hall, John (1982) 'Family Legends: Their Significance for the Family Therapist', in Bentovim, A., Gorell-Barnes, G. and Cooklin, A. (eds) *Family Therapy: Complementary Frameworks of Theory and Practice*, London, Academic Press, 213–28.

Callois, Roger (1961) *Man, Play and Games*, Glencoe, Free Press.

Callon, Michel (1986) 'The Sociology of an Actor-Network: The Case of the Electric Vehicle', in Callon, Michel, Law, John and Rip, Arie (eds) *Mapping the Dynamics of Science and Technology*, London, Macmillan, 19–34.

—— (1987) 'Society in the Making: The Study of Technology as a Tool for Sociological Analysis', in Bijker, W.E., Hughes, T.P. and Pinch, T.J. (eds) *The Social Construction of Technological Systems*, Cambridge, MIT Press, 83–103.

Carey, James W. (1975) 'A Cultural Approach to Communication', *Communication* 2 (2) 1–22.

—— (1989) *Communication as Culture: Essays on Media and Society*, London, Unwin Hyman.

Carrier, James (1990) 'The Symbolism of Possession in Commodity Advertising', *Man*, 25 (4) 693–706.

Caughie, John (1991) 'Adorno's Reproach: Repetition, Difference and Television Genre', *Screen*, 32 (2) 127–53.

Cheal, David (1988) *The Gift Economy*, London, Routledge.

Cockburn, Cynthia (1985) *Machinery of Dominance: Women, Men and Technical Knowhow*, London, Pluto Press.

Comstock, George, Chafee, Steven, Katzman, Natan, McCombs, Maxwell and Roberts, Donald (1978) *Television and Human Behaviour*, New York, Columbia University Press.

Cowan, Ruth Schwartz (1987) 'The Consumption Junction: A Proposal for Research Strategies in the Sociology of Technology', in Bijker, W.E., Hughes, Thomas P., and Pinch, Trevor (eds) *The Social Construction of Technological Systems: New Directions in the Sociology and History of Technology*, Cambridge, MIT Press.

—— (1989) *More Work for Mother* (2nd edition), London, Free Associations Press.

Curran, James (1990) 'The "New Revisionism" in Mass Communications Research', *European Journal of Communication*, 5 (2/3) 135–64.

Czikszentmihalyi, Mihaly and Rochberg-Halton, Eugene (1981) *The Meaning of Things: Domestic Symbols and the Self*, Cambridge, Cambridge University Press.

Dayan, Daniel and Katz, Elihu (1992) *Media Events: The Live Broadcasting of History*, Cambridge, Harvard University Press.

Debord, Guy (1977) *The Society of the Spectacle*, London, Practical Paradise Productions.

—— (1990) *Comments on the Society of the Spectacle*, London, Verso.

De Certeau, Michel (1984) *The Practice of Everyday Life*, Berkeley, California University Press.

Dittmar, Helga (1992) *The Social Psychology of Material Possessions*, Hemel Hempstead, Harvester Wheatsheaf.

Doane, Mary Ann (1990) 'Information, Crisis, Catastrophe', in Mellencamp, Patricia (ed.) *Logics of Television: Essays in Cultural Criticism*, London and Bloomington, BFI Publishing and Indiana University Press, 222–39.

Donzelot, Jacques (1979) *The Policing of Families*, London, Hutchinson.

Douglas, Mary (1973) *Natural Symbols*, Harmondsworth, Penguin.

Douglas, Mary and Isherwood, Baron (1979) *The World of Goods: Towards an Anthropology of Consumption*, Harmondsworth, Penguin.

Dunn, Robert (1986) 'Television, Consumption and the Commodity Form', *Media, Culture and Society*, 3 (1) 49–64.

Durkheim, Emile (1971) *The Elementary Forms of the Religious Life*, London, George Allen & Unwin.

Eco, Umberto (1972) 'Towards a Semiotic Enquiry into the Television Message', *Working Papers in Cultural Studies*, University of Birmingham, 3.

—— (1979) *The Role of the Reader: Explorations in the Semiotics of Texts*, Bloomington, Indiana University Press.

Eisenstein, Elizabeth (1979) *The Printing Press in an Age of Social Change*, 2 Vols, Cambridge, Cambridge University Press.

Elliott, Philip (1982) 'Intellectuals, the "Information Society" and the Disappearance of the Public Sphere', *Media, Culture and Society*, 4 (3) 243–53.

Ewen, Stuart (1984) *All Consuming Images*, New York, Basic Books.

Ewen, Stuart and Ewen, Elizabeth (1982) *Channels of Desire*, New York, McGraw Hill.

Featherstone, Mike (1990) 'Global Culture: An Introduction', *Theory, Culture and Society*, 7 (2/3) 1–14.

—— (1991) *Consumer Culture and Postmodernism*, London, Sage.

Fejes, Fred (1984) 'Critical Mass Communications Research and Media Effects: The Problem of the Disappearing Audience', *Media, Culture and Society*, 6 (3) 219–32.

Ferguson, Marjorie (1990) 'Electronic Media and the Redefining of Time and Space', in Ferguson, Marjorie (ed.) *Public Communication: The New Imperatives: Future Directions for Media Research*, London, Sage, 152–72.

Feuer, Jane (1992) 'Genre Study and Television', in Allen, Robert C. (ed.) *Channels of Discourse Reassembled*, London, Routledge.

Fiske, John (1989a) 'Moments of Television: Neither the Text nor the Audience', in Seiter, Ellen, Borchers, Hans, Kreutzner, Gabrielle, Warth, Eva-Maria (eds) (1989) *Remote Control: Television, Audiences and Cultural Power*, London, Routledge, 56–68.

—— (1989b) *Reading the Popular*, London, Unwin Hyman.

Flink, James L. (1988) *The Automobile Age*, Cambridge, MIT Press.

Fontaine, J.S. (1988) 'Public or Private?: The Constitution of the Family in Anthropological Perspective', *International Journal of Moral and Social Studies*, 3 (3).

Forty, Adrian (1986) *Objects of Desire: Design and Society 1750–1980*, London, Thames and Hudson.

Foucault, Michel (1977) *Discipline and Punish*, Harmondsworth, Penguin.

Frith, Simon (1983) 'The Pleasures of the Hearth', in *Formations of Pleasure*, London, Routledge & Kegan Paul, 101–23.

Galtung, J. and Ruge, M. (1965) 'The Structure of Foreign News', in Tunstall, Jeremy, (ed.) *Media Sociology*, London, Constable.

Gane, Mike (1991) *Baudrillard: Critical and Fatal Theory*, London, Routledge.

Gans, Herbert (1967) *The Levittowners: Ways of Life and Politics in a New Suburban Community*, London, Allen Lane.

Garfinkel, Harold (1967) *Studies in Ethnomethodology*, Englewood Cliffs, Prentice Hall.

Garnham, Nicholas (1986) 'The Media and the Public Sphere', in Golding, Peter, Murdock, Graham and Schlesinger, Philip (eds) *Communicating Politics: Mass Communications and the Political Process*, Leicester, Leicester University Press, 37–53.

—— (1991) *Capitalism and Communication: Global Culture and the Economics of Information*, London, Sage.

Gell, Alfred (1986) 'Newcomers to the World of Goods: Consumption among the Muria Gonds', in Appadurai, Arjun (ed.) *The Social Life of Things: Commodities in Cultural Perspective*, Cambridge, Cambridge University Press, 110–38.

—— (1988a) 'Technology and Magic', *Anthropology Today*, 4 (2) 6–9.

—— (1988b) 'Anthropology, Material Culture and Consumerism', *Journal of the Anthropological Society of Oxford*, 19 (1) 43–8.

Geraghty, Christine (1990) *Women and Soap Opera*, Cambridge, Polity Press.

Gerbner, George *et al.* (1986) 'Living with Television: The Dynamics of the Culturation Process', in Bryant, J. and Zillman, D. (eds) *Perspectives on Media Effects*, Hillside, N.J., Lawrence Erlbaum, 17–40.

Gershuny, Jonathan (1982) 'Household Tasks and the Use of Time', in Wallman, Sandra *et al.* (eds) *Living in South London*, Aldershot, Gower, 149–81.

Giddens, Anthony (1984) *The Constitution of Society*, Cambridge, Polity Press.

—— (1989) 'A Reply to My Critics', in Held, David and Thompson, John B. (eds) *Social Theory of Modern Societies*, Cambridge, Cambridge University Press, 249–302.

—— (1990) *The Consequences of Modernity*, Cambridge, Polity Press.

—— (1991) *Modernity and Self-Identity: Self and Society in the Late Modern Age*, Cambridge, Polity Press.

Gill, Roger (1984) 'In England's Green and Pleasant Land', in Alexander, Peter and Gill, Roger (eds) *Utopias*, London, Duckworth, 109–18.

Girouard, Mark (1985) *Cities and People: A Social and Architectural History*, London and New Haven, Yale University Press.

Goffman, Erving (1969) *The Presentation of Self in Everyday Life*, Harmondsworth, Penguin Books.

Golding, Peter and Murdock, Graham (1991) 'Culture, Communications and Political Economy', in Curran, James and Gurevitch, Michael (eds) *Mass Media and Society*, London, Edward Arnold, 15–32.

Goldthorpe, John H., Lockwood, David, Bechofer, Frank and Platt, Jennifer (1969) *The Affluent Worker in the Class Structure*, Cambridge, Cambridge University Press.

Goodhardt, G.J., Ehrenberg, A.S.C. and Collins, M.A. (1975) *The Television Audience: Patterns of Viewing* (2nd edition 1986), Farnborough, Saxon House.

Goodman, Irene F. (1983) 'Television's Role in Family Interactions: A Family Systems Perspective', *Journal of Family Issues*, 4 (2) 405–24.

Gordon, Colin (ed.) (1980) *M. Foucault: Power/Knowledge*, New York, Pantheon.

Gray, Anne (1987) 'Behind Closed Doors: Women and Video', in Baehr, Helen and Dyer, Gillian (eds) *Boxed In: Women on and in Television*, London, Tavistock Books, 38–54.

—— (1992) *Video Playtime: The Gendering of a Leisure Technology*, London, Routledge.

Grossberg, Larry (1987) 'The In-Difference of Television', *Screen*, 28 (2) 28–46.

Gunter, Barry and Svennevig, Michael (1987) *Behind and in Front of the Small Screen: Television's Involvement with Family Life*, London, John Libbey.

Habermas, Jürgen (1989) *The Structural Transformation of the Public Sphere: An Inquiry into a Category of Bourgeois Culture*, Cambridge, Polity Press.

Haddon, Leslie (1988) 'The Home Computer: The Making of a Consumer Electronic', *Science as Culture*, 2. 7–51.

—— (1992) 'Explaining ICT Consumption: The Case of the Home Computer', in Silverstone, Roger and Hirsch, Eric (eds) *Consuming Technologies: Media and Information in Domestic Spaces*, London, Routledge, 82–96.

Hall, Edward T. (1973) *The Silent Language*, New York, Anchor Press.

Hall, Stuart (1977) 'Culture, the Media and the Ideological Effect', in Curran, James *et al.* (eds) *Mass Communication and Society*, London, Edward Arnold, 315–48.

—— (1981) 'Encoding/Decoding in Television Discourse', in Hall, Stuart, Hobson,

Dorothy, Lowe, Andrew and Willis, Paul (eds) *Culture, Media, Language*, London, Hutchinson, 128–38.

Hannerz, Ulf (1988) 'American Culture: Creolized, Creolizing', in Asard, Erik (ed.) *American Culture: Creolized, Creolizing and Other Lectures from the NAAS Biennial Conference in Uppsala, May 28–31, 1987*, Uppsala, Swedish Institute for North American Studies.

—— (1990) 'Cosmopolitans and Locals in World Culture', *Theory, Culture and Society* 7 (2/3) 237–51.

Haralovich, Mary Beth (1988) 'Suburban Family Sitcoms and Consumer Product Design: Addressing the Social Subjectivity of Homemakers in the 1950s', in Drummond, Phillip and Paterson, Richard (eds) *Television and its Audience: International Research Perspectives*, London, British Film Institute, 38–60.

Hartley, John (1987) 'Invisible Fictions: Television Audiences, Paedocracy, Pleasure', *Textual Practice*, 2. 121–38.

Haug, W.F. (1986) *Critique of Commodity Aesthetics: Appearance, Sexuality and Advertising in Capitalist Society*, Cambridge, Polity Press.

Harvey, David (1989) *The Condition of Postmodernity*, Oxford, Blackwell.

Hawkins, R.P. and Pingree, S. (1983) 'Television's Influence on Social Reality', in Wartella, Ellen and Whitney, D.C. (eds) *Mass Communication Review Yearbook*, 4, London, Sage, 53–76.

—— (1990) 'Divergent Psychological Processes in Constructing Social Reality from Mass Media Content', in Signorielli, Nancy and Morgan, Michael (eds) *Cultivation Analysis: New Directions in Media Effects Research*, London, Sage, 207–24.

Hayden, Dolores (1984) *Redesigning the American Dream: The Future of Housing, Work and Family Life*, New York, W.W. Norton.

Heath, Stephen (1990) 'Representing Television', in Mellencamp, Patricia (ed.) *Logics of Television*, Bloomington, Indiana University Press, 267–302.

Heath, Stephen and Skirrow, Gillian (1977) 'Television: A World in Action', *Screen*, 18 (2) 7–60.

Hebdige, Dick (1988) *Hiding in the Light*, London, Routledge.

Heideggar, Martin (1977) *The Question Concerning Technology and Other Essays*, London, Garland.

Heller, Agnes (1984) *Everyday Life*, London, Routledge & Kegan Paul.

Hill, Stephen (1988) *The Tragedy of Technology*, London, Pluto Press.

Himmelweit, H.T., Vince, P. and Oppenheim, A.N. (1958) *Television and the Child*, Oxford, Oxford University Press.

Hirsch, Eric (1989) 'Households and the Domestication Process: Some Preliminary Thoughts on Family Culture and ICT', Brunel University, mimeo.

Hobson, Dorothy (1982) *'Crossroads': The Drama of a Soap Opera*, London, Methuen.

—— (1989) 'Soap Operas at Work', in Seiter, Ellen, Borchers, Hans, Kreutzner, Gabrielle and Warth, Eva-Maria (eds) *Remote Control: Television, Audiences and Cultural Power*, London, Routledge, 150–67.

Hodge, Bob and Tripp, David (1986) *Children and Television*, Cambridge, Polity Press.

hooks, bell (1991) *Yearning: Race, Gender and Cultural Politics*, London, Turnaround.

Horkheimer, Max and Adorno, Theodor (1972) *The Dialectic of Enlightenment*, New York, Seabury Press.

Horton, Donald and Wohl, R. Richard (1956) 'Mass Communication and Para-Social Interaction', *Psychiatry*, 19 (3) 215–29.

Hughes, Thomas P. (1989) *American Genesis: A Century of Invention and Technological Enthusiasm*, New York, Viking.

Huizinga, Jan (1959) *Homo Ludens: A Study of the Play Element in Culture*, London, Routledge & Kegan Paul.

Hunt, Pauline (1989) 'Gender and the Construction of Home Life', in Allen, Graham and Crow, Graham (eds) *Home and Family: Creating the Domestic Sphere*, London, Macmillan, 102–21.

Ignatieff, Michael (1984) *The Needs of Strangers*, London, Chatto & Windus.

Innis, Harold A. (1972) *Empire and Communications*, Toronto, Toronto University Press.

Jensen, Klaus Bruhn (1990) 'The Politics of Polysemy: Television News, Everyday Consciousness and Political Action', *Media, Culture and Society*, 12 (1) 57–78.

Kantor, David and Lehr, William (1975) *Inside the Family*, San Francisco, Jossey-Bass.

Katz, Elihu and Dayan, Daniel (1985) 'Media Events: On the Experience of Not Being There', *Religion*, 15. 305–14.

Katz, Elihu and Lazarsfeld, Paul F. (1955) *Personal Influence: The Part Played by People in Mass Communication*, New York, Free Press.

Katz, Elihu and Liebes, Tamar (1986) 'Mutual Aid in the Decoding of Dallas: Preliminary Notes from a Cross-Cultural Study', in Drummond, Phillip and Paterson, Richard (eds) *Television in Transition*, London, British Film Institute, 187–98.

Keen, Ben (1987) '"Play it Again Sony": The Double Life of Home Video Technology', *Science as Culture*, 1, 7–42.

Kellner, Douglas (1989) *Jean Baudrillard: From Marxism to Postmodernism and Beyond*, Cambridge, Polity Press.

Kerr, Paul (1984) 'Drama at MTM: Lou Grant and Hill Street Blues', in Feuer, Jane, Kerr, Paul and Vahimagi, Tise, *MTM: "Quality Television"*, London, British Film Institute, 132–65.

King, Anthony (1980) *Buildings and Society: Essays on the Social Development of the Built Environment*, London, Routledge & Kegan Paul.

Kohon, Gregorio (ed.) (1986) *The British School of Psychoanalysis: The Independent Tradition*, London, Free Association Books.

Kopytoff, Igor (1986) 'The Cultural Biography of Things: Commoditization as Process', in Appadurai, Arjun (ed.) *The Social Life of Things: Commodities in a Cultural Perspective*, Cambridge, Cambridge University Press, 64–91.

Langer, Suzanne (1951) *Philosophy in a New Key*, Oxford, Oxford University Press.

Laplanche, L. and Pontalis, J-B. (1973) *The Language of Psycho-analysis*, London, The Hogarth Press.

Lasch, Christopher (1977) *Haven in Heartless World*, New York, Basic Books.

Lash, Scott (1990) *Sociology of Postmodernism*, London, Routledge.

Lash, Scott and Urry, John (1987) *The End of Organized Capitalism*, Cambridge, Polity Press.

Laslett, Peter (1965) *The World We Have Lost*, London, Methuen.

Law, John (1987) 'Technology and Heterogeneous Engineering: The Case of the Portuguese Expansion', in Bijker, W.E., Hughes, T.P. and Pinch, T.J. (eds) *The Social Construction of Technological Systems*, Cambridge, MIT Press, 111–34.

Leal, Ondina Faschel (1990) 'Popular Taste and Erudite Repertoire: The Place and Space of Television in Brazil', *Cultural Studies*, 4 (1) 19–29.

Lefebvre, Henri (1984) *Everyday Life in the Modern World*, New Brunswick, Transaction Publishers.

—— (1991) *Critique of Everyday Life*, London, Verso.

Leiss, William, Kline, Stephen and Jhaly, Sut (1990) *Social Communication in Advertising: Persons, Products and Images of Well-Being*, London, Routledge.

Lévi-Strauss, Claude (1968) *Structural Anthropology*, Harmondsworth, Penguin Books.

—— (1969) *The Raw and the Cooked: Introduction to a Science of Mythology Vol.1*, London, Jonathan Cape.

Lewis, C.A. (1942) *Broadcasting From Within*, London.

Liebes, Tamar and Katz, Elihu (1986) 'Patterns of Invovement in American Fiction: A Comparative Analysis', *European Journal of Communication*, 1 (2) 151–71.

—— (1988) 'Dallas and Genesis: Primordiality and Seriality in Popular Culture', in Carey, James W. (ed.) *Media, Myths and Narratives: Television and the Press*, London, Sage, 113–25.

—— (1991) *The Export of Meaning*, Oxford, Oxford University Press.

Lindlof, Thomas A. (1988) 'Media Audiences as Interpretive Communities', in Anderson, J.A. (ed.) *Communication Year Book 11*, London, Sage.

Lindlof, Thomas and Meyer, Timothy (1987) 'Mediated Communication as Ways of Seeing, Acting and Constructing Culture', in Lindlof, Thomas (ed.) *Natural Audiences: Qualitative Research of Media Uses and Effects*, New Jersey, Ablex Norwood.

Lindlof, Thomas and Traudt, Paul (1983) 'Mediated Communication in Families: New Theoretical Approaches', in Mander, Mary S. (ed.) *Communications in Transition*, New York, Praeger, 260–78.

Livingstone, Sonia M. (1990) *Making Sense of Television: The Psychology of Audience Interpretation*, Oxford, Pergamon.

—— (1992) 'The Meaning of Domestic Technologies: A Personal Construct Analysis of Familial Gender Relations', in Silverstone, Roger and Hirsch, Eric (eds) *Consuming Technologies: Media and Information in Domestic Spaces*, London, Routledge, 113–30.

Lodziak, Conrad (1986) *The Power of Television: A Critical Appraisal*, London, Frances Pinter.

Lull, James (1980a) 'The Social Uses of Television', *Human Communication Research*, 6 (3) 197–209.

—— (1980b) 'Family Communication Patterns and the Social Uses of Television', *Communication Research*, 7 (3) 319–34.

—— (1988) *World Families Watch Television*, London, Sage.

—— (1990) *Inside Family Viewing*, London, Routledge.

Mackenzie, Donald (1987) 'Missile Accuracy: A Case Study in the Social Processes of Technological Change', in Bijker, W.E., Hughes, Thomas P., and Pinch, Trevor (eds) *The Social Construction of Technological Systems*, Cambridge, MIT Press, 195–222.

McKracken, Grant (1988) *Culture and Consumption*, Bloomington, Indiana University Press.

McLuhan, Marshall (1964) *Understanding Media*, London, Routledge & Kegan Paul.

McQuail, Denis (1987) *Mass Communication Theory: An Introduction*, London, Sage.

Mander, Jerry (1978) *Four Arguments for the Elimination of Television*, Brighton, Harvester Press.

Marsh, Margaret (1990) *Suburban Lives*, New Brunswick, Rutgers University Press.

Martin, Bernice (1981) *A Sociology of Contemporary Cultural Change*, Oxford, Blackwell.

Martinet, Andre (1969) *Elements of General Linguistics*, London, Faber & Faber.

Marvin, Carolyn (1988) *When Old Technologies Were New: Thinking about Communications in the Late Nineteenth Century*, Oxford, Oxford University Press.

Mason, Jennifer (1989) 'Reconstructing the Public and the Private: The Home and Marriage in Later Life', in Allen, Graham and Crow, Graham (eds) *Home and Family: Creating the Domestic Sphere*, London, Macmillan, 102–21.

Massey, Doreen (1992) 'A Place Called Home?', *New Formations*, 17. 3–15.

Mattelart, Armand, Delcourt, Xavier and Mattellart, Michelle (1984) *International*

Image Markets: In Search of Alternative Perspective, London, Comedia.

Mayer, M. (1977) 'The Telephone and the Uses of Time', in de Sola Pool, Ithiel (ed.) *The Social Impact of the Telephone*, Cambridge, MIT Press, 225–45.

Mellencamp, Patricia (1990) 'TV Time and Catastrophe: Or Beyond the Pleasure Principle of Television' in Mellencamp, Patrica (ed.) *Logics of Television*, Bloomington and London, Indiana University Press and British Film Institute, 240–66.

—— (ed.) (1990) *Logics of Television: Essays in Cultural Criticism*, Bloomington and London, Indiana University Press and British Film Institute.

Meszaros, Istvan (1970) *Marx's Theory of Alienation*, London, Merlin Press.

Meyrowitz, Joshua (1985) *No Sense of Place: The Impact of Electronic Media on Social Behaviour*, New York, Oxford University Press.

Miller, Daniel (1987) *Material Culture and Mass Consumption*, Oxford, Blackwell.

—— (1988) 'Appropriating the State on the Council Estate', *Man*, NS 23. 353–72.

—— (1992) 'The Young and the Restless in Trinidad: A Case of the Local and the Global in Mass Consumption', in Silverstone, Roger and Hirsch, Eric (eds) *Consuming Technologies: Media and Information in Domestic Spaces*, London, Routledge, 163–82.

Minuchin, Salvador (1974) *Families and Family Therapy*, London, Tavistock.

Modleski, Tania (1983) 'The Rhythms of Reception: Daytime Television and Women's Work', in Kaplan, E. Ann (ed.) *Regarding Television*, Los Angeles, AFI, 67–75.

—— (1984) *Loving with a Vengeance: Mass Produced Fantasies for Women*, London, Methuen.

Moore, Sally Falk and Myerhoff, Barbara (1977) (eds) *Secular Ritual*, Amsterdam, Van Gorcum.

Moores, Shaun (1988) '"The Box on the Dresser": Memories of Early Radio and Everyday Life', *Media, Culture and Society*, 10 (1), 23–40.

—— (1990) 'Texts, Readers and Contexts of Reading: Developments in the Study of Media Audiences', *Media, Culture and Society*, 12 (1) 9–31.

—— (1993) 'Satellite TV as Cultural Sign: Consumption, Embedding and Articulation, *Media, Culture and Society*, 15 (4) 621–40.

Morgan, Michael and Signorielli, Nancy (eds) (1990) *Cultivation Analysis: New Directions in Media Effects Research*, London, Sage.

Morley, David (1980) *The 'Nationwide' Audience*, London, British Film Institute.

—— (1986) *Family Television: Cultural Power and Domestic Leisure*, London, Comedia.

—— (1989) 'Changing Paradigms in Audience Studies', in Seiter, Ellen, Borchers, Hans, Kreutzner, Gabrielle, Warth, Eva-Maria (eds) *Remote Control: Television, Audiences and Cultural Power*, London, Routledge, 16–43.

—— (1992) *Television, Audiences and Cultural Studies*, London, Routledge.

Morley, David and Silverstone, Roger (1990) 'Domestic Communication – Technologies and Meanings', *Media, Culture and Society*, 12 (1) 31–56.

Morris, Lydia (1990) *The Workings of the Household*, Cambridge, Polity Press.

Morris, Meaghan (1988) 'At Henry Parkes Motel', *Cultural Studies*, 2 (1) 1–16.

—— (1990) 'Banality in Cultural Studies', in Mellencamp, Patricia (ed.) *Logics of Television*, Bloomington and London, Indiana University Press and British Film Institute, 14–43.

Morse, Margaret (1990) 'An Ontology of Everyday Distraction: The Freeway, the Mall and Television', in Mellencamp, Patricia (ed.) *Logics of Television*, Bloomington and London, Indiana University Press and British Film Institute, 193–221.

Moyal, Ann (1989) 'The Feminine Culture of the Telephone: People, Patterns and Policy', *Prometheus*, 7 (1) 5–31.

—— (1992) 'The Gendered Use of the Telephone: An Australian Case Study', *Media, Culture and Society*, 14 (1) 51–72.

Mumford, Lewis (1938) *The Culture of Cities*, London, Martin Secker & Warburg.

Murdock, Graham (1982) 'Large Corporations and the Control of the Communication Industries', in Gurevitch, Michael, Bennett, Tony, Curran, James and Woollacott, Janet (eds) *Culture, Society and the Media*, London, Methuen, 118–50.

—— (1990) 'Redrawing the Map of the Communications Industries: Concentration and Ownership in the Era of Privatisation', in Ferguson, Marjorie (ed.) *Public Communication: The New Imperatives: Future Directions for Media Research*, London, Sage, 1–15.

Murphy, Robert F. (1972) *The Dialectics of Social Life*, London, George Allen & Unwin.

Newcomb, Horace (1982) 'Toward a Television Aesthetic', in Newcomb, Horace (ed.) *Television: A Critical View* (3rd edition), New York, Oxford University Press, 478–94.

Newcomb, Horace and Hirsch, P.M. (1984) 'Television as a Cultural Forum: Implications for Research', in Rowland, W.D. and Watkins, B. (eds) *Interpreting Television: Current Research Perspectives*, Beverley Hills, Sage, 58–73.

Oakley, Anne (1974) *The Sociology of Housework*, London, Allen Lane.

Oliver, Paul, Davis, Ian and Bentley, Ian (1981) *Dunroamin': The Suburban Semi and its Enemies*, London, Barrie & Jenkins.

Ong, Walter J. (1971) *Rhetoric, Romance and Technology: Studies in the Interaction of Expression and Culture*, Ithaca, Cornell University Press.

—— (1977) *Interfaces of the Word: Studies in the Evolution of Consciousness and Culture*, Ithaca, Cornell University Press.

—— (1982) *Orality and Literacy: The Technologizing of the Word*, London, Methuen.

Pahl, Jan (1989) *Money and Marriage*, London, Macmillan.

Pahl, R.E. (1984) *Divisions of Labour*, Oxford, Blackwell.

Palmer, Patricia (1986) *The Lively Audience: A Study of Children Around the TV Set*, London, Allen & Unwin.

Park, Robert (1940) 'News as a Form of Knowledge', in Turner, R.H. (ed.) *On Social Control and Collective Behaviour*, Chicago, Chicago University Press, 32–52.

Parkin, Frank (1972) *Class, Inequality and the Political Order*, London, Paladin.

Parry, Jonathan and Bloch, Maurice (1989) *Money and the Morality of Exchange*, Cambridge, Cambridge University Press.

Philo, Greg (1990) *Seeing and Believing: The Influence of Television*, London, Routledge.

Piore, M. and Sabel, C. (1984) *The Second Industrial Divide*, New York,

Pitkin, D.S. (1985) *The House that Giacomo Built*, Cambridge, Cambridge University Press.

Pool, Ithiel de Sola (ed.) (1977) *The Social Impact of the Telephone*, Cambridge, MIT Press.

Postman, Neil (1987) *Amusing Ourselves to Death*, London, Methuen.

Putnam, Tim and Newton, Charles (1990) *Household Choices*, London, Futures Publications.

Radway, Janice (1984) *Reading the Romance: Women, Patriarchy and Popular Literature*, Chapel Hill, University of North Carolina Press.

Rakow, Lana (1988) 'Women and the Telephone: The Gendering of a Communications Technology', in Kramarae, Ceris (ed.) *Technology and Women's Voices*, London, Routledge & Kegan Paul, 209–28.

Real, Michael R. (1982) 'The Super Bowl: Mythic Spectacle', in Newcomb, Horace (ed.) *Television: The Critical View*, New York, Oxford University Press, 206–39.

Redfield, Robert (1960) *The Little Community, and Peasant Society as Culture*, Chicago, Chicago University Press.

Reiss, David (1981) *The Family's Construction of Reality*, Cambridge, Harvard University Press.

Relph, Edward (1976) *Place and Placelessness*, London, Pion.

Richards, Lyn (1990) *Nobody's Home: Dreams and Realities in a New Suburb*, Melbourne, Oxford University Press.

Ricoeur, Paul (1984) *Time and Narrative, Vol.1*, Chicago, Chicago University Press.

Roberts, Robert (1973) *The Classic Slum: Salford Life in the First Quarter of the Century*, Harmondsworth, Penguin.

Robins, Kevin and Cornford, James (1992) 'What is Flexible about Independent Producers?', *Screen*, 33 (2) 190–200.

Robins, Kevin and Webster, Frank (1988) 'Cybernetic Capitalism: Information, Technology, Everyday Life', in Mosco, V. and Wasko, J. (eds) *The Political Economy of Information*, Madison, Wis., 44–75.

Robinson, John P. and Converse, Philip E. (1972) 'The Impact of Television on Mass Media Usages: A Cross-National Comparison', in Szalai, Alexander (ed.) *The Use of Time: Daily Activities of Urban and Suburban Populations in Twelve Countries*, The Hague, Mouton, 197–212.

Rogge, Jan-Uwe and Jensen, Klaus (1988) 'Everyday Life and Television in West Germany: An Empathetic-Interpretive Perspective on the Family as System', in Lull, James (ed.) *World Families Watch Television*, London, Sage, 80–115.

Rudd, David (1992) 'Children and Television: A Critical Note on Theory and Method', *Media, Culture and Society*, 14 (2) 313–20.

Sahlins, Marshall (1974) *Stone Age Economics*, London, Tavistock.

—— (1976) *Culture and Practical Reason*, Chicago, Chicago University Press.

Saunders, Peter and Williams, Peter (1988) 'The Constitution of Home: Towards a Political Agenda', *Housing Studies*, 3 (2) 81–93.

Scannell, Paddy (1988) 'Radio Times: The Temporal Arrangements of Broadcasting in the Modern World', in Drummond, Phillip and Paterson, Richard (eds) *Television and its Audience: International Research Perspectives*, London, British Film Institute, 15–31.

—— (1989) 'Public Service Broadcasting and Modern Public Life', *Media, Culture and Society*, 11 (2) 135–66.

Scannell, Paddy and Cardiff, David (1991) *A Social History of British Broadcasting, Vol. 1 1922–1939: Serving the Nation*, Oxford, Blackwell.

Schiller, Herbert (1989) *Culture Inc: The Corporate Takeover of Public Expression*, New York, Oxford University Press.

Schneider, David M. (1980) *American Kinship: A Cultural Account*, Chicago, Chicago University Press.

Schramm, Wilbur, Lyle, Jack and Parker, Edwin B. (1961) *Television in the Lives of Our Children*, Stanford, Stanford University Press.

Schutz, Alfred (1973) 'On Multiple Realities', *Collected Papers, Vol.1.*, The Hague, Martinus Nijhoff, 207–59.

Schwach, Victor (1992) 'L'integration des Objets Techniques dans la Vie Quotidienne', in *Sociologie des techniques de la Vie Quotidienne*, Paris, Editions l'Harmattan, Collection Logiques Sociales, 103–8.

Seaman, William R. (1992) 'Active Audience Theory: Pointless Populism', *Media, Culture and Society*, 14 (2) 301–12.

Seamon, David (1979) *A Geography of the Life World*, London, Croom Helm.

Seeley, J.R., Sim, R.A. and Loosley, E.W. (1956) *Crestwood Heights*, London, Constable.

Seiter, Ellen, Borchers, Hans, Kreutzner, Gabrielle, Warth, Eva-Maria (eds) (1989) *Remote Control: Television, Audiences and Cultural Power*, London, Routledge.

Sennett, Richard (1986) *The Fall of Public Man*, London, Faber & Faber.

Sheldon, Roy and Arens, Egmont (1932) *Consumer Engineering: A New Technique for Prosperity*, New York,

Shields, Rob (ed.) (1992) *Lifestyle Shopping: The Subject of Consumption*, London, Routledge.

Shils, Edward and Young, Michael (1953) 'The Meaning of the Coronation', *Sociological Review*, 1 (2) 63–82.

Shotton, Margaret (1989) *Computer Addiction? A Study of Computer Dependency*, London, Taylor & Francis.

Silj, Alessandro (1988) *East of Dallas; The European Challenge to American Television*, London, British Film Institute.

Silverstone, Roger (1981) *The Message of Television: Myth and Narrative in Contemporary Culture*, London, Heinemann Educational Books.

—— (1988) 'Television, Myth and Culture', in Carey, James (ed.) *Media, Myths and Narratives: Television and the Press*, Newbury Park, Sage, 20–47.

—— (1990) 'Television and Everyday Life: Towards an Anthropology of the Television Audience', in Ferguson, Marjorie (ed.) *Public Communication: The New Imperatives: Future Directions for Media Research*, London, Sage, 170–89.

—— (1991a) 'Beneath the Botttom Line: Households and Information and Communication Technologies in an Age of the Consumer', *PICT Policy Papers 17*, Swindon, ESRC.

—— (1991b) 'Television, Rhetoric and the Return of the Unconscious in Secondary Oral Culture', in Gronbeck, Bruce E., Farrell, Thomas J. and Soukup, Paul A. (eds) *Media, Consciousness, and Culture: Explorations of Walter Ong's Thought*, Newbury Park, Sage, 147–59.

—— (1993) 'Time, Information and Communication Technologies and the Household', *Time and Society*, 2 (3) 283–311.

Silverstone, Roger and Hirsch, Eric (eds) (1992) *Consuming Technologies: Media and Information in Domestic Spaces*, London, Routledge, 15–31.

Silverstone, Roger, Hirsch, Eric and Morley, David (1992) 'Information and Communication Technologies and the Moral Economy of the Household', in Silverstone, Roger and Hirsch, Eric (eds) *Consuming Technologies: Media and Information in Domestic Spaces*, London, Routledge, 15–31.

Silverstone, Roger and Morley, David (1990) 'Families and their Technologies: Two Ethnographic Portraits', in Putnam, Tim and Newton, Charles (eds) *Household Choices*, London, Futures Publications, 74–83.

Siune, Karen and Truetzschler, Wolfgang (eds) (1992) *Dynamics of Media Politics: Broadcast and Electronic Media in Western Europe*, London, Sage.

Sixsmith, Judith and Andrew (1990) 'Place in Transition: The Impact of Life Events on the Experience of Home', in Putnam, Tim and Newton, Charles (eds) *Household Choices*, London, Futures Publications, 20–4.

Smith, Anthony (1976) *The Shadow in the Cave*, London, Quartet.

Sorenson, Knut (1990) 'The Norwegian Car: The Cultural Adaptation and Integration of an Imported Artefact', in Sorenson, Knut H. and Berg, Anne-Jorunn (eds) *Technology and Everyday Life: Trajectories and Transformations*, Oslo, NORAS, 109–30.

Spigel, Lynn (1990) 'Television in the Family Circle: The Popular Reception of a New Medium', in Mellencamp, Patrica (ed.) *Logics of Television*, Bloomington and London, Indiana University Press and British Film Institute, 73–97.

—— (1992) *Make Room for TV: Television and the Family Ideal in Post-War America*, Chicago, Chicago University Press.

Sreberny-Mohammadi, Annabelle (1991) 'The Global and the Local in International Communications', in Curran, James and Gurevitch, Michael (eds) *Mass Media and Society*, London, Edward Arnold, 118–38.

Stephenson, William (1988) *The Play Theory of Mass Communication*, New Brunswick, Transaction Books.

Stirratt, R.L. (1989) 'Money, Men and Women', in Jonathan Parry and Maurice Bloch (eds) *Money and the Morality of Exchange*, Cambridge, Cambridge University Press, 94–116.

Strathern, Marilyn (1987) 'Producing Difference: Connections and Disconnections in two New Guinea Highland Systems', in Collier, Jane Fishburne and Yanagisako, Sylvia Junko (eds) *Gender and Kinship: Essays Toward a Unified Analysis*, Stanford, Calif., Stanford University Press, 271–300.

—— (1993) 'Future Kinship and the Study of Culture', in Cohen A. and Fukui, K. (eds) *Humanising the City? Social Contexts of Life at the Turn of the Milliennium*, Edinburgh, Edinburgh University Press, 184–200.

Swingewood, Alan (1975) *Marx and Modern Social Theory*, London, Macmillan.

Taylor, Ella (1989) *Prime Time Families: Television Culture in Postwar America*, Berkeley, University of California Press.

Thomas, W.I. (1966) *On Social Organization and Social Personality*, (edited by Maurice Janowitz), Chicago, Chicago University Press.

Thompson, E.P. (1968) *The Making of the English Working Class*, Harmondsworth, Penguin.

—— (1971) 'The Moral Economy of the English Crowd in the Eighteenth Century', *Past and Present*, 50, 76–136.

Thompson, John B. (1990) *Ideology and Modern Culture: Critical Social Theory in the Era of Mass Communication*, Cambridge, Polity Press.

Thorns, David C. (1972) *Suburbia*, London, McGibbon & Kee.

Thrall, Charles A. (1982) 'The Conservative Use of Modern Household Technology', *Technology and Culture*, 23 (2) 175–94.

Tomlinson, Alan (1990) 'Home Fixtures: Doing-it-yourself in a Privatised World', in Tomlinson, Alan (ed.) *Consumption, Identity and Style: Marketing, Meaning and the Packeting of Pleasure*, London, Routledge, 57–63.

—— (ed.) (1990) *Consumption, Identity and Style: Marketing, Meaning and the Packeting of Pleasure*, London, Routledge.

Tunstall, Jeremy (1977) *The Media are American*, London, Constable.

Turkle, Sherry (1986) *The Second Self: Computers and the Human Spirit*, London, Granada.

Turner, Ralph *et al.* (1986) *Waiting for Disaster: Earthquake Watch in California*, Berkeley, California University Press.

Turner, Victor W. (1969) *The Ritual Process*, London, Routledge & Kegan Paul.

Ure, A (1835) *Philosophy of Manufacturers*, London.

Vaihinger, Hans (1924) *The Philosophy of As-If*, London, Kegan Paul Trench Trubner.

Veblen, Thorstein (1925) *The Theory of the Leisure Class: An Economic Study of Institutions*, London, George Allen & Unwin.

Virilio, Paul (no date) 'The Overexposed City', *Zone 1/2*, 14–31.

Voloshinov, V. (1973) *Marxism and the Philosophy of Language*, New York, Academic Press.

Wallman, Sandra (1984) *Eight London Households*, London, Tavistock.

White, Mimi (1992) 'Ideological Analysis and Television', in Allen, Robert C. (ed.) *Channels of Discourse Reassembled*, London, Routledge, 161–202.

Whyte, William A. (1956) *The Organization Man*, Harmondsworth, Penguin.

Williams, Raymond (1974) *Television: Technology and Cultural Form*, London, Fontana.

—— (1986) *Keywords*, London, Fontana.

Willmott, Peter and Young, Michael (1960) *Family and Class in a London Suburb*,

London, Routledge & Kegan Paul.

Wilson, Patricia and Pahl, Ray (1988) 'The Changing Sociological Construct of the Family', *The Sociological Review*, 36 (2) 233–72.

Winner, Langdon (1985) 'Do Artifacts Have Politics?' in Mackenzie, Donald and Wajcman, Judy (eds) *The Social Shaping of Technology: How the Refrigerator Got its Hum*, Milton Keynes, Open University Press, 26–38.

Winnicott, D.W. (1965) *The Maturational Processes and the Facilitating Environment: Studies in the Theory of Emotional Development*, London, The Hogarth Press.

—— (1974) *Playing and Reality*, Harmondsworth, Penguin.

—— (1975) *Through Paediatrics to Psycho-analysis*, London, The Hogarth Press.

Wober, J. Mallory (1990) 'Does Television Cultivate the British? Late 80s Evidence', in Signorielli, Nancy and Morgan, Michael (eds) *Cultivation Analysis: New Directions in Media Effects Research*, London, Sage, 207–24.

Wober, J. M. and Gunter, B. (1987) *Television and Social Control*, Aldershot, Gower.

Woolgar, Steve (1988) *Science: The Very Idea*, Chichester, Ellis Horwood.

Wright, Charles R. (1968) 'Functional Analysis and Mass Communication', in Dexter, Lewis and White, David Manning (eds) *People, Society and Mass Communication*, New York, Free Press, 91–109.

—— (1974) 'Functional Analysis and Mass Communication Revisited', in Blumler, Jay and Katz, Elihu (eds) *The Uses of Mass Communication*, Sage, Beverly Hills, 197–221.

Young, Robert M. (1986) 'Life Among the Mediations: Labour, Groups, Breasts', paper delivered to Department of History and Philosophy of Science, University of Cambridge, February.

Zelizer, Viviana (1989) 'The Social Meaning of Money: "Special Monies"', *American Journal of Sociology*, 95 (2) 342–77.

Zone 1/2, (no date) New York, Urzone Inc.

Index